This book is dedicated to:

Brian O'Callaghan Westropp, who left an imprint on my
heart and soul that I will carry for the rest of my days.
Thank you for the gifts of love, laughter
and adventure.

And

Colm Holohan, for a lifetime of wonderful memories
and some mighty gems of advice.
Gone but never forgotten.

As the

Smoke Clears

9/3/22

As the SMOKE CLEARS

Zoe Holohan

Gill Books

Gill Books

Hume Avenue

Park West

Dublin 12

www.gillbooks.ie

Gill Books is an imprint of M.H. Gill and Co.

© Zoe Holohan 2021

978 07171 9024 9

Print origination by O'K Graphic Design, Dublin

Copy-edited by Rachel Pierce

Proofread by Djinn von Noorden

Printed in Dublin by Sprintprint

This book is typeset in 11.5/17.5 pt Sabon.

The paper used in this book comes from the wood pulp of managed forests. For every tree felled, at least one tree is planted, thereby renewing natural resources.

5 4

CONTENTS

PROLOGUE

t's spring 2020 and the world is caught in the grip of the coronavirus pandemic. Stuck on lockdown, I find myself totally glued to the TV, waiting to hear news of when we've finally won the war against this virus. Life is temporarily on hold and while solitary confinement may be tedious, I've become accustomed to change over the last few years and firmly believe that much of what is mapped out for us in this lifetime is out of our control. I take comfort in that thought. We never truly know what path we are on and can only attempt to make plans for the future. Inevitably, our fate will still bring surprises, so it's best to make the most of the present, and recognise and embrace the good stuff while we can. I've had my own struggles to overcome, though I hope my worst times are now over and done with. My name is Zoe Holohan and this is the story of my own private battle, how I beat the odds and lived to tell the tale.

My 'worst time' began on 23 July 2018 when the path I was happily travelling on crumbled beneath my feet. On that scorching midsummer's day, a series of wildfires broke out across the coastal areas of Athens, Greece. A major disaster ensued, the deadliest of its kind in Europe so far this century, and the fires eventually took 102 lives and destroyed so many others in its wake. Amongst those killed was an Irishman, my husband, Brian O'Callaghan Westropp. We were on our honeymoon at the time, just four days after our wedding. Devastated to find myself suddenly widowed and alone, I also had severe injuries to contend with. I was rescued, seconds from death, by a volunteer fireman who risked his own life to save mine, but I still suffered life-threatening burns all over my body. I was considered one of the lucky ones to have survived at all.

This book is my recollection of the events from that hellish time to the present day. What occurred was a traumatic and painful journey, a true fight for life with many cruel twists of fate. Yet amongst all that darkness there were still glimpses of beaming light. I encountered the very finest that humanity has to offer – from the phenomenal surgeons and therapists who saved my life to the nurses who soothed me during my bleakest moments. These amazing people offered me comfort when I believed there was no consolation to be had; when the tide of grief was determined to drown me, they held my head above the waterline and kept me breathing.

One surprising thing I learned on this journey is that when you least expect it, in the midst of physical and mental anguish, there can still be laughter, often at the most inappropriate of times. Life is strange that way. You'd be amazed what funny things occur in intensive care, what instruments of torture (more commonly known as medical devices) can provide hilarious moments of relief. I discovered that my obstinate and mildly deranged nature couldn't stay hidden forever, and no doubt I tested the patience of numerous health professionals during the various stages of my recovery. There were times when I was particularly unhinged, notably my post-coma phase when I couldn't tell hallucination from reality. The coma state was the birthplace of my living nightmares and they were reluctant to release their grip on me, even when I was conscious.

There were also many physical challenges, which began when I emerged from that post-coma haze. Much like an infant, I had to learn how to walk, talk, eat and use my dysfunctional limbs once more. Starting from scratch, with everything I had ever known or taken for granted gone, I coped by focusing on tiny daily victories. When the bigger picture is too terrifying to face, I found that you have to concentrate on the small steps that will eventually take you to the finishing line.

Nearly two years on from that terrible day, I've found that while time can't heal everything, it certainly gives it a good try. The grief from losing someone you love doesn't disappear, but you learn to carry it with you. I've absorbed help and kindness from some amazing people and learned how to live with pain and deal with PTSD. I am now pushing forward to the next step in my life. My wish is that my story will offer hope and strength to anybody suffering sudden loss or life-altering situations. If nothing else, it might reignite faith in human nature, even at the worst of times. That's what I want to take from this period in my life, and hopefully you will too.

Zoe Holohan
April 2020

PART ONE

Miss your kisses
Miss your touch
C'mere till I tell you,
I miss you much
(ZH)

1

THE FIRST DATE

first met Brian in my local café on a breezy October afternoon in 2014. I know that it was blustery because it was nearly impossible to maintain composure in my sleek leather outfit and four-inch heels while desperately holding onto my freshly styled hairdo on the walk to my destination. Back then, I wore long, sumptuous hair extensions that were my pride and joy. My hair was spectacularly long – I could have given Rapunzel a run for her money. It was so windy, however, that I cursed my mane under my breath, arriving at the café virtually strangled by my tangled tresses. Needless to say, the whole 'dragged through a bush' look was not the first impression I had intended to make.

I'd connected with Brian a few days earlier on a dating site for professionals looking to find true love and a genuine relationship. I may have slightly misled some people (namely my mother) when I described how I first met Brian, leaving the website part out entirely. Having had no success on this site for over a year, I'd finally resolved that this meeting would mark my last foray into digital dating. I'd met my share of 'interesting' characters during that time – Lord knows I'd kept my friends highly entertained with stories of my dating mishaps – but I'd come to the conclusion that enough was enough. I'd met them all, from the mildly psychotic narcissists to those obsessed with seeking revenge on ex-wives or partners, and I was disenchanted with the whole process. I'm not suggesting for one minute that I myself was perfect, but at very least I was honest on my profile. There was one deluded chap, for instance, who 'accidentally' lied about his age, knocking off at least a decade and using a photo that was probably taken at school. Bizarrely, he assumed I wouldn't notice that he was considerably older than he'd claimed to be when we met face to face. Even the comb-over couldn't disguise that fact!

So up until that fateful day in October, this site had not exactly matched me with the man of my dreams. I had secretly vowed that this rendezvous would be my last. Little did I know how prophetic that vow would turn out to be.

Brian had my curiosity piqued from his first communication. While his profile was promising in that he seemed genuine, intelligent and looking for a real relationship, the photo he had used was not the most flattering shot. God only knows why he chose what was, quite simply, the worst headshot I've ever seen of him. He was such a handsome guy in reality, with the most beautiful, twinkling blue eyes. Luckily, unflattering blurred picture aside, he won me over in his emails with his wit and charm, and the fact that he took the time to read my profile carefully really impressed me. He convinced me that this dating malarkey could be worth one last try, so I agreed to meet him.

I entered the café with my 'windswept' hair, looking for the guy from the profile pic. Immediately I encountered a problem: there were two men, each sitting alone, at opposite sides of the café, and either could be the guy from that photo. Neither looked exactly like the picture, but both were approximately the right age and both looked up expectantly as I walked in the side door and to the middle of the room.

The first of the two men, the one sitting by the window, was just my type – dark hair, a well-groomed beard and smiling blue eyes. The other guy, sitting by the back door – well, in truth I can't remember what he looked like, other than clean-shaven and, in my opinion, the less attractive of the two. But the profile photo showed a clean-shaven man, so I assumed that he must be Brian. He caught me staring at him and seemed to rise from his chair, as if to greet me, so I started to walk in his direction. Instantly I felt disappointed, wishing that my coffee date was with the other guy with the beard.

Perhaps reading my mind, at that very moment Brian – yes it was him, the cute, blue-eyed, bearded wonder – stood up and called my name. I know I blushed then, not only because I had been saved from a potentially embarrassing situation but also because I quite liked the way the real Brian was looking at me. I even liked the way my name sounded when he called it. He smiled, chuckled a little and beckoned me to join him. My cheeks reddened a deeper shade and my stomach started to do that churning thing it does when I feel giddy, which was definitely a good omen.

Brian introduced himself properly, we shook hands and sat down. I quickly overcame my initial awkwardness as he complimented my outfit and even my disorderly hair. Conversation came easily. Not to get schmaltzy about it, but I definitely knew from the get-go that this date was special. My first instincts are rarely misleading, and I liked him straight away. Although I couldn't tell for sure if the feeling was absolutely mutual, he certainly seemed interested in getting to know me better. If nothing else, he wasn't offended by my tangled bouffant or my confused entrance and what was meant to be just a coffee date quickly grew into something more substantial.

I'm sure millions have experienced those wonderful first-meets, when you literally want to know everything about the other person. That was it for us. We finished our coffee, decided to order lunch and ended up sitting in that café, talking, for hours. We shared our life stories, our achievements, failures, joys and challenges. Brian had led a fascinating existence up until then. He appeared smart and ambitious but exuded warmth, too. We had both been married before but, unlike some of my recent dates, Brian only had nice things to say about his ex-wife, demonstrating his true character. Between us, we certainly shared a wealth of life experience and a passion for travel and adventure. I'd had the travel bug for years, even wrote the odd review in certain newspapers, and was fascinated to hear of places I had not yet visited. Brian had been everywhere from Australia to South Africa, the Middle East to the Great Wall of China.

The lunch turned into dinner, still in the same café, though I'm not sure if I actually consumed any food, such was my excitement. I do recall doing a little victory dance in the Ladies', when I had a moment to gather my thoughts. For those of you unfamiliar with this concept it mainly consists of silent, delighted screams, air punches, butt wiggles and approximately half-a-dozen jumping jacks, which I recommend you only ever perform when nobody else is around. Once I was more composed, I checked my phone and was astounded to see that six hours had passed since we'd first met. Obviously time literally does fly when you're having fun.

The café closed, but neither of us wanted this date to end so we ventured off to my local bar, a stone's throw away. More wine consumed, more stories shared. We laughed when a rather drunk old man decided to crash our date, attempting to sit at our table. He announced that he could tell we'd been married for many years by how comfortable we looked together. Brian nodded and said that it was indeed our tenth wedding anniversary. Cheekily, I winked at my 'husband' and said I hadn't had my anniversary kiss yet. Brian seized his chance, pulled me into his arms and kissed me for the first time. You can tell a lot from a first kiss. This was a toe-curling, passionate kiss and it continued for so long that the drunken old geezer got bored and moved on to the next table. I'm pretty sure in that moment I made up my mind: from that day on I only ever wanted to be kissed by Brian. To put my theory to the test and not be hasty about it, I continued to kiss him for the rest of the evening. Just to be sure …

I often joked with Brian down through the years that our first date was actually three in one because in just twelve hours we had a coffee, lunch and dinner date. We couldn't get enough of each other and it turned out we had started as we meant to go on. I saw Brian again the following day and virtually every day after that. We moved in together just a couple of months later and began our life together. Sadly, it was destined to be a short life, but it was oh so sweet nonetheless.

2

TIME PASSES

t's 18 December 2018, a few days before Christmas and nearly five months since Brian passed. I prefer to use the word 'passed' because 'death' conjures up a cold and defined ending, while 'passed' feels gentler, like the person I've lost is just elsewhere for a while, in an ethereal waiting room, hanging around in limbo until I'm ready to join him. I've considered myself a vehement atheist since my early teens but for the first time, in my mid-forties, I find myself questioning everything I've ever believed in, including an afterlife, or lack of one. I certainly don't believe in any god (if I did, he or she would be the cruellest of gods to take Brian that way), but I do sometimes indulge in a spot of make-believe, imagining Brian and my dad chilling out together somewhere divine. I dream they are both spending their days filled with laughter and joy, someplace considerably lovelier than where they left me behind.

My dad also passed away during this time, just three weeks after Brian, and I've had a lot of time to question why this happened, a lot of hours staring at hospital walls wondering why they're both gone and why I'm still here. So much pensive time, in fact, that I decided to write down all my recollections, hoping to make some sense of what has occurred. I'm sitting at my dining-room table, typing at a painfully slow pace (my defective left hand battles with me daily) and my home is now my office. I'm surrounded by piles of post from well-wishers on one side, and bigger piles of bills from those with less kindly intentions on the other.

My hope is that writing will kick-start the healing process, will help mend my mind, if nothing else. Physically, my reflection is changed beyond recognition. The skin I never truly appreciated before is marred and scarred all over. My 'canvas' is a patchwork quilt of burns and skin grafts from head to toe. My chest and upper back carry slash-like scars and my legs look, to all intents and purposes, as though they have been cooked. At least I can walk, though, even if it is at a much slower pace than before, and I'm exceedingly grateful my legs work at all. There is a lot of pain to manage, but I'm also making constant improvements. Some days are better than others.

All around me are memories of a past life that now seems to belong to somebody else, someone I once knew. Smiling photos on the shelves mock my broken heart and my dad's joyful paintings, which always brought me such happiness, now only cause pain. All these things that were here before remain as they always were. Nothing much has changed in my home (bar the deafening silence) and my life, in whatever form it now takes, stubbornly continues on. That doesn't sit well with me. The only telltale sign to an observer that anything is off-kilter is the calendar on my fridge that proudly shows our wedding day, circled in red: 19 July 2018. No other entries are made after that date, as if time froze on that day.

But time has a way of moving forward, whether I like it or not.

On 1 December 2018 we finally held the memorial service for Brian. I missed his cremation, which took place back in August in his hometown of Shannon, because I was still in hospital in Greece. Brian's mum, Rosemary, and his best friend, Adey (his brother from another mother), had the torturous task of organising Brian's final journey home, without me there to hold their hands. The decision to fly Brian home ahead of me was an agonising one to make but it was, in my opinion, the right thing to do. I couldn't bear the thought of my beautiful husband stuck in the mortuary in Athens for months on end, while I lay nearby in a hospital bed. Cremation isn't practised in Greece and in the days after the fire the mortuary was packed to capacity with all those who lost their lives in the tragedy. Truthfully, back in August I had no idea of the sheer volume of people who had been killed in that disaster and would only learn months later that a wildfire like this hadn't occurred in over a century.

Given the circumstances of Brian's death, we thought it best to send him home ahead of me. Arranging the transportation of his coffin from Greece to Ireland was a traumatic task, one undertaken primarily by Adey. Months later he described Brian's final flight to me, detailing the sensitive manner of the flight crew, the delicate handling of the coffin and the immense respect shown to Brian, Adey and Rosemary when they finally arrived back in Ireland. It was a complicated process, made all the more difficult by the media interest. It took clever planning to ensure no cameras or journalists intruded on this private moment. Already many reporters had got it wrong about how he died, saying that we had been separated in the confusion of the fire, but thankfully those articles were kept hidden from me for some time. We knew there would be considerable interest in Brian's final journey home to Shannon. Adey and Rosemary called in more than one favour to ensure they avoided the awaiting photographers and reporters at the airport. Adey works in the travel industry, as Brian's own father had done decades before, so they knew who to call upon for assistance in this matter.

Brian's cremation took place with just Rosemary, Adey and a handful of close friends in attendance. I begged them to delay Brian's proper funeral ceremony until a time when I was able to join them and, true to their word, they kept their promise. I started making plans in my head for Brian's memorial service while lying immobile in the ICU and it spurred me on to get better as quickly as possible. From the very beginning I told myself that I needed to get well enough to walk on my own two feet, and properly honour the memory of the man I loved.

Bizarrely, I knew exactly what Brian wanted for his final send-off because just a few days before our wedding we'd had an idle conversation about our funerals and what our last wishes were. That was how, amongst other things, I learned that Brian preferred cremation to burial. Little did I know how portentous that conversation would turn out to be, for a week after it occurred, four days after our wedding, Brian was dead.

3

THE WEDDING DAY

Our wedding took place in the beautiful country estate of Clonabreany House in rural County Meath on 19 July 2018. To say it was the happiest day of my life sounds like a cliché, but it's a simple truth. We opted for a garden ceremony and with the sun beaming down, a factor you could never take for granted in Ireland, my heart danced with excitement from the moment I woke that morning.

This was the second time around the rodeo for both of us and for that reason we chose to have a small gathering of about 80 people, just immediate family and close friends. Having already been married before, you may be forgiven for thinking that this time must have been a piece of cake. It was not. I am not exactly what you would call the most organised individual. In fact, like most brides-to-be, I reckon I was a bit of a nightmare in the run-up to the big day. I dubbed the bridesmaids, my pals Ornaith and Caroline, my 'bride-slaves' in the weeks before the main event. It was a joke, of course, but these two ladies certainly went above and beyond in their duties, taking on many tasks to get me ship-shape. They also had the patience of saints, a virtue I was never blessed with, and there were some days I felt they were the master planners for the wedding and I was just along for the ride!

Ornaith even made our wedding cake in her spare time, though everybody knows there's no such thing as 'spare time' for a mother of three kids who also holds down a full-time job. Perhaps, like most mums with young children, the whole 'there are only 24 hours in each day' rule doesn't apply. The cake was a spectacular creation, incidentally, with three delectable tiers – each a different flavour to keep everybody satisfied. There was the traditional fruit layer (for Brian and Dad to divide in two), a salted caramel sponge (my favourite salty-sweet treat) and the great crowd-pleaser – the finest chocolate biscuit rocky road on earth. Caroline drove me around in whirlwind fashion to a myriad of appointments, everything from dress fittings to hair trials and florist consultations. Those final weeks were all a bit of a stress-blur, but with my bride-slaves in tow, or rather in control, we pretty much got it all covered.

Amazingly, we found the time to squeeze in a couple of hen-do's during those chaotic few weeks – one in Dublin, which actually merged with Brian's stag and turned into a brilliant night for the whole gang, and one more exotic trek to Marbella for just us little gang of gal-pals. We partied our socks off in the Spanish sun and it was an utterly memorable trip, not least because it will probably be the last ever sun holiday I'll enjoy in this lifetime. If that turns out to be the case – well, at least I went out with a bang, so to speak.

Finally, it was the big day. This experience was very different from the first time around. When I'd married my first husband, I'd had a sense of foreboding that we weren't meant to be, that we were a mismatch. My gut feeling turned out to be right. This time was completely different. I had no doubts at all. I was deeply in love and trusted my intuition that we made a good team. The wedding itself sealed the deal on paper, but the proof had been in our life together since our first date nearly four years earlier. I can't remember a day when we didn't laugh together, and I loved every second we shared. My favourite time was eating dinner and running through our day. It was just us three sitting together, me, Brian and Meow the cat (though she wasn't allowed to sit at the table, of course), and those evening meals became a nightly ritual. Brian taught me how to work through my daily stresses, showed me that no problem was so great it couldn't be eased with a decent meal, and most evenings we'd end up forgetting our minor tribulations and making plans for our future. We didn't claim to be the perfect couple, we weren't perfect individuals for that matter, but we were truly happy together. So happy, in fact, that I was raring to go on that sunny afternoon in July and had to be virtually restrained by my bridesmaids so that I didn't actually run up the aisle. Apparently, it doesn't do to look too eager! I no longer cared what anyone thought. I simply could not wait to marry Brian.

Stephen, my younger brother, agreed at the very last moment to walk me up the aisle in place of my dad, who was feeling unwell on the day. That was not a surprising turn of events because Dad had been undergoing treatment for bowel cancer and did not feel physically up to the task. The chemo had really taken its toll on him and he looked feeble and fragile, not his usual cheerful self. The fact that he was there at all was sufficient for me, as I was aware the weeks prior to the wedding had been particularly difficult for both him and Mum. She had warned me that he had been anxious the previous night and I didn't want to put him in a situation that would make him uncomfortable. So just a few minutes before I was due to walk up the aisle, Stephen stepped in and took his place.

The ceremony was performed in a picturesque walled garden set in the grounds of the country estate. Stephen and I hid around the corner from the gathering, just out of view behind some trees, waiting for the procession of flower girls and bridesmaids to set off. I was so excited, I couldn't contain my nervous giggles and it wasn't the most mysterious of entrances – the entire congregation could hear my laughter. I've never been accused of being too quiet for my own good and before long my giggling started a wave of laughter that carried through the guests. By the time Stephen finally led me up the garden path to the altar we were skipping and laughing to the joyous sound of whoops and chuckles from everyone present. Needless to say, that moment set the mood for the day.

Brian looked so handsome in his blue suit (he always looked best in that colour, highlighting his deep sea-blue eyes) that I broke with all traditions and kissed him straight away before the formalities had even begun. By now even the celebrant was laughing and any minor nerves that may have been hanging in there were utterly dispelled. We shared our personal vows, I cried as I said mine, Brian winked as he said his and the next time we kissed, just some short minutes later, we did so as husband and wife. I thought my heart would burst with happiness.

What followed was the most wonderful celebration amongst our much-loved family and friends. The sheer joy of our day will be forever ingrained in my memory and heart. For the reception we ate great food, drank fine wine and made terrible speeches – and I include my own in that honourable list. We danced to swing music in the marquee in the sweltering evening heat. Well, at least I did, insisting on dancing with everybody in attendance. Our first dance was a not-so-traditional bounce around the dance floor to Pharrell Williams' 'Happy'. Brian and I were big kids at heart and we both loved the movie *Despicable Me*. One of the first gifts he ever gave me was a giant, singing Minion and when he presented me with it, I took it as a sign that I had met my true match. Beneath that serious exterior, he was just as daft as I was underneath. Even though the choice of song may have surprised some, it had sweet significance to us and we happily made right royal fools of ourselves, twirling around the floor without a care in the world.

After the reception we carried on celebrating until the wee hours in a little 'shebeen' bar on the grounds. This was a highlight of the event: an epic sing-song after-party. Stephen brought the house down with his spectacular vocals, Gerry (my old boss and friend) played guitar till his fingers were raw and we even discovered a piano in the back room that also got a good workout – who knew my pal Lincoln was such a pianist. It was a session to beat them all. Eventually, Brian and I snuck off to the bridal suite at about 4 a.m. and left the remaining revellers, of which there were quite a few, to continue the music until nigh-on breakfast time.

To this day the euphoria of our wedding is the most difficult thing to bring to my mind. It's the sweetest memories that hurt the most. Stupidly, I assumed then that our joy would never end, but four days later our happiness was totally erased and the wedding laughter that rang out on 19 July would quickly become a thing that belonged in the past.

4

THE FIRE

Athens was my choice of honeymoon destination. My name has Greek origins and I've long felt a connection to that country. I even studied classical studies in college, though I wasn't exactly a diligent student. I basically attended the odd class, honed my 'borrowing notes' skills and pretty much crammed my way into attaining a degree. However, I truly loved the mythology, literature and historical magic of that country and had wanted to visit Athens since I was a student, but had never got around to it, so I persuaded Brian that we should go there for the honeymoon and use it as a base to explore the neighbouring islands. He wasn't a fan of strong heat in the summer, but he agreed. For that act of persuasion I will carry guilt for the rest of my days. My never-ending list of guilty regrets that keep me awake at night begins with my choice of honeymoon location.

On Saturday 21 July, two days after the wedding, we flew to Athens, where we planned to holiday for two weeks. We booked a stunning house, Villa Aliki, in Mati, a little seaside town not far from the port of Rafina. The owner, Aliki, greeted us upon arrival with some delicious home-cooked moussaka and proudly took us on a tour of the villa. She could not have been more hospitable, describing the local amenities, recommending beaches and restaurants. Given that it was our honeymoon, she even offered to cook us a special Greek feast on a night of our choosing. Upon leaving, Aliki warned us that on some rare occasions the electricity could be cut off in Mati and in that case we would need to manually open the electric gates that surrounded the property. I distinctly remember thinking that a little electrical shortage wouldn't infringe upon our honeymoon and must confess that I didn't really listen to her instructions. Thankfully, Brian, being the sensible one, did. The funny thing is that I believed that a power cut would be somewhat romantic: surely there are worse things than being locked in the villa in darkness with your new husband?

We enjoyed our first day there together, relaxing, swimming and eating tasty local cuisine and then passed our first evening exploring the port. We were on cloud nine.

The next day, Monday 23 July, we woke up late and Brian made us a delicious brunch that we decided to eat in the shady part of the garden, behind the kitchen. We had stocked up on lots of local delights that first day in the supermarket and now we feasted on tzatziki, stuffed vine leaves, salads, meats and olives. Like silly teenagers we giggled as we excitedly changed our Facebook status from 'In a relationship' to 'Married'. We also planned how we would spend the next few days, discussing what historical sites took our fancy, which islands we would travel to and explore.

It was incredibly hot that day. I imagine the temperature had to be in the late 30s by noon. We decided to cool off in the pool after our meal, the water providing much-needed refreshment from the burning heat. It wasn't exactly what you'd call a vigorous swim, more a lazy dip, and when we climbed out it took us just minutes to dry off in the sun. Soon the heat became too much, even for a sun-worshipper like me, and we took shade in the porched patio area at the side of the house.

I reminded Brian that it was his mother Rosemary's birthday and suggested he give her a call. Brian called her on speakerphone and as he contentedly puffed on a cigar, we both wished her the best. The conversation was brief as Rosemary was in the middle of a celebratory lunch with her friends. Brian finished the call by sending his love. This was the last time they ever spoke to each other. There is some small consolation, I suppose, in that his parting words to his mother were, 'I love you.'

The O'Callaghan Westropp family were no strangers to tragedy. Brian's father, Denis, passed away at just 46 years of age (bizarrely, exactly the same age that Brian was when he was killed). Denis died from complications of the blood condition haemochromatosis, an illness that his son inherited, though in Brian's case it was more easily treated compared to the early 1990s, when it took his father's life. Brian's younger brother, Colin, died just five years after their father, at the tender age of 21. He was killed in a motorbike accident. Rosemary also survived her second husband, Patrick (Pat) Gleeson, so Brian was not only her eldest son but her last living blood relative.

After the birthday call, we decided to retreat back inside the air-conditioned villa. Inside, the house was deliciously chilled after the intense heat of the garden and we decided to take an early afternoon 'siesta'. We made love, the last time we would ever do so, and afterwards I fell into a deep sleep for at least an hour.

I woke up to find Brian was no longer in the bed beside me. In fact, I woke up to the sound of him calling to me urgently to get out of bed and get dressed.

I walked out of the bedroom, pulling on my still damp bikini, which I found strewn on the bedroom floor, and took tentative steps down the staircase. At that stage my greatest fear was that I might slip on the heavy wooden steps and take a tumble. At the bottom of the stairs I found Brian standing, transfixed, by the open patio doors, staring out into the garden and pool area. I was instantly hit by a sheet of blindingly intense heat. The fence along the side of the garden, just a few metres from where we were standing, was ablaze. Brian snapped out of the shock that had held him there and immediately closed the patio doors. He told me to shut the door in the kitchen that led out to the back fence (which was also by then on fire) and I promptly did as he asked.

We knew then that we had to leave immediately.

I cannot explain the panic I felt as I ran back up the stairs to throw on some clothes. I grabbed the first things I could find: a long, white, embroidered dress that I had purchased especially for the honeymoon and a pair of wedge sandals. I believed a long dress might protect my legs and it was the only item made of heavy cotton that I could find in those few terror-stricken moments. Next, I went to the safe and took out our passports, cash and jewellery and threw them into my large white handbag. It probably took seconds, it felt like hours. My body appeared to be moving in slow motion but my heart was beating so quickly it felt as though it was attempting to burst its way out of my chest wall – as it is doing right now as I recall those moments.

By the time I ran back downstairs I could see through the patio doors that the fire was already engulfing the whole back area of the villa and was quickly catching every shrub and tree around the side of the garden. Ominously, although it was still early afternoon, the light was surprisingly dim, the air becoming smokier by the second.

We grabbed the keys to the hire car and bolted from the villa. Once outside the front door, we were hit by the sheer intensity of the raw heat. I had never experienced a temperature like that in my life before, nor do I ever want to again. It felt as though we were breathing in molten air, an unnatural thing to do, like swallowing acid.

We ran to the car, which was parked in the driveway, and jumped in. Brian tried to open the electric gates with the beeper, and for just one fleeting moment I thought we were safe. But the beeper didn't work. The tall electric gates shutting us off from the road outside, from our escape route, weren't budging. It was only clear to us then that the electricity, just as Aliki had warned two days previously, had indeed been cut off. Brian told me to wait in the car while he ran back inside to find the Allen key we had been given for this exact circumstance, to help us open the gates manually. He found the key in seconds and in the blink of an eye was at the gates, trying to winch them open.

Nothing happened.

The gates, which were at least 9 feet tall, didn't budge an inch. I jumped out of the car to see if I could help and we wasted crucial minutes trying to push and pull, cranking the key in the lock, all to no avail. This was our only way out and it was fast becoming evident, as the flames were now surrounding the car and encroaching on where we stood, that there was nothing for it … we could either stay there and be trapped in the burning garden or make a run for it on foot.

I'm not entirely sure how we managed to climb over the gates. I scrunched the long dress up over my knees and Brian helped push me up over the gate, but as I jumped down on the other side I felt my left knee pop out of its socket as I landed awkwardly in my wedge sandals. Later I'd discover that I had dislocated my kneecap. It felt wobbly and unstable, but the adrenaline coursing through my veins at that moment outweighed the pain. There was no time to feel anything, no time to think or delay further. We knew that we were running for our lives.

Like a child I turned to Brian and begged him to assure me that we were both going to survive. He took my hand and told me that we were going to get through this together, promised me that we would make it. We started to run then, scuttling up the main road in front of the villa, but managed just a few hundred metres before we ran straight into an inferno. We were blocked by what I can only describe as a scorching wall of fire. Instantly we turned around and headed downhill in the direction of what we assumed was the sea. It was getting blacker and smokier by the second and it was nearly impossible to ascertain which direction we were running in, or where we would end up. The winds were picking up with whipping force and it felt like we were at the centre of a searing tornado, with burning pieces of fiery debris spinning in the air all around us.

All of a sudden we bumped into a small group of people in swimsuits running up the hill that we were trying to navigate down. They quickly explained that they too had tried to make it to the coast but couldn't reach the sea as the burning trees made the path impassable. We warned them not to take the route we had just come from, but they ignored us and kept moving forward. A woman in the group shouted back to us that the direction we were taking would bring us to our doom – well, she used words to that effect – and we were frozen in our tracks, for what could only have been seconds, trying to work out what our next move should be. It was like being stuck in a living nightmare. The people in swimsuits were suddenly gone and we were terribly alone again. They had literally disappeared into the dark and it was now just us two, surrounded by fire, breathing boiling air that burned our throats and handicapped by the thick, smoggy smoke that stung our eyes.

The next few minutes were horrifically confusing. We turned again uphill, to try a different route up yet another road. It was so dark now that it was getting even more difficult to find our way. In truth, I'm not even sure if we were going in a new direction or back on the original path we had taken just minutes before. It was hot, so terribly hot. I suddenly realised that the end of my long dress was alight. The pretty white embroidery was now a hellfire red and the flames that were curling around my ankles and calves were biting at my skin and lapping swiftly towards my thighs. I screamed and stopped in my tracks. Brian instantly bent down and put out the flames with his bare hands. My legs were badly singed, Brian's hands must have been burned too, and I wanted to cry, but we couldn't stop, there wasn't time. We had to keep running.

We were now back on what seemed to be the main road, possibly the same road we had started out on. In the midst of the clouds of smoke and flames we encountered a small group of children, maybe four, maybe five of them, standing in the middle of the road. It was as though they had appeared by magic, materialising out of the smoke. The children looked so small and petrified and they were staring directly at us. One of them was in a nappy, a mere toddler, dazed and confused. The smog was so dense, we couldn't see if they had any adults with them. The shock of seeing such vulnerable little people made us forget our own predicament. We ran to them, the instinct to rescue kicking in.

At the very moment we reached the children, a car miraculously emerged on the road, chugging in our direction. It was first vehicle we had seen since we'd left the villa. Like the people in the swimsuits and the children we were now trying to comfort and protect, the car seemed to appear out of thin air, as if it had been hiding all along behind the thick, smoky clouds. It was crawling up the hill and our muddled little group happened to be standing directly in its path. The motor looked very old and barely roadworthy and was moving so cautiously that I could make out the two people in the front, an elderly man and woman and another adult sitting in the back seat. We stood still, waved and begged the driver to stop. He did. Brian and I scooped up the children in our arms and barrelled them into the back seat. It was only then we realised that with the car full to the brim, there wasn't enough room for us. I shouted to the driver to open the boot, as that was the only place Brian and I could now fit. Behind and all around us the fire was quickening. The boot of this car was our best chance of survival.

The driver did as I asked; he popped the boot and we climbed in. It was a small space and we were too big for such a confinement. We couldn't shut the cover completely over our bodies, so we had to hold it half closed with our hands, curling ourselves into an uncomfortable position. The car took off, at a greater speed than before, and we desperately clung to the edge of the boot cover with our fingers in an attempt not to fall out. At this stage I realised that my dress was once again on fire, eating ferociously into my legs, torso and arms. My long hair had also caught fire and as it burned and stuck to my face, I could feel my skin melt. The pain was excruciating. The driver was now moving at a considerable pace and Brian was doing his best to comfort me, attempting to stamp out my smouldering dress with his free hand, while still holding onto the boot cover with the other. I also tried to batter out the flames that were cooking my hair and face and I remember thinking that the pain in my face was so extreme, I was surely melted beyond recognition.

Brian was muttering something to me, or was he praying? I couldn't tell. I couldn't hear properly, the sound of the raging fire roaring in my ears was so loud. If I had known a god, perhaps I would have prayed too, but the burning agony all over my body was all I could focus on and the fear of what would come next was all-consuming.

The driver was racing up the hill now, trying to escape the searing fire that was chasing us, the flames lashing us through the half-open boot. And then suddenly the car crashed. It ran straight into a large, burning tree that, like everything else in this hell, seemed to emerge suddenly from nowhere. The entire tree collapsed on top of the car, its huge, flaming branches falling directly into the now wide-open boot, and Brian and I were smothered in a blanket of burning debris. My poor darling husband got the brunt of it. His clothes instantaneously burst into flames and in a split second he rolled out of the boot, screaming in shock and agony, onto the open road. I tried to grab him, tried to pull him back into the boot, but he rolled too quickly and much too far from my grasp. There, right in front of me, he was engulfed in fire.

The last word he screamed out, a long, agonised scream of sheer terror, was: 'Why?'

And then he was gone. He vanished before my eyes, into thick black smoke.

There was nothing more to do then. It was over. I gave in to the heat and believed this was my final moment, too. I lay in the car boot that had become a searing oven with my legs, arms and face all cooking now. With the only breath I had left in me I called out for Brian, hoping the last thing he would hear was his wife, the woman who adored him above all others, calling out his name. I could no longer see him, no longer hear him, but I kept calling out to him, with all the strength I could muster.

Perhaps it is because I called out for Brian that I was discovered in the boot of the car and rescued.

Through the wall of fire that was now surrounding the vehicle, I could faintly make out the shape of a big man in firefighter gear. He reached down and carefully but swiftly lifted me from the boot of the car. I was informed much later that at first he thought I was dead, so badly burnt and so very still was I in my metal coffin. It was only when I let out a whimper and opened my right eye (my left was melted shut) that he realised I was still alive. Had he arrived a few seconds later, I'm sure that I would indeed have died. The man who pushed through the burning inferno that had engulfed the car is called Manos Tsaliagos. It is to him that I owe my life.

Manos valiantly carried me out of the wreckage, through more flaming trees, protecting my face with his arm, until we eventually reached safety, just metres away on the other side of that burning wall of fire. Brian had been just metres away from survival. All the while the fireman spoke to me gently in Greek, in a comforting tone, but I couldn't understand what he was saying. I begged him to turn back and find Brian, knowing that he was so close by, but I was requesting of him an impossible task. There was no going back there, not on that day. In my heart of hearts I already knew that Brian was lost to me, knew what I had seen with my own two eyes. But my mind was desperately trying to delete that image and deny the truth, so I kept begging, just in case I'd got it wrong.

I was carried out of danger's way and eventually lifted into the front seat of a fire engine that was waiting further up the hill. We took off at a serious pace, with Manos hanging on outside the vehicle, gripping the window. There mustn't have been room for him inside, though I couldn't tell you how many people were in that front seat. I think shock must have begun to set in. I recall staring at my left hand, watching the skin begin to fall off, like a piece of overcooked meat. We raced through more flames with my rescuer still hanging on outside, still speaking to me through the crack in the window. At one stage I turned my head towards him and he smiled and nodded as if to reassure me that soon I would be safe. Right then I believed that I would never be safe again.

Petrified, I continued to stare down at my left hand and soon it no longer resembled a hand at all. It was the stuff of horror movies: the skin and flesh were melting off right in front of my eyes, creeping away to reveal bone and tissue underneath. All I could smell was my singed hair, which was now matted in a gluey consistency against the side of my face. The long, white embroidered dress was unrecognisable. What was left of it was black and tattered and it was burnt off right up to my thighs. I wondered if my face was as unrecognisable as my clothing.

The fire engine eventually reached a small hut on the outskirts of the town and Manos very gently carried me inside and placed me on a wooden bench against the back wall. He handed my care over to a young woman and left. I guess she was a volunteer as she wasn't wearing a uniform of any kind. Unfortunately, she didn't speak English and I had no Greek, so communication was an immediate problem. I realised that my dress was still smouldering and even if I hadn't seen the flickering embers of fabric melting into my stomach, I could certainly feel them burn. I begged the woman to quench my burning clothes, to cut them off my body, but she didn't seem to understand what I was saying. My body was so badly burnt at that stage that I couldn't move, otherwise I would have torn the fabric away from my flesh. The woman found a small bottle of water and offered me a drink, but I gestured to my burning torso with my good hand and finally she seemed to understand. She poured the contents of the bottle over me, but it wasn't enough to douse the burning and I began to truly register the pain that was all over my body. I became hysterical, begged her to stop the burning, pleaded with her to cut off my clothes. I could feel the hot fabric eating into my skin, burrowing into my flesh. I made a scissors sign with my fingers. She understood. In seconds, she had cut off all my clothes, my bikini top and wedge sandals.

I looked down at my body. The raised embroidery pattern that I had initially loved so much on the dress was imprinted on my arms, my chest and my stomach. My sandals likewise had left their mark. In fact, I still wear the scars on my left foot, the woven print from the sandal permanently singed into my flesh. I am forever branded with a reminder of this nightmare day.

Gently the volunteer proceeded to pour water from more small bottles over my body, hair and face, as I lay exposed on that wooden bench. Once she had properly doused me, I was covered in a tinfoil blanket, to protect what was left of my modesty. Like Manos before her, she tried to comfort me as best as she could, but with the language barrier there was little more she could do or say to help me. My body temperature was peaking and plummeting at an alarming rate; I was boiling one second, then freezing to my core the next. I started to shake uncontrollably. The only distraction from this torture were the people, fire-fighters and some local volunteers, who kept coming in and out of the hut every few minutes. Each time somebody new entered I'd look up expectantly, praying that it would be Brian. But of course he never appeared. I beseeched anybody who would listen to go back and find my husband. I don't think the language barrier was the obstacle. There simply was no going back to where I had been rescued from.

Eventually a man entered the hut and explained to me in broken English that once the road was clear they would take me to hospital. He also responded in a firm tone, to my continued pleas for Brian, that the road from which I had come was now closed off. He told me it was forbidden to go back there that day and then turned on his heel and left the cabin. I learned many months later, however, that Manos did in fact go back, with some other men, to that particular stretch of road and saved several other lives. They were true heroes that day. This I only discovered many months after the fire, and it would be a long time before I had the chance to thank the man who saved my life.

After some time, how long I couldn't guess, the ambulance arrived to transport me to hospital. That journey seemed like the longest of my life, not least because of the mental anguish and physical pain I was enduring without any medications to numb the symptoms. I couldn't peel my eyes away from my left arm and hand, once again transfixed by the grotesque image before me. It now looked skeletal, with bare bones visible and scraps of flesh clinging on here and there. My fingers had begun to curl into a claw-like fist. My face felt like melted wax and I couldn't help thinking that if my hand was this badly damaged, how deformed must my face be? I had now lost all vision in my left eye as it had sealed up entirely.

The two men in the ambulance – I'm assuming they were paramedics – appeared at first not to speak any English, although it probably wouldn't have made much difference if they had. I expect I was raving at that stage because I was in absolute agony, yet they didn't offer anything to alleviate the pain. I started to cry. I didn't know how else to demonstrate my anguish. They ignored me. They seemed far more interested in carrying on a conversation than helping their patient. One of them even told me to 'shut up' now and then, in perfect English, when my cries became too loud and interrupted their exchange. At one stage they actually started to giggle. That very nearly brought me to breaking point. I thought to myself: I have lost everything I love, my life and my future have been stolen from me, and these men are laughing. I was incensed. I wanted to scream at them, to make them be quiet, but quickly my fury evaporated into resignation. I stopped wailing. It really made no difference if these total strangers laughed or not. They didn't care what I felt and, frankly, it really didn't matter. Even if they had been kind to me, it wouldn't have changed anything because nothing would ever feel right again. Just four days ago I had married the love of my life: now he was dead, and I was alone. I closed my eyes and tried to envisage Brian's face on our wedding day, his cheeky grin, the way he kept winking at me as we exchanged vows … I drifted away.

When we eventually reached the public hospital, it was clear to me that while I felt very much alone, I certainly wasn't the only person injured from this wildfire. It was evident, as I was stretchered into the hospital, that this fire had consumed a much bigger area than that one small patch of road in Mati.

The emergency department was in pandemonium. Everywhere I looked, I saw men, women and children laid out on beds and stretchers. Like me they were burned and bleeding, many with faces so damaged it was as if they were made of melted wax. The stench of stale smoke and cooked flesh made me gag. The sound of people wailing was deafening.

I was placed on a gurney in the corner of the emergency department. As I lay there for what must have been several hours, with swarms of other victims around me, I found my mind wandering, trying to work out how I had ended up there and why this had happened to us. I began to create a self-admonishing list of 'what ifs':

What if I hadn't insisted on Greece as our honeymoon destination? It was my fault we were there in the first place!

What if I hadn't slept so long after we made love, maybe we would have escaped quicker, before the electricity was cut off. It was my fault because I had delayed our escape!

What if I hadn't let go of Brian's hand as he rolled out of the burning boot and fell into the flames?

It was too much to bear, the thought that I could have rescued Brian by holding on to him tighter.

My fault, my fault, everything was my fault!

The guilt was overwhelming. I couldn't catch my breath. I started to panic and must have cried out loud because suddenly there was a man by my side, hushing me and trying to comfort me. The great blessing was that he spoke English. He was the first person I had encountered who could understand me. That realisation calmed me down. The stranger asked me where I came from and I explained that I was Irish. I gave him my name and asked for help in finding my husband. I was still in a total state of denial as to what I had witnessed on that road in Mati. He explained that he was a social worker and that he would endeavour to get me some help. His parting shot was that he knew somebody in the Irish embassy who could assist me. And then, as so many people had done the whole day long, he too disappeared.

5

A FACE STRANGELY FAMILIAR

I spent several hours on the gurney in A & E, although I couldn't say exactly how many as I was slipping in and out of consciousness. I do remember a young doctor cleaning my face and body with some liquid solution that temporarily cooled my burning skin and I overheard him discuss my condition with another medic. I got the distinct impression, from their grave expressions, that amputation of my hand may have been the topic of conversation. He asked me about medical coverage, and it was only in that instant I realised that I had the insurance card in my purse. Incredibly, even with all the mayhem of the fire, from the moment I was rescued to my arrival in that hospital I had managed to hang onto my handbag. I hardly believed it myself! There it was beside me, tucked under the tinfoil sheet. Inside the partially melted white leather were both of our passports, my phone, our jewellery and my wallet, along with some other items. In my wallet the medic found the lucky ticket that would transport me out of A & E: my health insurance card.

Once I had produced proof of coverage, I was moved swiftly to a floor high up in the hospital, away from the chaos of the emergency room. However, this was not the saving grace it appeared to be. Placed in the corner of a room, by a window, I was immediately hidden from view by a long translucent curtain that the nurse pulled shut. There I was left to my own devices, without any assistance or pain relief, for what seemed like an eternity. The pain, the burning sensation all over my body intensified aggressively. It was torture heaped upon torture.

I caught a glimpse, out of my right eye, of a frightening reflection in the window by my bed. It was a terrifying vision, my *Phantom of the Opera* mask moment. My face was unrecognisable to me. My left eye was still sealed shut behind a melted, blackened char down the left side of my face. I called out for a nurse, begging for some pain relief. Whatever cooling solution the medics had used in A & E had long since worn off. No longer able to move my arms or legs, it was as though they were set in cement; every motion I attempted to make was agonising. I called repeatedly for a nurse, even spotted several walking up and down the wards, but no one came. Hours passed …

There was a nurse in my ward. She was tending to numerous patients quite close to me but was purposely giving me the deaf ear. Eventually she pulled back the curtain and explained in a terse manner that no medication would be given until I was seen by a doctor. I begged for a simple paracetamol, anything to help dull the excruciating pain. She refused, closed the curtain behind her and stomped away.

It now had to be very late at night, perhaps the early hours of the morning, as it was pitch-black outside the window. Closing my good eye, I tried to will away the day, to make it all untrue. More time passed. Still no doctor and still no pain relief. I wondered if I had simply been left to die alone in agony, hidden behind the curtain. Actually, that wasn't such an unappealing thought. I could be released from my torment and be with Brian once more. I allowed myself to drift off and imagined joining him on the other side.

Suddenly, quite surprisingly, I was awoken from my delirium by a woman's voice gently calling my name. Opening my right eye to check if she was real or just a figment of my imagination, I observed a pretty woman, about my age, standing by my bed, smiling anxiously at me. She said my name again and I cleared my throat and quietly confirmed that, yes, I was indeed Zoe. The amazing thing was that, though she was a stranger to me, she possessed a face that was strangely familiar. That face was the first comforting thing I had seen since ... well, since we had left the villa.

I soon realised that the woman was not alone, that she had a companion and that they were speaking to me in an effort to wake me. It turned out the social worker I had met in A & E had done as he had promised and tracked down two people from the Irish embassy. They had come to my rescue. One was a local called Aliki (by curious coincidence, the same name as our villa owner) and the other was an Irish woman called Marianne. It was Marianne's smiling face that I seemed to recognise, but I couldn't put my finger on how I knew her. It was much later, many weeks after that night, that we finally worked it out: we'd studied ancient Greek civilisation in college together over two decades earlier. Life seemed to be throwing coincidence upon coincidence at me that night, though at the time I didn't made that connection. All I registered was a feeling of incredible relief. Marianne and Aliki were there to help me; somebody had finally come to my aid. The comfort of hearing an Irish accent and seeing a gentle, kind, faintly recognisable face brought me more solace than I can explain.

Interestingly, when my embassy visitors arrived, the nurse who had consistently ignored me for hours displayed a sudden and dramatic change in attitude. All at once she appeared by my bedside, checking my vitals and feigning concern. I explained to Marianne and Aliki that I had been refused pain medication up to this point, and we worked out that I had been there for over eight hours by then. This was when I discovered the power of having an official in your corner. Marianne and Aliki went to work at lightning pace, finding a doctor and ensuring I finally received blessed pain relief. That task was completed within minutes and once the injection began to take effect, I finally began to think more clearly.

I showed Marianne my handbag and asked her to retrieve my phone. Dawn had broken by that stage, and I was aware that my family, Brian's mum Rosemary and our close friends might soon hear of the fire on the news. I needed Marianne to make contact and explain the circumstances. In confidence I whispered that I believed Brian probably had not survived and gave her a description of my husband, of his tattoos and scars, that would aid identification. In my heart I desperately hoped that he too had been rescued and was perhaps in this or some other hospital, but in my head I knew that was simply not true. Marianne wrote a list of people to call, beginning with my brothers. Due to my father's fragile state of health, I knew the news of this event would be best coming from one of them. Marianne took care of everything, making a note of all the essential phone numbers straight away in case my phone died. I entrusted her with my handbag and its contents, happy to have one less thing to worry about.

Clearly the public hospital was overrun with patients, such was the magnitude of the fire, but still Marianne was horrified to hear that I had been left so long without any medication. She believed that I would receive better care elsewhere and, given the serious nature of my injuries, suggested that the Mitera private hospital would be better equipped to help me. She gently persuaded me to make the move. The doctor who had just appeared and the nurse who had ignored my pleas for help all night long suddenly became uncooperative when they realised that we wanted a transfer. Now they were terribly eager to keep me here, telling me that with my level of medical insurance I would have excellent care at their facility. I couldn't help wondering what happened to those without healthcare in that hospital. They refused to sign my discharge papers and a whispered argument began at my bedside.

All the while I looked to Marianne. She was the person I'd decided to trust with my life. It was clear she knew the lay of the land locally and I was relieved to make no more decisions for the time being. As I had done with my handbag and its contents, I handed over my care to her and agreed to the transfer and whatever else she advised.

Within an hour I was on the move again, this time with Marianne beside me, in a private ambulance hurrying to the Mitera intensive care unit. This ambulance journey was very different to the one I had experienced the previous day, with Marianne and the paramedics by my side comforting me and tending to my wounds all the way. Once we reached the second hospital, for the first time since this terrifying ordeal had begun, I started to feel safe at long last.

Safe enough at least to finally close my eyes and sleep, just for a minute or two ...

6

A SAFE COCOON

have vague memories of those first few hours in the Mitera hospital. I can certainly recall being given some serious medication upon arrival: the blessed relief was heaven-sent. Marianne eventually left my bedside and I was brought into theatre almost immediately. I was placed under the care of one of the hospital's leading surgeons, an expert in plastic surgery, Mr Georgios Moutoglis. It was clear from the get-go that he was eager not to waste any time and for my first procedure I wasn't fully sedated. Mr Moutoglis explained, as he began to examine my left hand, that he needed me to be somewhat responsive to determine how extensive the nerve and tissue damage was. I remember him moving my fingers – I think I saw bones poking through as he did so – and manipulating the hand and wrist. I felt very little pain with all of the medication I had under my belt, but I remember the unnatural sensation as he worked. Even in my semi-delirious state I understood he was doing all he could to ensure the hand could be salvaged.

By then, after everything that had occurred in the past 24 hours, I'd actually begun to accept the possibility of losing my hand. My mind kept wandering off to thoughts of my eldest nephew, John's son Theo. Then 15 years old, he had been born, for some unexplained reason, without hands. As a family, watching him grow and thrive over the years, we didn't see a child with a disability but an amazing young man who could overcome any obstacle thrown in his path, once he put his mind to it. In truth, I often forgot that Theo was without hands and though he had to deal with some huge challenges that other children and adults would never encounter, I never tagged him as 'disabled'. That just wasn't a term I could apply to my nephew. I preferred to see him as he was: a mighty, brave warrior.

Theo was stubborn (a Holohan trait for sure) and constantly refused assistance, even as a baby, working out ways to overcome the many problems he had to learn to solve. I watched him with fascination for the first few years, my heart bursting with admiration as he learned how to do everything his friends and younger brother could do, occasionally with prosthetics but for the most part without. That was probably the reason I regularly forgot that he had this impediment. I just saw him as an ordinary, yet extraordinary, teenage boy.

I suppose then that in my family missing a limb wasn't inconceivable and perhaps, because of Theo, it wasn't as terrifying a concept as it could have been. His coping skills and phenomenal attitude to life in general had always been inspirational. I lay there, while recuperating from that first stint in surgery, and I came to the conclusion that if my incredible nephew could survive and thrive without hands, then surely I could cope with just one. I reckoned he could even teach me a trick or two along the way.

Mr Moutoglis gently explained to me that he believed they could save my hand, or at very least he promised to try his very best to do so. Looking at his earnest face, I decided to trust him. I felt safe under his care and reckoned he would do everything in his power to keep me that way. Perhaps it was the air of authority he carried that inspired my trust. It was clear he was highly respected amongst the doctors and nurses. More likely, though, it was the fact that he was a thoroughly likable guy. For one with such a responsible role, Mr Moutoglis always had a little glint, a smile behind those eyes. He exuded warmth and kindness and I believe that was the main reason he was so well regarded by his staff. During my time at the Mitera, he showed me immense sensitivity and compassion yet also displayed a lovely sense of humour. He became the person I relied upon above all others. As it turned out, my confidence in him was well founded.

I was immediately placed on a rota of surgeries, one every two to three days and each focusing on a different area: my face, chest, arms, hand and, of course, legs. My legs and hand were the worst afflicted, with third- and fourth-degree burns. It was a constant blur of surgery and recovery, but with a little help from my new best friend morphine, my pain levels were kept well under control. Mr Moutoglis was always there, surgery or no surgery, keeping the closest eye on his patient. His reassuring presence and cheery manner always made me smile – even on the scarier days. Before this time in my life I had surgeons typecast, and his kindness and gentle nature weren't what I expected from a man in his position. I had always assumed that great surgeons would have even greater god complexes. Mr Moutoglis quickly dispelled that theory and changed my opinion. Yes, he knew my tragic position, and that could have been the reason he showed me such empathy and humanity, but I have no doubt he treated every patient that crossed his path with the same dedicated care.

Soon I became accustomed to the ever-revolving door between ICU and the surgical theatre. I lost count of how many surgeries occurred in those first couple of weeks. My legs were so severely damaged that walking was impossible, so I was transported everywhere on a gurney. Even moving my legs in the bed was hopeless, as they were so heavily bandaged. Likewise, both arms were an immovable feast under all their swaddling and my left hand was banjaxed. Initially my face was charred to such an extent, with my left eye closed over, that it was anybody's guess if I would ever see through that eye again. Even in my semi-sedated state, the thought of going blind frightened me. I still hadn't recovered from the shock of seeing my reflection on that first night in the other hospital – that image had been haunting me ever since, so I thought it best not to know what I looked like. Having always been quite image-conscious (some call it vanity, I call it insecurity), now I couldn't bear to look in a mirror. I was terrified that what lay beneath the blackened char was an utterly disfigured face, so all reflective surfaces were banned from ICU. Anyway, for now there were more important things to concern myself with, survival being top of the list. The face stuff – well, maybe I was better off not knowing for the time being.

While I was recouping my strength after surgery, I was placed in recovery, safely cocooned in the ICU. My injuries were so severe that I couldn't have even the lightest of sheets touching my skin, so for my protection I was placed in a metal frame that was basically a loose cage around my body. Attached to one end of my cage was a tubed contraption that constantly pumped warm air over my limbs. This kept my topsy-turvy body temperature – sometimes hot, sometimes freezing cold – under control. Anybody who has experienced burns knows that maintaining an even temperature is difficult, so the air pump resolved this issue and gave me great comfort.

I became quite attached to my special cage and christened it my little cocoon. Maria, one of my nurses, told me the Greek word for cocoon was *koukoúli*. We often joked, when it was time to change my burn dressings or when I had to be prepped for surgery, that I had become a little too fond of my *koukoúli*. I was not only accustomed to the warm air that was continuously pumped over my skin but also to the security of being hidden away in my cage. Tucked away in there, my entire body was concealed, with only my head poking out at one end, though my right hand did occasionally have a public viewing. In a childish way it became my armour and I believed my little fortress would keep me safe from any further pain. Sadly, not even my precious *koukoúli* could protect me from the agonising news that was coming.

On the afternoon of Tuesday 24 July, I was having a quiet moment alone in ICU and my mind wandered back to the fire and to the moment the car crashed. I started to question my own memories and pose an alternative view on what could have happened. Suppose I was wrong about what I thought I had witnessed, then perhaps Brian hadn't died there on that smoky path? If I had been rescued from the boot of a burning car, moments from death, then surely it was entirely possible that Brian could also have been saved at the last second? It wasn't beyond the realms of possibility that, in the confusion of the crash and with such dense smoke all around, I could have missed another volunteer rescuing my poor husband and saving him from the inferno. I banished the memory of Brian screaming out in agony when he fell out of the boot, deleted the vision of him rolling into the deadly flames and conjured up a new, wonderful reality of Brian, alive and recuperating elsewhere, in some other ward, perhaps even in this very hospital. I worried then that he may have been badly injured or suffering in pain. I knew that he would be as anxious about me as I was about him and so was desperate to get a message to him, to let him know that I was alive.

My worry became fear as I envisaged him seeing my face in its current condition, and I hoped I wasn't so deformed that he wouldn't recognise his bride. Even with all of these emotions whirling around in my mind, hope still won out. My fantasy (or delusion) of his rescue outshone any of my fears and secretly I convinced myself that Brian was still alive.

I recall speaking to my family that evening, with one of the nurses kindly holding the phone to my ear as I couldn't manage to do it myself. I reassured them that I was going to make it. I also told them that there was still a distinct chance that Brian would be found. Yes, he had been declared missing like many others in the chaotic aftermath of the disaster, but he hadn't been found, and that meant he could still be alive and recovering in a hospital somewhere.

Marianne had contacted my family as soon as I was settled in the Mitera hospital. My older brother, John, immediately caught a plane to Athens as soon as there was one available. My parents were unable to travel to Greece. Dad was simply too ill to make the journey and my mum stayed by his side, caring for him as she had done through every step of his illness. I'd no comprehension at that time just how seriously ill my father had become, believing, once those last sessions of chemo were complete, that he'd be finally cured. During the days and weeks after the fire, Mum did everything she could to hide the gravity of Dad's deteriorating health from me. That's what mums do: they protect their children (even as adults) from the worst.

It was well over a year before I discovered the truth about what had gone on at home during that period. While Mum acted as though everything was fine in Ireland, at the same time I did my best to put a positive spin on my situation in Greece. As emotional as that first call with my parents was – it was the first time I'd spoken to them since my wedding day less than a week before (a lifetime ago) – it was also one filled with false positivity on both sides.

John arrived in Greece on Wednesday 25 July, just two days after the fire, and unbeknownst to me was taken straight to the Irish embassy and then directly to the morgue. While I was busying myself with daydreams about Brian's rescue, John was identifying my husband's body.

That Wednesday evening, John finally arrived at my bedside in the Mitera. I was overjoyed to see my big brother; there simply aren't words to describe how happy I felt having him there. We spoke about my injuries and I told John all about the fire, detailing those final moments before my rescue. It was when I started to speak about Brian and my theory of how he was lost out there somewhere, probably in another hospital, that John realised he was in an impossible position. He knew he had to deliver the worst news that anyone can ever break.

He said, 'Actually, I have some news about Brian.'

I knew then the awful truth – although if I'm honest, I had always known it. My brother's face and the tone of his voice said it all. He kept talking, but I don't remember anything he said after that; my ears started to whistle and the room began to spin. I know John must have said something comforting, but there was no comfort to be had. Not then, not now. My lovely imaginary parallel universe, where Brian and I got to live happily ever after, was obliterated once and for all. My husband was dead.

About a year later I learned that Brian's body had been located exactly where I had seen him last, on that road in Mati, metres from where the car had crashed. John told me that he had been easily identifiable because of his distinct tattoos, but I begged him not to share any more details with me.

Brian's mum, Rosemary, and Adey flew out to Athens the day after John and they also went to confirm identification of Brian's remains in the morgue before coming to visit me. I hadn't wanted Rosemary to see her son in that state, but she had insisted that it was her right as his mother, and that fact I couldn't argue with. I can't recall much of our first meeting, other than their anxious faces and obvious attempts not to cry in my presence. Like John, Rosemary mentioned something about Brian being easily recognisable, but again I shut down that conversation. I suppose that fact should have brought some relief. It meant he must have died from smoke inhalation, a quick and relatively painless death, though really, who can know if this is true?

Rosemary brought up Brian's identification several times over the days that followed, before they all returned to Ireland on the Saturday, but each time I changed the subject. It was a road I just couldn't go down with her or anybody. It wasn't merely the thought of Brian lying on a cold slab in the mortuary, it was the manner in which he had died. Only I had heard his long, agonised cry, the sound that still rung out on my ears every night when I closed my eyes. It was also the fact that I was still alive and that he had been so close to being rescued. It just wasn't a place I could go. I wanted to think of Brian as he was that last morning, splashing around in the pool, laughing and gossiping about the wedding. This was where I always went to in my mind when I needed to regain composure, so it was a place I frequently visited.

If only I had as much control over my subconscious at night-time. Once Brian's death was properly confirmed, my nightmares began in true, vivid horror. Every time I fell asleep, visions of Brian's brutal death would crash into my dreams. This marked the beginning of a long, horrendous spell where I returned nightly to my own version of scorching hell, with flames all around, eating at my body and devouring the faces and forms that surrounded me. Most harrowing was the sight of my poor husband, melting in front of me, reaching out, begging me to hold his hand, begging to be rescued. Try as I might, I never managed to grasp his hand, and so he would die before me, over and over and over. The only way to escape this diabolical persecution was by waking up. Sleep equated torture, so I began to fight it with all my will, doing everything I could to stay awake and avoid those nightmares.

During those long sleepless nights, I lay in my cocoon and wept silently. I became quite good at crying without making a sound, as I didn't want to draw attention. Even when I eventually did sleep, usually from sheer exhaustion, my eyes still seemed to seep water. By morning, my pillows were always drenched with my salty tears.

Beyond my traumatic grief, there was also a physical reason for my tears. The fire had caused considerable damage to both eyes. Mr Moutoglis had ordered a strict regime to salvage my sight during those first few crucial days in intensive care. Every hour, on the hour (night and day), the nurses cleansed and applied ointments and drops to both eyes. I give those nurses and their tender care total credit for saving my eyesight. I've no doubt it is thanks to their dedication that I can see in both eyes to this day.

I cannot say for sure what day my left eye finally opened. I know it was about a week after John confirmed the news of Brian's death, but eventually it cracked open. That was a bitter-sweet moment. My vision, blurred and foggy for the first few seconds, soon became clearer, like a heavy veil slowly lifting. For the first time since I had arrived in the Mitera hospital, the tears that fell from my eyes were ones of joy. I had vision in both eyes.

7

DR TSOPELAS

Apart from Mr Moutoglis, one other figure really stood out in the first few days. His name was Dr Tsopelas, he was my assigned psychiatrist and I met him not long after I was admitted to the ICU. A tall, thin, bespectacled man, he exuded wisdom and intelligence, much like a Greek scholar but in modern clothing. He spoke in a low, calm tone, not quite whispering but quiet enough to make you feel as though your secrets were safe with him. While genteel in manner, Dr Tsopelas didn't pussyfoot around and right on that first evening he asked me some very probing questions to ascertain exactly where my mind was at, beginning with my recollections of what had occurred in Mati. I told him as best I could all that had happened and was even honest enough to reveal the truth about Brian's last moments. The whole conversation was a little surreal, describing my emotions like I was talking about somebody else, a mere observer to my own story.

Naturally, much of that first consultation is now a foggy memory, but I know that we talked for well over an hour, possibly two, while I lay in my bed and Dr Tsopelas sat beside me. We discussed my family, my concern over my father's illness, and mostly Brian. As if in a dream I even described our wedding day and how we came to choose Greece for our honeymoon. Every now and then Dr Tsopelas would ask a question, but for the most part I did the majority of the talking.

When he did intervene, he was direct and got straight to the point, addressing me as one adult to another. He said that I appeared to be of sound mind, given what had just occurred, and reassured me that I was now safe, away from harm. Clearly, as he gauged my response to the tragic events, he was curious to see if I posed any harm to myself. Although, given that I couldn't move my limbs at this stage, I very much doubt I would have been able to do anything to myself, even if I had wanted to. I was honest with him from the get-go, even mentioned that I had suffered from depression on and off for most of my life, commencing in childhood. I told him about my dark days, as I called them, and revealed that there were times in the past that were so overwhelming, suicide had entered my thoughts. That was something I had worked hard to overcome and I was now sufficiently clued in to the workings of my own mind to recognise the warning signs. I promised that if he helped me survive this, I would be completely truthful in every aspect for as long as I remained in Greece. It was almost like making a secret pact in that moment. I was taking him into my trust and I knew he would be keeping a very close eye on me.

Grateful for that close eye on me, I often found myself watching the big clock hanging on the wall outside my room, waiting for Dr Tsopelas' evening visits. Even though I knew I was secure in the ICU, I still found myself in a state of internal terror. This was something I could reveal only to him. His very presence calmed me during those petrifying moments when my psyche echoed and sometimes even relived events from that horrific day of the fire. Haunted by the memory of Brian's death and those last seconds in the car boot when I was convinced I was about to die, I found night-time the worst time, and it was then that I was often blessed with the doctor's company. He would sit by my bedside and we would talk quietly, often for many hours. I know now, as I'm sure he did then, that I was suffering from post-traumatic stress disorder. For the most part the hauntings occurred when I was asleep, but the most terrifying events were those that happened in waking hours. These I called my living nightmares.

My first living nightmare occurred when a young nurse (not one of my usual angels) was attempting to insert an IV line directly into my stomach. For some days the doctors had been having difficulty inserting IVs into the veins in my right arm and my left arm was off-limits, so the nurse had to find another way in. She was, in my humble opinion, a bit of a numpty, not because she chose my abdomen as the location to insert the IV – she was only following orders on that – but because she decided to do it while I was asleep.

Now I'm not a medical professional, but even I would have guessed this was not the smartest approach, as inserting an IV into the stomach is a rather unpleasant, painful process and one guaranteed to wake up any patient, unless they are heavily sedated. I was not sedated, but after fighting the urge to sleep for so many nights, I had finally fallen into a deep slumber.

The nurse appeared to have some difficulty in inserting the IV and, whatever she did, the vein on my side started to spray blood at an alarming rate. I woke abruptly to a sharp pain in my abdomen and the horrific sight of blood spurting out of my stomach. She was clearly panicking, as my blood sprayed all over her white scrubs, and she tried everything to stem the flow. She was stammering in Greek, probably calling for assistance, but I couldn't understand anything she was saying. In a split second, the shocking awakening and the spurting blood triggered my first hallucinatory flashback from the fire ...

My cocoon cage, my safe *koukoúli*, suddenly transformed into the car boot in which I'd been so severely burned on that fateful day. No longer able to see or hear the nurse, the entire ICU disappeared from sight and I was transported back to my own personal hell. The cool glass walls of my cubicle were replaced with scorching flames curling all around me and a burning tree loomed over my head, awaiting its moment of collapse. I froze with terror. I tried to curl my legs upwards, as I'd done before to protect them from burning, but they wouldn't cooperate. I'd lost the ability to move. I was trapped and there was no escape. Burning trees sprung up all around me as the poor nurse was desperately trying to stem the puncture site. I feel quite sorry for her, looking back, because I must have been hysterical at this stage. The blood that continued to spurt appeared to me like fire erupting from my body. Screaming for help, I called for Brian and begged for a release from this agony. My eyes were wide open but all I could see was red, all I could hear was that whirling wind, a tornado of fire screaming in my ears ...

Eventually, a doctor came to the rescue and solved the leaking vein issue. He, like the nurse, tried to calm me down, calling my name, but it was as though his voice was calling to me from very far away, from behind the wall of fire. I'm not sure if he understood what was going on, but his voice finally reached me. Soon the shadows of the doctor and nurse became apparent in the corner of my eye, emerging from the background of my living nightmare like apparitions, wispy figures appearing out of the smoke. I presume at that stage I must have been sedated because I know I stopped screaming and the flames that had covered my body were quenched and disappeared.

When I woke from a deep, drug-induced sleep some hours later, with the IV line firmly inserted into my stomach I might add, I knew what had occurred had been merely a vision. The fact that it had been so realistic was petrifying, though, and I was utterly terrified that this scenario would reoccur. Already afraid of sleep, now I knew there was a chance my nightmares could invade my waking hours, too.

The following day I told Dr Tsopelas what had happened. He listened intently and agreed that the shock of my waking in that manner had probably induced the vision. He promised it would never happen again. I began to understand that Dr Tsopelas must have been quite an important figure in that hospital, as that nurse never came anywhere near my cubicle after that evening and there were no more 'waking surprises'. All procedures were completed when I was either wide awake or under sedation. To assist my rest and help me overcome my fear of sleep, Dr Tsopelas prescribed various different types of medication. It wasn't a straightforward process: some simply didn't work, while others sent me straight to sleep but locked me into my deep traumatic nightmares. There is nothing more terrifying than being trapped in a vivid nightmare, unable to wake up.

In the end, he cracked it. The only way I felt safe enough to sleep and the only thing that really worked for me was good old-fashioned talking it out, so Dr Tsopelas visited virtually every night. He encouraged me to speak about my fears, my past, my lost dreams and hopes for some kind of future. Metaphorically he held my hand and those nightly chats became my lifeline. I'd like to say they stopped the torment, but unfortunately that wasn't the case, although the nightmares did become less gruesome and I, for my part of the deal, allowed myself to succumb to sleep.

I must confess that, looking back on this time, I miss our little chats. We covered so many topics beyond what had brought me to his door: literature, religion (not usually a favourite topic of mine, but I do enjoy the odd philosophical debate), the past and the present. We even delved into my first marriage, family history and my previous episodes of depression. He often asked me if I had suicidal thoughts, and I answered honestly that it wasn't an option for me at that time. I was scared out of my mind for sure but, bizarrely, not suicidal. That baffled me, that at the most calamitous moment of my life I hadn't yet considered ending it all. This topic had been in the shadows of my mind many times in the past, during much less stressful periods than the one I was now living through, yet right then it wasn't even a consideration. Maybe that was because I was in survival mode and had no choice but to keep pushing forward. Or maybe it was because I had that watchful eye and dedicated care of Dr Tsopelas at the most crucial of times. Perhaps that's what made all the difference.

8

THE CALLERS AND THE CAPE

y brothers jetted to and fro, between Dublin and Athens, for the entire duration of my recovery, like a fraternal tag team. We three had always been close and though our life choices and paths differed, I always thought of us as more than mere siblings. We were friends. John, the eldest, took what I suppose one could call the traditional role in life: he was married, with two fabulous teenage boys. To an observer he seemed like the sensible one, but I knew better – he would always be my daft big bro. John was the one I had looked up to in my teens, the dude who knew everything there was to know about 'cool' music and culture. He grew into a wonderful, nurturing father and is the sort of bloke who, like our dad, could always tell a damn good story or a joke with style and ease.

Stephen, the youngest and eternally the baby of the family, even though we're all in our forties, is the sweet, kind, caring one. He has considerable flair, is instantly likable and has entertainer's blood in his genes. Steve also has the sensitive heart to make him my most excellent, lifelong confidant. Like our mum, he has a cracking singing voice and the ability to bring the roof down when he hits the big notes.

I am the middle child of the Holohan siblings and I play the part of loving sister and daughter, secret-keeper, negotiator and problem-solver. Divorced and remarried (and now widowed), I guess I would have been described as a little wayward in my younger years, though I mellowed considerably in middle age. Always independent, a little too loud sometimes (to mask crippling anxiety) and fiercely loyal to those in our inner circle, that's the person I think my brothers had come to know.

As with any family, each of us had assumed roles and even though this tragedy further sealed our sibling solidarity, my position was, at very least, thrown off-course. It was a strange feeling knowing that I may need to rely on my brothers for the rest of my life in a way I'd never done before. I didn't know what health issues and challenges lay ahead and having always thought that, out of us three, I was the one to come to with problems, I was uneasy knowing I was now the problem that required solving. I liked to help, not to be helped. I enjoyed being the organiser. Occasions like Christmas, Easter and birthdays fell under my remit. When Brian was in my life, he joined in celebrating these happiest moments and, being the chef extraordinaire, took over the culinary duties with ease. That would all change now because I was changed. Up until 23 July I had known my place in the pecking order, but now that too would be altered. In fact, it had already begun to change.

John stepped into the big-brother shoes straight away. He took charge of multiple tasks with amazing capability, ensuring that my medical and travel insurance covered my needs, communicating with my work, officials in the embassy and indeed anybody that urgently required an update. He assumed the communicator/managerial role he was born to carry out. It was a relief to know there was somebody whom I trusted with my life there to take charge. Likewise, Stephen demonstrated his greatest skill by taking care of my parents with love and gentleness when the shocking news of the fire broke. He also helped with all the organisational matters, like liaising with the embassy, hospital and my close friends at home. Stephen kept everybody in the loop.

They were the marvellous brothers I had always known them to be, and in this time of crisis they couldn't have made me prouder. The funny thing is that although they had never exactly drifted apart, John and Stephen hadn't spent a lot of time together for some years. It brought me joy (perhaps my only joy at that time) as I watched them become again the team of brothers and true pals they used to be. In the hospital I could see that they started to gel as they had done in their younger years, communicating in ways that only brothers do, delegating and dividing duties and teasing their way through the most delicate of situations. I watched on as they took care of business, grateful that I had them in my corner.

Mr Moutoglis asked me to draw up a list of trusted visitors I would like to see. At that time, I had no idea that there was a media frenzy about the story of the honeymooners caught in the fire, so I didn't know he was doing this to protect me from journalists trying to gain access to the hospital. I drew up a short list of friends, who had to adhere to a rota.

Caroline and her fiancé Fearghal (better known as Ferg) were the first people outside of family to visit. They arrived not long after I was admitted to the ICU. At home, back in Ireland, the four of us – Caroline and Ferg, Brian and me – practically lived in each other's pockets. We were neighbours and as a little posse we were inseparable, wining and dining together at least once a week. We went on holidays, enjoyed ridiculous games nights and were simply partners in crime. Caroline and Brian had studied Chinese medicine together, years before I even met him, and were close friends. When I became his partner, we all became pals, to such a degree that I even chose Caroline as my bridesmaid.

It was a wonderful moment when Caroline and Ferg first arrived in the ICU, as though I was seeing them properly for the first time. I remember thinking what a beautiful couple they made. Though they demonstrated great strength, smiling throughout that first visit, I knew what immense grief lurked beneath. Caroline looked as though she'd wept an ocean and it registered with me that she now had a huge loss in her life to contend with. As a friend, Brian would be simply irreplaceable. I must confess, I wondered then what impact four becoming three would have on our little gang in the future. Would it force us to drift apart? Would I become merely a painful reminder of good times gone bad? Or would I find it too difficult to be around them, now that I no longer had Brian by my side? With these thoughts spinning around in my head, I looked closely at my friends and asked Ferg to take Caroline's hand. I told him to hold it tight and never let her go. Really, I was thinking that if I'd held onto Brian's hand just a little tighter, perhaps we would still be a group of four.

By the time they visited again a couple of weeks later, I had been moved to a private room. They looked truly pleased this time around: by their accounts, my face had much improved. They brought with them stories from home and it was good to hear normal, gossipy nonsense. Brian would have loved it: no matter how hard he protested, we all knew Brian was the biggest gossip amongst us.

Rosemary and Adey also returned after a couple of weeks, accompanied by Adey's gorgeous wife, Lisa. She had also been a lifelong friend of Brian's, knowing first his brother Colin and then Brian himself since their teens. From the moment I met Lisa, just a month after Brian and I started dating, I knew we would get on. She and Adey greeted me with such warmth and I quickly understood why they and their three children were like family to Brian. They were a happy, hardworking, fun family. The nicest quality Lisa possessed was that while she was extremely pretty and graceful, she didn't have an ounce of vanity and was quite shy in demeanour, although that shyness evaporated when we got to know each other properly. Brian had always said that Adey and Lisa were the perfect couple and I had to agree. If nothing else good came from the calamitous situation that befell us that summer, I at least inherited them and their children as my extended family for life.

Lisa certainly didn't arrive empty-handed: I had requested lip gloss for my parched mouth and I reckon she must have purchased every gloss in duty free. It'll take me a lifetime to work through them all! Her luggage was also filled to the brim with get-well cards made by their three adorable children, Callum, Evan and Natasha. My room was instantly transformed into a sparkling kaleidoscope of colour. Let's just say the kids didn't scrimp on glue and glitter. One of the nurses commented that it was like a glitter bomb had exploded, but nobody complained as it was amazing what joy those shimmering cards brought. Callum, Evan and Natasha adored Brian, were grieving in their own right and it saddened me to think they should be touched by death at such young ages. Still, they put all their energy into cheering me up with their magnificent artwork. It also amused me when Adey revealed that they'd adopted a stray cat and named him Brian. The kids were convinced Brian's spirit lived on in this straggly creature. It amused me because anyone who knew Brian would tell you he would have only been reincarnated as a dog, never a cat! Still, I knew it represented the children's desire to stay connected to their uncle.

Soon more cards, letters and parcels reached me from home, though many I didn't open until I returned to Dublin. Mr Moutoglis didn't want me becoming overwhelmed, so their number was kept to a limit each day. Beyond my own family and friends, many had heard of Brian's tragic death and my plight in Greece and I received sackfuls of post from all over the world containing kind messages of support. Some were from total strangers, those who had been touched by tragedy themselves and wanted to reach out; others from people I had known in childhood or relatives that lived as far away as America. It was really strange to receive a letter from a long-lost cousin who has seen my face on American TV. The one thing they all had in common was positivity and love. Their energy boosted me, willed me to keep going. The written word is truly a powerful thing and often during sleepless nights those messages were my only comfort, seeing me through the dark hours until the morning sun would peek through the blinds.

Another constant source of support was the staff from the Irish embassy, led by the Irish ambassador to Greece, Orla O'Hanrahan. She was a warm, charismatic woman who was extremely competent in that time of crisis. Orla, Marianne and the rest of the embassy team kept a close eye on me, managing all the chaos that followed in the wake of the fire. They were on hand to assist in locating and identifying Brian's body, certifying his death and tending to all the official paperwork. The embassy also took extremely good care of my brothers and friends when they came to Athens, helping them with accommodation and transport. When the time came, they even located and retrieved my property from the villa, which miraculously had not burnt to the ground. They saw to the miles of red tape when Brian's remains were to be eventually repatriated and made that emotionally charged process so much easier. Most importantly they ensured that Brian's last journey home was handled in a dignified and private manner. In short, the work that the embassy performed on our behalf was a tour de force and without their help we wouldn't have known where to begin. Orla was even kind enough to drop by frequently to my room for a chat, always with gifts of books or flowers. Her orchid was the only floral gift that I was allowed to keep. Knowing that she and her team were in charge of all the legalities there in Greece brought huge comfort to us all.

Then there was Marianne. She'd been there for me from the very beginning and had become my beacon of hope. To add to my 'glitterati' collection of cards, Marianne's children sent in their own creations. In fact, by the end of my stay an entire wall in my room was plastered with the iridescent glory of these works of art. I know some people detest glitter, but at that time there was nothing that lit up my day more than a piece of card covered with glue and sparkly stuff. It was a guaranteed cheerer-upper. Marianne's kids' creativity didn't end there; they also sent in a bag of gifts that included a Supergirl cape and mask in the most fetching and patriotic shade of green. Marianne told me it was their idea, to remind me of the super-strength I possessed. Now this present may not necessarily have given me the power of flight or X-ray vision, but it certainly smacked a super-smile on my face!

Try as I might, I cannot explain how indebted I felt to Marianne for taking charge of my care that first night. I'll never forget the moment I caught a glimpse of her smiling face out of my 'good' eye and knew that somebody had come to my rescue. She was that one bright light on my darkest night. Like Orla, Aliki and Michelle, the other members of this embassy taskforce, Marianne went way above the call of duty. Naturally, back then I hadn't a clue just how much the embassy did on my behalf, but eventually I learned of the lengths they went to for me.

John and Stephen, Adey and Rosemary had been the first people to arrive from home and immediately it became evident that difficult decisions had to be made with regard to Brian's body and the plan to fly his remains home. I knew I wasn't going to make that last journey back with Brian, but I wanted to ensure that everything was as organised as it could be. I was especially grateful to those four for taking those terrible duties off my shoulders. And, in turn, I was very grateful to the embassy staff for supporting John and Stephen, Adey and Rosemary. They were the rock we all leaned on in those dark days.

9

AN 'EGGSCEPTIONAL' MEAL

The nurses who carefully tended to my visible wounds also saw to those that were less visible: they calmed my haunted soul and held my hand when I cried out in the night. I was grateful to all the nurses for their tender devotion, but there were two in particular that I had a soft spot for, Anna and Maria. These two were my primary caretakers and often went above and beyond the call of regular duty. Like all of their colleagues, they were truly angels on earth.

Anna and Maria were both in their early twenties and to me were beautiful inside and out. Anna had a warm nature and such good humour that she brought huge comfort to all the patients in ICU. She smiled all day long and though her tasks were frequently intensely gruelling and the crucial care unit was packed to capacity after the fire, she still always seemed to have a skip in her step. Her light brown curls, pinned up, of course, bounced along behind her. Even on the worst days I found myself smiling back at Anna. Maria was quieter and had a gentle, caring nature. A mum with a young baby, she was really quite the stunner, with model good looks – silky blonde hair and sparkling blue eyes – but she didn't display any signs of the vanity that usually goes with such advantage. Maria sat by my bedside and talked for hours on the nights when I was most distressed. She would tell me about her life away from the hospital, describing the village where her family lived, distracting me from my own reality. I was delighted that most of the nurses, like Anna and Maria, spoke excellent English, so these chats were a true joy. (And it was lucky because Greek was pretty much all Greek to me!)

Between them, they covered most shifts while I was in the ICU and I quickly became utterly reliant on them. In my little cocoon I felt childlike. It was unfamiliar territory, requiring complete care from people close to half my age when I'm a person who has often been accused of being much too independent by nature. Now I was being spoon-fed and soothed, bathed and bandaged, counselled and comforted by these women, and was totally dependent on them for everything. It's impossible to describe, in retrospect, how much their extra little gestures meant to me. When I couldn't sleep, for instance, Anna would show me pictures of her dogs and describe their naughty escapades. Guiltily, I'd find myself amused for just a few moments. It was akin to telling a child a bedside story, a diversion from my own unique version of the bogeyman.

Sleep wasn't the only thing I was avoiding. Since I'd been admitted, my appetite had completely deserted me. I was so disinterested in food that I would have happily stopped eating and drinking entirely. Mr Moutoglis ordered extra protein in my diet to aid my recovery and begged me to eat more, to help regain strength. I wasn't trying to be difficult, I just had no hunger, and soon found it increasingly difficult to swallow food. As a result, food had become number two on my list of things to avoid. Sleep was number one, top of the heap.

Anna attempted numerous tactics (again, as you would with a child) to coerce me into eating. One evening I took pity on her and promised I'd try my best to consume whatever she served me – well, served and spoon-fed me. She boasted that she made the best cheese omelette in Greece and I gave her my word that I'd attempt to devour the lot. With that promise, she went off to the kitchen to create her masterpiece.

There was an elderly man who lay unconscious in the bed opposite mine in the ICU. I could just about make out his masked face (oxygen mask, that is) over the edge of my *koukoúli* and spent hours, day and night, watching the lights on his monitor dance up and down, like a hypnotic game of Pac-Man. I couldn't turn my head, so his bed, directly facing my cubicle, was my constant view. Sometimes I imagined I was his secret carer and that by observing his monitor, I was ensuring that he continued to breathe with an even rhythm and that his ping-pong, coloured lights kept bouncing around as they should.

That evening, as Anna busied herself making the 'omelette extraordinaire' in the kitchen, the alarm attached to this man's monitor started to beep loudly. The lights began to zip frantically left and right at a much faster pace. Something was terribly wrong, but in the blink of an eye Anna was there by his side, tending to him. I watched silently, praying my old pal (whom I never actually met) would survive. I couldn't bear the thought of watching somebody else die in front of my eyes, but

I couldn't stop looking nonetheless. There was quite a bit of activity around that cubicle for the next while, with numerous doctors and nurses rushing to his aid and blocking my view. Thankfully, they did whatever was needed to alleviate the problem and within minutes, or maybe hours (time is measured differently in the ICU), the old man went back to his regular rhythm of breathing and the Pac-Man machine returned to its even ping-pong pace. I thanked whoever or whatever I had been silently praying to and closed my eyes with relief.

There were always at least six nurses silently and efficiently tending to the patients on that ward. They communicated in low tones so as not to disturb those sleeping and moved as if on wheels, gliding around in circles from bed to bed. Each patient had their own glass cubicle, with a door for privacy when needed. I preferred to keep my door open as much as possible, partly because I was scared something bad would happen if it was shut, but mostly so I could see and hear enough to keep me awake and avoid the dreaded sleep. That night, I observed that the nurses on duty were considerably noisier than usual. There was an air of joviality among them, as if they were trying to smother their own laughter. When I asked one nurse, Aspa, if I could speak to Anna, she swallowed a snigger and told me that she was otherwise occupied. Two nurses close by, hearing Aspa's explanation, burst into a fit of giggles and disappeared in the direction of the kitchen.

Curiosity began to get the better of me, especially when a grinning Anna emerged minutes later and, in ceremonious fashion, presented the omelette. Try as she might to suppress her chuckles, she couldn't quite manage it, and as she placed my dinner on the tray before me it soon became clear that it was the source of all the amusement. I looked at the food, baffled. It appeared to be a perfectly ordinary omelette, yet when I asked what was so funny, Anna looked at my plate and instantly erupted into laughter. The other nurses, who were looking on, likewise started cracking up. When Anna finally regained her composure, she revealed what was so hilarious. In the moments before she tended to the elderly man's needs, she had placed my dinner in the microwave to heat up. It was a new microwave and the time settings were different from the old one. She had intended to set the dial to heat up my omelette for one minute, but having never used this machine before, unwittingly set the timer for one hour. So while she was tending to more serious matters, the microwave containing her precious creation continued to happily nuke my omelette at full heat.

The end result was detonative. In the time it took for her to retrieve the dinner, she had managed not only to eliminate my omelette (she was presenting me with her second creation, it turned out), but also to blow up the brand-new microwave in the process. There was now egg splattered all over the walls of the smoke-filled kitchen. Not so much omelette extraordinaire, more omelette explosive. She even showed me a photo on her phone as evidence of the 'eggstraordinary' disaster. I couldn't help myself, it was one of those ridiculous moments when one has to give in. I burst out laughing. We all did. And so Anna's famous omelette became my most memorable meal in Greece, perhaps not for the reason she would have liked, but because I got to share a moment of much-needed glee with all the nurses. That was almost as nourishing as the omelette itself.

10

HAIR TODAY,
GONE TOMORROW

My hair extensions were my crowning glory, especially those I had inserted for my wedding day. My hairdressers, Jen and Jenny, had painstakingly applied them a few days before the wedding (for the uninitiated, the process takes approximately three hours to complete) and the result was a long, lustrous golden brown- and caramel-toned mane. Less than two weeks later, all their hard work had gone up in smoke, literally. Much of my hair had caught fire and frankly didn't smell too delightful. There is really no stench like burnt hair. The tufts that remained had melted into a solid tangled mass, like a brittle bird's nest on my head. The lengths that had hung in there had matted into chunky dreadlocks, so much so that I christened myself Bob – after the late, great Bob Marley, of course – though his dreads were legendary while my stinky, barbed-wire version most certainly was not.

Anna, Maria and some of the other nurses thought it would cheer me up if they tried to restore my hair to its former glory, or at least try to salvage what they could and make me look relatively human. It was quite the challenge and, I have to admit, almost like a game after a while. First, they had to properly wash the hair. It had been washed in surgery, but that was more a necessary cleansing task as opposed to a wash and blow dry. To be fair, I think the surgical team were more concerned with saving my life than faffing around with my bouffant.

As I could hardly move any of my body, I had to be washed twice daily in my bed by the nurses. They would cautiously bathe me, then gently pat me dry and apply soothing ointments and bandages to my wounds, dressing all the areas bar those off-limits as per Mr Moutoglis' instructions. Bathtime took a long time and we would contentedly while away the time gossiping. My little glass cubicle served me well: it was not only my bedroom but also dining room and bathroom, and now it would become my hair salon as well.

Anna had a genius plan to address the nest on my head. It involved basins of warm water, metres of plastic coverings and, the sweetest part of all, scented shampoos and conditioning treatments she had brought from home. She inveigled two other nurses to assist in this mammoth task and their generosity of spirit simply blew me away. I knew that grooming my hair wasn't essential, and that the nurses were doing all they could to lift my spirits. Their mission: to disentangle, cleanse, moisturise and hopefully save whatever was left on my head. They went to work with gusto, spending hours scrubbing my hair, combing through lotions and potions. We laughed when we actually found a twig (probably from the tree on the night of the fire) deeply embedded in one of my dreadlocks. It really did resemble a nest after all.

Anna's mum kindly sent a honey-based treatment that smelt divine to coat my hair. Although this magic elixir didn't quite restore its former glory, it certainly smelled a lot better afterwards. As well as the scent, the treatment had another surprising side effect. 'Bob' was ready to take on a whole new persona. Anna had managed to divide the hair in two sections at the back of the head, but for some reason it matted again, this time separating into two large pigtails that insisted on turning upward at a bizarre angle. Now, for all intents and purposes, I looked like Pippi Longstocking on a bad-hair day. To be fair, at least my head was twig-free, so I was happy to adopt a new nickname. No longer Bob, I would now only answer to Pippi.

It may seem strange to be concerned with silly vanities like hairstyles at such a terrible time. My reality was not lost on me. I was very aware that my husband was dead, that I was severely burned all over and incapacitated to such a degree that I didn't know if I'd ever use my hand or be able to walk again. There was no denying any of this, but in the midst of all of that hell, ridiculous moments, like attempting to style my deranged hair, actually kept me going. I almost felt normal again when the nurses fussed and attempted to groom my unruly mop and as we nattered, as one does in a regular salon, swapping lessons in Greek and English (though I'm ashamed to admit I hardly remember any Greek words), I was distracted, if only for a moment, from my reality. I can still recall with true warmth the sound of their gentle laughter as they splashed around with buckets of water.

While my hair was challenging, it wasn't the only issue that needed to be addressed in my little 'beauty salon'. My fingernails were also a big problem. I was due for a serious surgery on my left hand. Mr Moutoglis had explained that he was operating on the damaged bones, tendons and skin and by the look on his face as he broke down the procedure, this was the big one. But before anything could happen, my talons had to be dealt with. For the wedding I'd had acrylic nails applied (vanity, thy name is woman!) and the end result would be best described as two-inch long, rock-hard claws. The nails were created from a liquid acrylic that solidifies as hard as cement when set. They were painted a faint, shimmering rose-gold colour to match my wedding dress, and on the day they had looked utterly beautiful. Sadly, my fabulous claws, like my hair, had caught fire and melted into a vicious curl on my left hand. They cut into my nail-bed and the tips of my fingers on both hands and frankly they hurt like hell. More importantly, in order for the surgery to take place, Mr Moutoglis needed the nails filed right down or else they would have to be removed entirely. Regular acetone would not dissolve the acrylic, so we decided to look to an expert for help.

That was when I was introduced to Paulina, the beautician. She worked in a local hair salon and the hospital called her to see if she could assist with my problem. Paulina was a stylish blonde from Poland, with the sort of sleek, silky hairstyle that only a woman working in her profession has. She inspected my nails and assured me she could help. She then disappeared for half an hour and returned with a large case, resembling a doctor's bag, bursting with goodies. From the magic bag she extracted what looked like an industrial sander – well, a smaller version but equally effective. Settling down to the task in hand, slowly she began to file each nail. Boy, was that hilarious! There was literally smoke coming from my cubicle for well over an hour, as my nails smouldered while she cautiously ground them down. Every now and then Vassilis, the big burly male nurse who worked the desk in the ICU, would take a peek into my cubicle and gasp, staring on in sheer horror. It was comical because with all the gruesome sights he must have witnessed regularly in his job, the filing of these virtually indestructible nails, and the gusts of smoke that ensued, seemed to totally freak him out. He probably thought it some medieval form of torture. However, as a woman who had endured far more painful beauty treatments, not to mention recent agonising injuries, this was a piece of cake. All I had to do was stay very still indeed.

When Paulina finished her Herculean task, she revealed my left hand with nails short enough for surgery. Her parting shot was that she would be back in a few days, once I was out of recovery, to address the 'Pippi Longstocking' situation. Well, those weren't her actual words, but she did promise to return and sort out my hair.

1 1

LET IT BLOW

t soon became clear that my path to recovery was going to be a slow and complicated process. Mr Moutoglis knew this and was determined to move me towards progress, and that meant getting out of my precious *koukoúli*. By the end of week two he had ordered the removal of my metal cage and raised the dreaded topic of physio. To be honest, I wasn't going to budge an inch while I had my armoured fortress to hide behind. Anna introduced me to the physiotherapist by declaring that I was about to meet the best-looking man in the hospital. Had she chosen a different career, Anna would have made an excellent salesperson, as she was evidently trying to sell me the concept of physiotherapy. They all knew that I was bound to be a reluctant mover – movement equalled pain and was to be avoided at all costs.

Enter stage left: the physio, Yiannis. By now it must seem like I thought everybody in the Mitera was beautiful. This wasn't a case of rose-tinted glasses or the fact that my eyesight was still a little blurry, it was simply true. Mr Moutoglis led the show with the sparkly-eyed charm of a 1980s TV star. He had the charisma of Magnum PI, Tom Selleck, combined with the handsome, tanned looks of Michael Douglas. It didn't end there. The doctors and nurses gave Dr Dreamy and the whole gang from *Grey's Anatomy* a run for their money. It was ridiculous. Either all Greeks are devastatingly good-looking, and I was getting a mere glimpse of their glory, or this hospital only employed people who belonged on *Greece's Next Top Model*. Of course, the irony of the situation, that I had never looked so hideous in my entire life, made me laugh to myself: I was the only beast amongst a batch of beauties. So when Anna introduced 'the best-looking man in the hospital', my first thought was that this one would have to be an absolute Adonis to claim that title.

Anna brought Yiannis into my cubicle, holding his hand (methinks there was quite a crush there) and giggling like a teenager. Yiannis (forgive me for saying this, Brian) was hot, it was true. He had that olive skin, dark-eyed, shaved-head look – a Mediterranean Bruce Willis, if you will. Anna was thoroughly justified in her crush and I secretly applauded her good taste. As we got acquainted, Yiannis all the while smiling from ear to ear, it occurred to me that the therapy I was about to undertake was bound to be agonising. They'd brought out the big guns, the best-looking therapist in town to distract me from the pain. These guys meant business!

To break me in gently, my first physio session was little more than a chat, but Yiannis explained that from this day forward he would be in twice daily, morning and evening, to work with me. There was quite a slog ahead. My arms, hands, legs and entire core had been effectively frozen – an ironic term considering what brought me there. I had little use of my right hand and arm and none at all of my left arm, which was off-limits due to ongoing surgeries. My legs were clearly going to be the biggest challenge. Thankfully, there was feeling in my toes, but it would take a hell of a lot of work to get me walking again. Before we started targeting any of my limbs there was the matter of those pesky lungs of mine. I had a spot of pneumonia due to smoke damage and my breathing capacity was not up to par. I was weak, wheezing and coughing a lot (sometimes drawing up clots of blood) and our number-one goal was to get those lungs functioning properly. Yiannis promised that he would return later that evening to commence breathing exercises and with that he left.

Unfortunately, what occurred before our next meeting could only be described as a rather unpleasant afternoon. To begin with, my sleep had been particularly bad the night before, disturbed by horrifically brutal nightmares. I tried to nap that afternoon to restore some energy, but it was an eventful day in ICU with monitor alarms going off frequently, so there was little or no peace. In short, I got no rest and was exhausted.

The other disagreeable occurrence is one that I'm rather embarrassed to relate and probably wouldn't except it's pertinent to this part of my tale. I was hooked up to a glorious intravenous morphine drip to deal with the constant pain. For those not in the know, a major side effect of morphine is severe constipation and, without going into too much detail, I hadn't managed to go to the bathroom since I had been admitted to hospital, two weeks before. Nothing was working to alleviate the problem and, believe me, I had tried them all: fruit, laxatives, copious amounts of fluid. It was a lost cause. I finally had little choice but to agree to my first ever enema. Don't worry, I have no intention of describing that exact torture. Let's just say it's no coincidence that *enema* and *enemy* are very similar words. Up until then I'd been bed-bathed, hand-fed and swaddled by the nurses, but now my very last vestige of dignity disappeared. Oh, the humiliation of having poor Nurse Aspa assist me in this most private of moments. (I can't imagine it was a barrel of laughs for her either.) The mortification lingers even now. By the time her mission was complete, I was very much depleted ... in every sense of the word.

It was just minutes after the enema procedure, while I was trying to overcome the utter humiliation of my 'public poopology', that Yiannis bounded into my little glass cubicle, proudly holding a small cardboard box. God love him, he'd no idea of the drama that had just transpired and with his beaming smile and without a word of explanation he proceeded to open the box and remove its contents. He produced a long, blue plastic tube, about 8 inches in length, and a red ping-pong ball. Bearing in mind what had occurred just minutes before, and still haunted by Aspa's implements of torture, I could not help myself. Observing the tube and ball with horror, I exclaimed: 'And where the hell do you think you're going to stick them?'

It was one of those moments, and I have had plenty of them, when the words that should have stayed in my head escaped my lips. I call it foot-in-mouth syndrome, when entirely inappropriate thoughts fly out before I can stop them. It's a lifelong affliction of mine, saying the wrong thing at the wrong time, and when Yiannis pulled out his gadgets, I boomed out those words with such force (for a gal with banjaxed lungs, it was fierce loud) that he just stood there in shock for about ten seconds before, thankfully, exploding into laughter.

Once he started, and I'm talking proper side-splitting laughter, I likewise began to crack up. It was contagious. As the tears flowed from his eyes, I too lost control. We both howled for a good five minutes, unable to speak. My exhaustion and embarrassment evaporated instantly and we were so noisy that Anna even popped her head in to see what all the commotion was about. Neither Yiannis or I could explain, and I certainly wasn't about to reiterate what I'd just said, but I can definitely confirm that laughter was the best medicine that day. You could say my first session of physio was a breath of fresh air! From that moment on, Yiannis and I became firm allies.

Incidentally, the tube and ping-pong ball belonged to a breathing device aimed to help my lungs. Once assembled, the apparatus was designed to make me inhale and exhale – the ping-pong ball moving up and down as I did so. Yiannis later told me that every time he had to give this apparatus to a new patient, he would forever think of me and laugh. I must confess, every time I see a ping-pong ball, I do the same.

12

A ROOM WITH A VIEW

Once Yiannis and I got the whole breathing malarkey mastered, there were bigger mountains to climb, like learning learn how to walk again on severely damaged legs. We knew I wasn't paralysed because I could feel sensation and move my toes slightly, but my legs had suffered intense burns from my thighs to my toes. Now that the cage had been removed, I could see some of the extent of the damage, but I was still too afraid to properly examine my body. Even during my baths and burn treatments, which occurred several times daily, I'd opt to look away and stare at the ceiling while the nurses and doctors did their thing. I desperately tried to think of anything other than my charred limbs.

Mr Moutoglis explained that I would require grafts all over both legs and on my left arm and hand, but naturally I didn't really understand what that would entail. Naively, back then I thought grafts would make it all instantly better, that I would have my old skin back as it used to be. That, alas, would not be the case. However, with constant surgeries, followed by days of recovery, there was little time to ponder these things. It was only at night, when I lay alone and my mind went to the darkest of places, that I'd allow myself to wonder about how physically damaged I truly was.

During the day Yiannis gave me plenty of breathing and flexing exercises to keep me preoccupied. My legs were completely bound in bandages and though I had excellent pain relief, even wiggling my toes hurt. It was a very difficult task to perform. My brain signals weren't reaching my toes at a normal pace. There was a time delay between the order and the action, reminding me of my dodgy old laptop at home, constantly rebooting at a frustratingly slow speed. I'd ask my toes to move and just a fraction of a second too much later they would. But move they did, and that in itself was a wondrous thing. The first time it happened I was both elated and incredibly relieved because in the back of my mind I had wondered if I was paralysed. That moment when they wiggled, even at a lethargic pace, I knew the signs were promising. If the toes worked, then, ultimately, I could make my legs work too.

Mr Moutoglis and Yiannis came up with a plan to get my feet on the ground sooner rather than later. The challenge was to get me taking steps before the huge task of grafting took place, as that would require a considerable period of recovery afterwards. Yiannis explained that the longer I remained in bed, the harder it would be to learn how to walk again, so the first stage of the plan was to move me from my cubicle in the ICU to a private room, where I would have sufficient space to move about.

Mr Moutoglis arranged for me to be moved to a room on the sixth floor. There were in fact a couple of reasons for this change of scenery. The obvious one was to give me more space to learn how to walk again. That made total sense. The second reason, concealed from me at the time, was a little more sinister. Unbeknown to me, my stay at the Mitera was causing security issues. Being in my safe little recovery bubble, protected by the staff, I was totally unaware that outside the hospital walls the story of the honeymoon tragedy had piqued the interest of the press, not only locally but also in Ireland and further afield. The wildfire disaster of 23 July in Athens was worldwide news. As each day went by, more and more bodies were being discovered amongst the burnt-out rubble and the death count was quickly increasing. Eventually the official number would reach 102 deaths, with many more people experiencing catastrophic injuries, the majority of those affected being locals. Many victims had not only lost their lives, or their loved ones, but also their homes, properties and businesses.

This fire was a tragedy of a scale not witnessed in Greece for over a century and as well as all-out grief, there was considerable fury amongst those who had been affected. As the months went by I would begin to understand how they felt and would eventually be consumed by anger, too, especially once I got a clearer picture of what had occurred in the lead-up to the wildfires in Mati and the surrounding areas. There were decisions made by those in charge, warnings ignored and acts of cowardice and self-service that caused many deaths on that fateful day. Much of the tragedy that ensued could have been avoided. So many lives were lost unnecessarily, including that of my darling husband, and locals had begun to gather and protest, demanding answers. While I was lying in my bed in the Mitera hospital, safe in my little cocoon, I knew nothing of the sheer volume of deaths nor the amount of lives destroyed in Athens. It was those same citizens – the very victims who demanded that the people responsible for this terrible event be held to account – who also had to commence the heart-breaking and cruel clean-up from the aftermath of the fires. They had little choice but to re-enter their homes and villages, many of which had been virtually wiped out from the catastrophe.

In the midst of all of this, the story of the ill-fated honeymooners resonated and seemed to capture the attention of journalists. Within days of my admittance, problems started to arise. Photographers and journalists tried every cunning tactic they could to gain entry to the ICU and take photos of the burnt bride. The hospital staff, on high alert, did all they could to protect me while keeping me closeted from that truth. Thinking back, I wonder how those doctors and nurses didn't resent me or my presence there. They had so many other seriously ill patients to take care of and yet they had to impose new regulations, on top of all the other added strains at that time, to prevent security breaches. No doubt many of them had relatives or friends affected by the fires themselves. This demonstrates how truly special these people were. I was totally oblivious to the media invasion and the problems caused by my presence. Perhaps I didn't need my *koukoúli* after all. I had an army of angels protecting me all the while.

I didn't know any of this, so when I heard I was to be moved from my familiar cubicle, I really didn't want to leave. I started to cry as I was wheeled off on a stretcher. Frankly, I was terrified of the unknown at that stage and couldn't bear to be separated from Anna and Maria, even though they both assured me they'd visit. I was only going up six floors, after all. They kindly kept their promise in the weeks to come.

I felt a bit of a fool for making such a fuss when I was presented with my new accommodation. The suite was luxurious and spacious, more like a five-star hotel than a hospital room, with a view overlooking the impressive Olympic stadium and the rolling hills of Athens shadowing in the distance. It was simply spectacular. My tears dried up quickly, I can tell you. Mr Moutouglis was there waiting to welcome me to my new abode and to reassure me that I would be not only very comfortable but also safe and secure. He explained that nobody was permitted to enter my room without his express permission. He asked me to compile a short list of visitors, made up of family members and close friends, including their descriptions, phone numbers and other methods of identification to ensure nothing untoward occurred. This was my first real inkling of the media interest outside the walls. I would later discover that these precautions were truly necessary as some journalists had already tried to gain access by impersonating members of my family, namely my brothers. One photographer had even been caught wearing doctor's scrubs, trying to get into my room. It was a surreal situation.

My new nurses on the sixth floor were introduced to me as Dimitra and Dimitrus. Dimitrus was a clean-cut hunk of a guy in his mid-twenties. Several of my visitors pointed out that he was rather easy on the eye, as if I didn't have eyes in my own head! However, it was Dimitra with whom I bonded immediately and she quickly became the person I relied upon. She had a calming presence that was in itself healing and, without sounding hippy-dippy, she exuded a soothing energy. I discovered that she practised holistic therapy when not working in the hospital, so healing was not only her trade but also in her very DNA. While Dr Tsopelas was my official counsellor, I came to understand that Dimitra, like Anna and Maria in ICU, had special qualities beyond medical training. They offered their own version of therapy.

It was around this time that I truly began to comprehend what I'd lost. The loneliness and all-encompassing sadness hit with full force. There's no word powerful enough to describe that emptiness. There were days that, try as I might, I couldn't stop the tears flowing and it was Dimitra who helped quell my anguish. She would sit and listen to my sobbing, tenderly drying my tears while holding my hand. Sometimes on recovery days she'd stay for hours and in an effort to distract me from my pain would, like Anna and Maria had done before, tell me all about her life outside the hospital. She'd talk about Greek food, local traditions and festivities and I'd listen intently, hoping to drown out the sad voices that cried out in my head. Some days passed me by in a sort of delirium. I guess the real shock set in once I had left the ICU. There, the focus had been all about survival in its most literal sense, but on the sixth floor I had more time to think about the next stage, like what would happen in the future. With no choice but to face the truths set before me, I was utterly overwhelmed and could spend days staring out the window, letting my tears wash over me until darkness fell. In an attempt to keep me from falling into a state of total despair, Mr

Moutoglis encouraged plenty of visitors. And so they came: John and Stephen, Adey and Lisa, Rosemary, Caroline and Ferg, and my pals from home, Katharine and Allie. There was somebody visiting practically the entire duration of my stay, which ended up being a full month.

My visitors often stayed quite late into the night, certainly past official visiting times, and once they had left Dr Tsopelas or Yiannis would usually drop by for a little chat, to check in and see how I was doing. Consistently, though, pretty much every single night it was Mr Moutoglis himself who would call into my room last thing at night. Such was his kind and caring nature, he never forgot his sad Irish patient on the sixth floor, even with so many others under his care at that time.

I recall one evening he arrived looking particularly exhausted. Mr Moutoglis always smiled at me, but even his smile couldn't mask his tiredness that night, so much so that I expressed concern for him. He explained that he had just completed two serious back-to-back surgeries on patients who had been severely injured in the fire, culminating in a fourteen-hour shift. Hard to imagine how shattered he must have been, and yet still he found a few minutes at the end of his day to check in on me. This is the perfect example of why I grew to adore the Greek people and, in particular, all those in the Mitera hospital. This generosity of spirit, kindness and total dedication was something I'd never experienced before. There was Mr Moutoglis, the head plastic surgeon, working himself to the bone during this catastrophic time, yet after another intensely gruelling day he still took the time to drop by, making sure I had eaten well, completed my exercises and, most importantly, had somebody to talk to that evening. It was his nightly visits I most looked forward to.

I felt that I had regressed and become almost childlike after the trauma. Stubbornly, I'd stay awake each night until Mr Moutoglis came by, as a young child would await a parent to say goodnight. And like a parent, if I was watching TV – which was, of course, simply a tactic to delay closing my eyes – he would order me to turn it off and go to sleep. He would then gently pat me on the forehead or on the side of my face and tell me I was safe and that everything was going to be alright. It is impossible now, in retrospect, to explain just how comforting those words and his presence were to me. On one hand, this man could take charge of intensely serious situations in a determined and resolute manner, performing life-saving surgeries day in, day out, and yet, on the other, he could demonstrate such personal tenderness and care to his patients. His visits at the end of a long day made me feel it was okay to close my eyes and even though I knew everything was indeed not going to be alright, they were the words I needed to hear at that time.

ONE SMALL STEP FOR WOMANKIND

n the weeks that followed I had intensive sessions with Yiannis, spent day and night working on my breathing, my core strength, my right-hand grip, and moving my feet and legs. In the hours between our sessions I would diligently do the exercises he had taught me. I became a master of the ping-pong device, my lungs became much stronger and I spent hours doing my version of sit-ups in the bed. It wasn't until week three that I actually had the strength to sit up in bed unassisted. My right hand began to cooperate. It was a tremendous moment when I fed myself for the first time, though I must confess it turned into a rather messy affair, with more food landing on me than in me. Nonetheless, I was pretty chuffed with myself. As one who'd never been the best student, I got an A+ for effort. I put my all energy into these therapies; every moment alone I pushed myself forward, to give my body the best possible chance of recovering.

It wasn't easy. Every motion was painful, from breathing (I was still coughing up blood) to moving, sitting and using that right hand. I continued to make progress, however, and soon Yiannis decided it was time to start working on the legs. That proved to be the most agonising, frustrating and sometimes damned impossible process yet, but fear drove me on. In the recesses of my mind I believed that, if I didn't put the work in, my legs would fail me. Ultimately, I was terrified I'd become wheelchair-bound or turn into 'Zimmer Zoe'. This was a term I'd stupidly joked about with my friends on every birthday since I'd hit forty – Zimmer frames representing impending old age. I vowed never to use that moronic joke again. I was frightened that I'd never again run in the Phoenix Park or dance like a maniac alone in my bedroom when nobody was looking, which were my own private, joyous moments. I knew that if I ever wanted to get back there, I'd have to start with learning how to walk.

Once I'd mastered toe-wiggling, Yiannis quickly got me to move my feet, pushing them back and forth, circling them round and round. If that was relatively easy, the next stage definitely was not. It started with moving both legs, slowly raising them up from the bed. That was incredibly difficult – it felt like they were superglued to the mattress. Then we moved onto bending my knees for the first time, which was an excruciatingly painful task. The problem was no longer my lazy brain sending delayed signals, it was simply working through the pain. Both Yiannis and Mr Moutoglis had warned me that it was going to be 'challenging', but this was off the Richter scale. It felt like I was self-harming, torturing my own limbs. However, I knew I had to push through to get to the next stage, so I bit my lip and persevered. 'No pain, no gain' took on a whole new meaning.

Yiannis was immensely patient and always encouraging. I confided in him that I needed a daily victory to get a sense of achievement, that even the smallest of triumphs, like raising my right leg an inch off the bed, made me feel as though I'd conquered Everest. For each one attained, I craved the next. That was how I overcame, and to this day still overcome, the obstacle of pain. There was no time off for good behaviour, no days without a new challenge – delays in my rehabilitation represented a step backwards.

In the past I had often used theme tunes if there was something significant going on. They were the backing tracks to my life. Dolly Parton's 'Nine to Five' was my support when I was being bullied in work and I'd listen to it every morning on the train without fail. The Killers' 'All These Things That I've Done' was another regular when life went off the tracks, reminding me that I was a warrior at heart. I even had my standard recovery tune for when a man did me wrong – they don't get much better than 'Cell Block Tango' from the musical *Chicago*. These were the songs that helped me through difficult times and the tune on constant play in my head during my 'learning to walk' period was that old ditty 'Dem Bones'. It was not so much a conscious choice, but one that just popped into my head and then refused to leave. It showed up one morning when I was working with my feet and stubbornly decided to hang around for several weeks. Those irritating lyrics (be warned, they're pretty hard to shake off once you start) rattled around in my mind day after day: *'The foot bone's connected to the ankle bone, the ankle bone's connected to the leg bone ...'*

'Dem Bones' was a pretty obvious choice. Nobody could have been more aware that my bones were connected. Hell, I could practically feel every single one each time I budged. I never sang it aloud – I didn't want to appear like a total lunatic – but I'd hum it in my head and I actually believe it helped me focus on getting my body parts to work in unison. I continued to work on my core, too, though I didn't have a theme tune for that. 'Let's Get Physical' would have worked, though somehow I don't think Olivia Newton-John was referring to sit-ups in her track! While my torso and stomach had been burned in the fire, they were not as intensely damaged as the rest of my body. The pneumonia left me weak, but I stuck at the sit-ups every chance I got.

I can practically visualise my friends laughing out loud at the very idea of me performing stomach crunches of any variety. I have never been one to commit to 'traditional' forms of exercise. So anti exercise-establishment was I in my younger years that I was once barred from my gym for causing a disturbance. We're not exactly talking riot action here, I was just kicked out for laughing hysterically during a cross-training class.

To be fair, I was put in an impossible position. The bloke I was paired with for the class had chosen not only to wear unfortunately gaping shorts but had, for some unimaginable reason, decided to go commando. The exercises were torture enough without the additional view of his jewels (pebbles, really) dangling over me as I attempted to do sit-ups, while he stood over me masterfully counting. Before long my sniggering erupted into all-out hysterics, which soon became contagious amongst the rest of the women in the class. I've often thought that women have an unspoken language, that we can communicate telepathically, without uttering a word. My laughter gave the game away and soon the rest of the class cottoned on to my flashing partner's antics. I may have also indicated that his private area was less than impressive. It wasn't long before there was mayhem in the class, with a dozen women bent over double laughing, as opposed to bent over double exercising.

The men in the room, including my gormless exercise partner, looked baffled. The butch trainer (his name might have actually been Butch) totally lost his temper with me for disrupting his precious class. He lifted me off the floor and physically hauled me over his shoulder, removed me from his class and dumped me in the changing room. All the while I was still in convulsions of laughter, not giving a damn! That was my first and last ever proper fitness class. After that I decided to create my own form of exercise, like dancing to show tunes with the bedroom door locked or stumbling around in the Phoenix Park pretending to be a proper runner. So my pals would have been astonished if they had seen me embrace my new exercise routine so diligently, following the rules for once in my life.

For the first time ever I was really working on improving my core strength, so that when by the time my legs were ready I'd be able to hold my entire body upright. Slowly, day by day, I got there, moving determinedly towards the ultimate task: putting my feet on the ground and taking some steps. That day finally arrived. I had mastered knee bends and swinging my legs over the edge of the bed, albeit somewhat clumsily, and it was time to put my feet on the ground at long last.

Yiannis, with Dimitra and Dimitrus assisting, stood close by, ready to help, as I gradually lowered my feet onto the floor and tentatively stood up. It was excruciating and exhilarating all in one – the sheer definition of ecstasy. My feet, adorned in fetching blue plastic socks that I called my hospital Louboutins, though sadly they didn't come with red soles, rested flat on the cool tiled floor. My toes straightened, my legs stretched out and I stood for the first time since the fire. If lifting my leg off the bed some time before had been my Everest, this victory was my Olympic medal-winning task. For the record, actual walking would be my triple gold medal victory, but this moment came pretty close. In my ears Yiannis, Dimitra and Dimitrus were cheering: 'Yes Zoe, yes, you did it!' There and then, I could almost say I was happy.

Every day after that we repeated this standing task, increasing the time from that millisecond stance to, finally, an entire minute. Then Yiannis announced that it was time to take my first steps. The four of us took our places. I was safely corralled, with Yiannis supporting me on the right, Dimitra on my left and Dimitrus standing behind me in case I should fall. It was like a military exercise and these three were my protectors, my own little army, and with their support I was sure I could succeed. They began to say my name in a rhythmic fashion, willing me to lift my feet off the ground, one by one, as if in a rallying cry to push me forward. Failure could not be an option, not for me and not for them. The pain was phenomenal, like burning electric shocks coursing through my limbs, but the adrenalin pumping through my veins and sheer determination won the day.

I took three steps that afternoon. This was my sweetest victory yet. 'Dem Bones' were working. I could walk again.

14

IN MEMORY OF AN ARTIST

On 12 August, three weeks after Brian passed, my father, Colm, died suddenly from a massive heart attack.

Dad had been suffering from bowel cancer for some years, with sporadic periods of remission. Assured that this last course of chemo would give him the best chance of survival, the most promising prognosis yet, it still seemed to be the cruellest medicine. While Dad had been a positive soul his whole life, in the last few months he became haunted by anxiety, sleepless nights and utter despondency. These were the torturous side-effects of that treatment. I hardly recognised the man I adored: physically he was weakened, but mentally he was tormented.

The last time I saw Dad was the day after my wedding when we hugged goodbye. We'd always been very close. He wasn't just my dad, he was also my pal and lifelong advocate. Colm's positivity was infectious. He always wore a cheeky grin and invariably had a funny story to cheer up the most miserable day. He was an entertainer and took great pride in telling the perfectly timed joke. Even if the jokes were awful, he was guaranteed a laugh because he had that way of telling them. My father was kind, wise, smart and always self-deprecating. One of my favourite pastimes was meeting him for a pint after work in the local pub. We would sit there mulling over the problems of the day, be they work, personal or political. To be fair, I was clueless about the latter but happy to listen to the expert. Often we spoke about nothing at all, or nothing of any great consequence. That was the sweetest thing – a father and daughter sitting quietly in the corner of the pub, happily passing an hour or two talking utter nonsense. We just liked hanging out together.

When I sought advice, Dad was great at offering sage tips like, 'Often the best course of action is taking no action at all.' Mind you, he also once told me, 'Always find somebody else to blame when you've been caught making a mistake.' I'm fairly sure he was joking when he shared that little titbit. Still, with that twinkle in his eye, you never could tell.

As an artist he demonstrated great talent, though he was only recognised in his later years. Colm saw the world around him in vivid colour and only ever painted aesthetically pleasing subjects, his magical eye for detail translating into beautiful works of art. His paintings were filled with joy and, much like the artist himself, were guaranteed to make you smile.

As a man, he was well loved and a bit of a character. Speaking to friends and collectors of his work at an event in his honour some months after his death, I learned a few things I didn't know about Dad. Through their eyes I caught a glimpse of Colm as a friend, an artist and a sportsman. Incidentally, his pals were made up of men and women ranging in age from 30 to 80: he had a way of reaching people of all ages and backgrounds. That day, everybody I met had a Colm story to share. He had touched so many lives and everywhere he went, he left his mark. I discovered good deeds of generosity that had been hidden, ridiculous jokes (most of which he'd deemed inappropriate to tell his daughter but were still bloody funny), and a mighty competitive spirit on the tennis court or golf course that always won out. I definitely inherited the spirit of competition, but, alas, I lacked the sporting prowess. I uncovered joyful little pieces of my dad's jigsaw that up until then I never knew existed. Each piece made sense, each had his distinct aura. This is the Colm Holohan that I wanted to and will always remember.

The last conversation I had with Dad was when I called to confirm Brian's death. It was a call that I had been dreading, but one I couldn't put off any longer. Given his fragile state of health, I was terrified that Dad wouldn't be able to handle the news of Brian's death and had asked my family to hide it from him for as long as possible, wanting to break it to him personally but fearing the consequences for his own health.

My father and Brian had come to be firm friends. In truth, Brian was the first man I brought to the door that Dad really approved of. Their relationship was sealed when my father got sick and was rushed to hospital. He had a very close brush with death and I was utterly terrified I would lose him. It was the first time I had to contemplate the idea that my parents were mortal. I wouldn't let Dad out of my sight, spending morning, noon and night in the hospital. Being the kind man that Brian was, he stayed with me and held my hand for that entire duration. Given that this was early days in our relationship and he was also studying for his MBA exams at the time, his support was much more than I had expected. That was it with Brian – if he was in it, he was in it for the long haul, good times or bad. Dad saw the qualities of the man I had fallen in love with, saw how he looked after me while I was looking out for my father.

Once Dad was discharged from the hospital, they got to know each other much better. They shared a love of golf – well, Dad loved golf and Brian enjoyed spending time with Dad. They would often escape for a long game together. At home they could talk up a storm, yapping about work, politics, sports – all the sorts of 'fascinating' topics that guaranteed Mum and I would leave them alone in the sitting room and busy ourselves in the kitchen. In short, beyond my relationship with Brian, he and Dad were friends in their own right. I knew Brian's death would devastate him.

I can still hear Dad's agonised cry down the phone to this day when I broke the tragic news, a tormented wail I'll never forget. It was the worst and the last conversation we ever shared. My only comfort is that the last words I ever uttered to my father were, 'I love you, Dad.'

A couple of days later, he too was dead.

His heart, in a weakened state, finally just gave up. He was at home with my mum when he collapsed on the floor. My poor distraught mum did all she could to keep him alive, holding and resuscitating him while she frantically phoned for an ambulance. I was trying to call at that exact moment from my hospital bed and receiving only an engaged tone; my mum was trying to save her husband's life. The ambulance eventually arrived and they managed to revive him several times as he was rushed to hospital. Instinctively, I knew something was wrong and phoned that night over and over. We had a set routine: a prearranged time to talk and Mum always answered my evening calls. I tried both my brothers, too, all with no response, and I couldn't shake that bad feeling. Even with my worst suspicions, though, I never thought life could be that cruel.

Eventually, Stephen answered the phone in the early hours and told me that Dad had been taken to hospital, but assured me that he was alright. He didn't give me the full story, nothing about a heart attack, only that he had taken ill and was being kept in hospital for checks. I'm not sure now, looking back upon that conversation, if my brother knew the full story or was just trying to allay my fears, or perhaps his own. I can only imagine how terrifying that night was for my mum, John and Stephen – how they would have been willing my father to survive with all their strength. But even with the best wills in the world, Dad's heart just wasn't strong enough. He passed away in the early hours of the morning, with his whole family – everyone except his daughter – by his bedside.

It wasn't until the following afternoon that my worst fears were confirmed. Nobody knew how to break the news to me, so John phoned and spoke to Mr Moutoglis. Upon learning that Adey was in Athens visiting me at the time, Mr Moutoglis asked him to help break the tragic news. It was by then Adey's third visit since the fire. As he had been so close to Brian, he was the one capable of bringing me some peace. We'd talk about him as though he were still alive. But when Adey entered my room that evening, as soon as I saw his teary eyes and strained smile, I knew that something terrible had happened. Behind him, in the shadows of the doorway, Mr Moutoglis stood with his head bowed as though in mourning.

It had been arranged that at that very time of Adey's arrival, John would phone me. I watched Adey's face break as he looked at the phone, now ringing insistently. He gently placed his hand on mine and I lifted the receiver. I said very little during that call. I heard my brother's voice and I understood what he was trying to say, but couldn't find any words in response. John continued to speak, I think he tried to comfort me, but I just lay frozen, all the while staring at Adey in disbelief. That was it. They broke the horrific news of Dad's death and in doing so broke whatever piece of my heart was still intact. I hung up the phone.

Mr Moutoglis now stood with Adey by my bedside and I heard echoes of gentle words but nothing that I could clearly make out. The pain was more than I could bear. Dad was dead, too. I wondered if I had stopped breathing, because all the air felt as though it had rushed out of my chest. I wished it would. I wanted it all to be over. Smothered by grief, I just wanted to be left to drown in my sea of loss.

I don't remember much else about that evening or the days that followed. I know I spoke to my poor heartbroken mum, but I don't think I found the right words to ease her distress and I was guilt-ridden for not being there to hold her hand. She had been so brave, doing everything in her power to help my father, and though she had her sons, it should have been me, her daughter, by her side in her hour of need. I have been told that many rallied around my family at that time to help. Adey delayed his flight home and stayed a few more days to keep an eye on me, but I don't remember any of that. That time disappeared into darkness.

My father's funeral took place days later in Dublin while I lay in my bed, thousands of miles away. The night before his send-off I stayed awake, staring out the window at the Olympic stadium beautifully lit against the dark night sky and thought about my darling dad. I managed to write some words that night, my eulogy for my dad, which John read to the funeral congregation. It was my dedication to a great light extinguished.

My family arranged for the mass to be recorded, but I have yet to watch the tape, not sure if I will ever be able to. I was not there in person to say goodbye, but my heart and soul were with my dad that day. And he was with me.

The morning of his funeral, I had surgery scheduled and Mr Moutoglis was anxious it should go ahead. For my own part, I was glad to spend that day anaesthetised, even though I knew it would just inevitably delay my pain. Nonetheless it would give me a few hours of blessed oblivion. As I counted down, waiting for the sedative to take effect, 10, 9, 8 ..., I looked down at the bracelet the nurse had strapped to my wrist. It was emblazoned with my name, date of birth, country of origin and next of kin. It had become my custom, just before I conked out for each operation, to look at my band and double-check the details. It was a nervous habit – if I didn't make it through, I wanted to ensure all my information was correct. It also reminded me that I still existed, that with all that had changed at least my name, birth date and nationality remained the same.

7, 6, 5 ...

I looked at my wrist and saw that one thing that morning had indeed changed. In place of Brian's name as my next of kin, which I had insisted on when I was first admitted, there, clearly printed, was my father's name instead. Colm Holohan. There he was, right with me after all. The hospital had replaced my husband's name with my father's name some days before, but of course the administrator hadn't yet realised that he too had died.

To me that morning, it was a sign, a wonderful sign. I truly believed Dad knew he was needed there, with his daughter, in whatever way he could be. He was there holding my hand as I went under and drifted away ...

15

THE FOG

The days that followed are masked in a dark mist. There's little I recall other than being informed by Mr Moutoglis that my surgery had gone very well. I couldn't say if it was for my hand, arms or legs, or all of the above, as I was bandaged all over and heavily medicated. Physically I was recovering well, mentally I was absent. It had all just got too much: first Brian, now Dad. The trip switch in my brain had blown. Emotionally, my power was out.

Vaguely I was aware of visitors, people walking in and out of my room. I was hardly left alone for a minute. Yiannis ensured I was back on my feet as soon as possible, to make more strides in my little blue socks. I worked hard every day and did my best to please my physio and surgeon, trying to demonstrate that I hadn't yet given up on life entirely. Internally, though, I was withered with grief and despair but anxious they didn't see that. I didn't want them to give up on me just yet. Dr Tsopelas' visits increased in frequency and Dimitra and the other nurses barely left my side. I was kept constantly occupied. A good thing, perhaps.

After some time, my friends Katharine and Allie visited. It was fortuitous timing that Katharine (or Lady C as she is better known in our little gang, partly because she carries herself with regal flair, partly due to her love of fine champagne) arrived when she did, as the day before their arrival Marianne informed me that our luggage had been rescued from Villa Aliki. The owner of the villa had contacted the embassy after she heard of my fate on the news and had returned all our belongings, hastily packed in their suitcases. Marianne proceeded to wash every item several times because everything reeked of smoke. There were, of course, things that could not be saved, so badly damaged were they by smoke or fire.

When at first Marianne told me about the luggage, I had mixed emotions. Naturally I was delighted to get our personal effects back, especially Brian's things, which I was desperate to rummage through, hold and treasure. But I can't pretend that I wasn't devastated to learn that some of our belongings had survived that inferno. I had assumed everything had gone up in flames. It turns out the villa, being made of sturdy stone, was not burnt to the ground like many of the surrounding properties. It was one of the few structures that appeared, at least from the outside, untouched by the disaster. This opened up the Pandora's box of what ifs once more. What if we had stayed in the villa – would Brian still be alive? Would I have escaped without injury? Our impulse had been to run to safety, but perhaps we had made the wrong decision? As if reading my thoughts – or maybe I wasn't as good at hiding my feelings as I thought – Marianne told me that death by smoke inhalation would more than likely have been our fate had we remained in the villa.

Given the stench of smoke and damage to our clothes, even after numerous washes, I try to believe that's true. Much of my honeymoon wardrobe and all of our suitcases had to be binned, the stench of smoke too overpowering. I held onto the majority of Brian's clothes, though, bar those that were badly damaged, unwilling to part with any of his belongings.

In the hospital I wasn't allowed to inspect our luggage – Mr Moutoglis' orders, for sanitary reasons – but Marianne kindly brought me a couple of items that had clearly been washed at least half-a-dozen times. Most importantly, she returned Brian's wedding ring, which I kept safely tucked away in my bedside cabinet by day and secretly nestled under my pillow for comfort and protection at night.

As I said, the timing of my friends' visit could not have been better as Lady C, in particular, had always been renowned for her superb organisational skills and that talent was about to come in very useful. Every item would need to be identified, logged, washed and packed, ready to be sent home. Katharine took on the task with gusto – being quite the domestic goddess, she was in her element – with Allie by her side as an able assistant. I was oblivious to their toil, however. I had numerous surgical procedures that week, so much of their running commentary passed me by.

Together with Brian's wedding ring, the embassy also returned some personal items, including both of our passports. I discovered much later, back in Dublin, that the handbag I had so covetously hung onto that night had survived, though it was melted in places and held a stench that would make you retch. Bizarrely, though, I found many items within virtually unharmed. My cosmetics were definitely cooked (foundation flambé anyone?), but all other items, while smelling of smoke, were otherwise fine. A bigger shock was when I found Brian's satchel bag that he had carried on the day of the fire. That was a shock because I'd assumed it had been obliterated. It was badly damaged, but again the contents were intact. Inside I found his wallet, car and house keys and at the very bottom of the bag, in a melted pocket, I found a packet of cigars that were unopened and remarkably unharmed. They remain today in his bedside cabinet. I haven't the heart to throw them away. They were his favourite vice.

It's difficult to describe how conflicted I felt about retrieving our personal effects. Perhaps the lingering fog, that intense sadness, smothered the joy I would have otherwise felt. It was good to have Brian's things close to me, yet I couldn't help objecting to the great injustice of it all: those things had survived so why hadn't he? There were moments when I wondered if I would ever be capable of experiencing true joy again.

Yet even then, in the darkest of days, there were still little glimmers that poked through the haze. Anyone who has ever spent long periods in hospital will tell you that you find light relief in the strangest of places. It's like laughter at a funeral, inappropriate but often inevitable. I have to confess that in the midst of my cocktail of despair and confusion, I still experienced some humorous moments. They were my little snapshots of temporary respite.

For instance, Katharine arrived early one evening to find me lying on my bed, coated from head to toe in a thick layer of what probably looked like snowy-white paint. My burns had just been bandaged, also in white gauzy strips, so to a passing observer I must have looked like an Egyptian mummy. Finding me there, lying on the bed, giggling hysterically with Dimitra, Katharine naturally asked what us was so amusing. In unison Dimitra and I responded: 'Ahhh, Pulvo!'

Smiling, the nurse explained that I was enjoying my favourite treat. She then winked at me and left the room. We had been laughing because Dimitra, like all the nurses, knew my favourite time was Pulvo time. Some people enjoy a nice chilled glass of wine at the end of their day, others indulge in a long bath to promote relaxation; but being the creature of simple pleasures I'd become, all I fancied was a good dousing all over in thick white Pulvo spray. I was obsessed with the stuff.

Pulvo is a burns coolant spray that acts as an icy anaesthetic. It cooled my scorched flesh and instantly eased the pain all over my body. It was heavenly stuff – nectar sent from the gods. Each morning and evening, after the nurses had bathed and bandaged my wounds, they would laboriously apply coats of Pulvo over any areas that were uncovered, including my face. The effects were so therapeutic that I found myself begging nurses for 'just a little more'. Naturally, they cottoned on to its usefulness in negotiations, such was my enthusiasm for the magic snow spray, and they sometimes used it as a bargaining tool or bribe. It was like offering a kid dessert if they finished their dinner. I was promised extra Pulvo if I promised to eat more than a few lousy morsels of food.

My enthusiasm provided amusement for the nurses, too. The dressing of my wounds was a long and arduous process, so it was a good thing there was something to look forward to at the end. Pulvo was the icing on the cake (literally, I was the cake) and on that particular evening, just as Katharine arrived, we were laughing because Dimitra had told me they'd just taken in a large delivery of fresh tins. I'd probably used up the whole hospital's supply. I literally squealed with glee at this news and then of course begged her to keep spraying until I was so heavily coated, I resembled a snow-woman. Perhaps the most surprising factor to Katharine was not my adoration for the white fluffy coating but the fact that I had spent the previous decade at the opposite end of the colour spectrum, coated in layers of fake tan. You may say I swapped one 'shady' addiction for another.

On the topic of appearance, there was still my hair situation to be resolved. Paulina returned, as promised, to sort out my matted locks. I was still rocking the Pippi Longstocking look, albeit with a new snow-queen flair. She came up to the sixth floor with a trolley of goodies and beauty gadgets to sort me out. Of the numerous tools of her trade, the ones I could no longer avoid, were the scissors. In the back of my mind I was still attached to my 18-inch hair extensions, but it was high time to say adieu to those upturned frazzled lengths and hello to a more manageable, shorter style. As previously with the nurses in ICU, it took Paulina hours of detangling, conditioning and a superhuman mix of strength and determination to work her magic. Finally, she transformed my mop into a chic, dramatically shorter hairdo. My new bob, no longer of the dreadlock Bob variety, was edgy and sleek. Less reggae, more 1920s flapper girl. Sadly, though, my stylish little haircut was not going to last.

When the time came at the end of that week for Katharine and Allie to return home, they brought my luggage back with them. I know they took the greatest care of that precious cargo, the memories of a honeymoon that never was. Unbeknownst to them, and indeed to me at the time, they would be my last guests from Ireland. Over the next few days the situation in Athens was about to take a sudden turn and I would be facing a whole new batch of challenges. My world was set to spin on its axis once more.

16

HELLO JELLO, GOODBYE GREECE

was making great improvements in the walking department. Every day, after dressings, we would knuckle down and it became a team effort. With Yiannis and the nurses' constant cheerleading, I started to make headway. It's hard to convey how agonising and yet elating each one of those tiny steps was. It was an unnatural feeling, walking on severely burned legs (like arm-wrestling with a broken wrist), and my body objected to every movement, screaming out in pain, yet I completely trusted in Yiannis' judgement. I understood that the longer I delayed learning how to walk again, the more difficult it would eventually be, so I persevered. Through it all, Yiannis still managed to make me smile. He had a wonderful knack for distracting the brain. And as I said before, laughter is truly the best medicine – well, after Pulvo, that is.

Unfortunately, my appetite continued to go downhill. Initially, I put my lack of desire to eat down to shock and trauma. I was drip-fed during the early days and thought perhaps my stomach was still readjusting. Nearly a month on, however, that was no longer a viable excuse. I could only swallow miniscule morsels. The hunger button in my brain was firmly switched off and not only had I lost the ability to enjoy good food, I had no yearning to eat at all.

My weight was decreasing and Mr Moutoglis pleaded with me on a daily basis to eat more, trying every trick in the book to entice me. He had delicious meals concocted in the kitchen to appeal specifically to my tastes, having asked my friends what I most liked to eat. Every day I was presented with a menu selection of delectable dishes to choose from, resulting in Caroline and Ferg dubbing my room 'the hotel suite'. The food was wonderful, I just couldn't consume it. At the end of his tether, Mr Moutoglis even offered me takeout pizza one evening, my favourite guilty pleasure, yet still I refused. As a compromise, he brought me delicious fresh fruit juices in the evenings from a restaurant, and I agreed to drink them. I was desperate not to disappoint him. I wasn't behaving like a spoiled child, I just physically could not eat.

As the pounds continued to drop away, I was placed on a fortified protein drink plan in between meals to bolster my weight. These drinks were called Fortimel and were pretty much like a modern but equally revolting version of Complan, that old-lady drink from the 1970s. It was like sucking leaden liquid through a straw. I hated to upset Mr Moutoglis and seeing how concerned he was and wanting to behave like a good patient, I agreed to suck down three bottles of that toxic gunk daily. Mind you, I wasn't entirely cooperative when the nurse brought the Fortimel. I said I was a good patient, I didn't claim to be a saint.

I insisted on calling the drinks my little bottles of lukewarm 'vom'. I'm sure you can work out what 'vom' stands for – the nurses did and English was their second language. Perhaps my less-than-enthusiastic face said it all and provided the translation.

My reward for consuming the vom was the only foodstuff I found appealing at the time – a little pot of jello. These glorious, multi-coloured confections came in all the shades of the rainbow and often quite mysterious flavours. It was like playing Russian roulette; you never knew what you were going to get. The yellow jello, for instance, was always a surprise flavour: sometimes lemon, sometimes banana, often indescribable. No matter, I enjoyed the guessing game and unlike other foods, jello slid easily down my throat. It was my favourite meal of the day.

In the meantime, my step count was on the up and up. My daily victories became more frequent and nearly four weeks after being admitted I finally took a full lap around my room. There, in my little blue socks, I managed thirteen glorious, agonising steps. I counted each one out loud with huge pride. It was a landmark day for me and a truly awesome moment to share with Yiannis, Dimitra and Dimitrus. It was a shared achievement and there wasn't a dry eye in the house. Without their determination and patient confidence in me, I would never have managed that lap. Yiannis never gave up on me: from that first day with the ping-pong fiasco to the miraculous circuit around my room, he was a constant by my side. He taught me how to breathe, sit up alone, feed myself, bend and straighten my legs. He held me up when I took my first step on that cool marble floor and, most importantly, knew exactly when to let go of my hand and watch me walk solo. It was like teaching a baby all the skills needed to survive. He retrained my body and my brain and, day by day, dissolved the fear that accompanied each life lesson. It was a euphoric moment and I couldn't wait to share the achievement with my family. We were all well overdue some good news.

Excitedly, I phoned John that evening to break the news, but that call did not go as planned. We had barely started the conversation when my brother interrupted. My health and travel insurers, who had been pretty amazing up until then, were calling time on my stay in Greece and wanted me to return home to Ireland urgently. A bed had become available in the specialist burns ward in St James' Hospital in Dublin, and my insurers wanted me to take up the offer post-haste. This came as a huge shock to me, although it seems silly now, looking back, that I hadn't expected the news sooner. Evidently, I had become totally dependent on the staff at the Mitera, had put my life in their hands and couldn't bear the thought of continuing this journey without them. They were my healers, my protectors and given the tragic circumstances and the special care they bestowed on me, I considered many of them to be my friends. This hospital had become my citadel and the thought of leaving and returning home – not to mention facing my new reality there – filled me with absolute dread.

As John tried to reason with me, I burst into tears, became inconsolable and point-blank refused to go. Even the thought of being back in Ireland gave me no solace. I had no intention of going anywhere. My victorious moment of taking those thirteen steps had evaporated into thin air and my joyful mood had well and truly disappeared. I knew that eventually I'd have to face life back in Ireland, without Brian and Dad, but I just hadn't seen that time arriving so soon.

Over the next 48 hours there were many phone calls with my brother, discussing the insurance company's requests and my own medical requirements. I obstinately argued with John, begging him to postpone my return trip. I cried constantly and in childish revolt ceased all exercises, walking, and any other elements of my daily regime. Desperate to stay put, my increasingly irrational state of mind saw any further progress as a route to hasten my homeward journey. Nobody was aware that my lack of appetite and refusal to cooperate were symptoms of something more serious than pure stubbornness.

Mr Moutoglis was so concerned by my reaction that he tried to intervene. He called John and the insurance company himself and explained that I was too ill for the journey. Both parties disagreed and reiterated that it had been difficult to get this room in St James' in the specialist ward dedicated to plastic surgery and severe burns. A private plane was organised to get me home, everything was already in motion and there was no guarantee that they would offer this transport again if I didn't follow their plan. In retrospect, this was an entirely reasonable request but, as I explained, I wasn't in a reasonable state of mind. I tried every stunt to buy extra time. Mr Moutoglis, concerned for his patient, went to the board of the hospital and such was his power of persuasion, and their tremendous generosity, that they agreed to let me stay a further twelve weeks, complete all my surgeries and the full grafting process at no added charge to the insurance company, something that would normally have cost a small fortune. They offered to complete all their work pro bono.

It was an incredible demonstration of goodwill and magnanimity and confirmed everything I already knew about Mr Moutoglis and the Mitera team. They had put their all into my recovery and were willing to do whatever it took to get me to the end of that road. For that and so much more I will be indebted to them forever.

With that offer on the table, I was convinced the insurers would let me stay, but offer or no offer the decision was out of my hands. My poor drained brother explained to me, in no uncertain terms, that the window for getting a private mediplane was closing fast. If I didn't do as he asked, they could withdraw the offer and I would have to travel home on a public flight. John beseeched me to cooperate, adding that Mum was in a bad way and desperate to see me.

That did it. It finally hit me, I had to go home. Entrenched in my own grief, I'd all but forgotten that my poor mum had lost her husband of nearly fifty years, too. I had to help her in whatever way I could. I thanked Mr Moutoglis for his incredibly generous offer but told him that I would have to decline. I was needed back in Dublin.

Within the blink of an eye, it was organised. The nurses carefully packed up my possessions – the boxes of letters and cards being the most precious items – and with that I was ready to travel. I was wheeled out on my stretcher on the morning of 23 August 2018. Hard to believe it was exactly a month since the day of the fire: it felt so much longer, a lifetime. I guess it was in some ways, certainly a period that had altered my existence forever. What stood before me now was another new and uncertain era.

The nurses and doctors from the ICU and the sixth floor all lined up in the corridor outside my room. It was an intensely emotional moment. Amongst them, Anna and Maria waited with Yiannis, Dimitra, Dimitrus, Dr Tsopelas and, of course, my saviour Mr Moutoglis. I held back my tears as best as I could, fiercely trying to be brave because I didn't want Mr Moutoglis to think that I doubted my decision to leave. I promised that it was not goodbye and that I'd return to my beautiful life-savers. Vassilis, the burly man who managed the ICU desk, told me that I could only return on one condition: I had to walk an entire lap of the ICU unassisted, on my own two feet. I looked at Yiannis (he too was fighting back tears), nodded, and with a gulp agreed it was a fair deal. I would come back, walk all the hospital corridors if needs be, and hug each one of my Greek friends with two functioning arms.

Mr Moutoglis, ever the surgeon, also made me promise that once my grafts were complete, I wouldn't budge an inch for at least 48 hours after the surgery. I promised him faithfully to do as he instructed. He reminded me to eat and insisted he wanted to see bigger arms and a stronger body the next time we met. Again I gave him my word, assuring him I'd eat well, stay as still as a statue after the surgery and, most importantly, come back as soon as I could to thank him in person for all that he had done for me.

His was the last face I saw as I was wheeled away on a stretcher. As they all disappeared from sight, I could at last let the tears flow. I was leaving my angels behind and with them another fragment of my broken heart.

17

JOURNEY TO NOTHINGNESS

The ambulance ride to the plane went without a hitch. It was a small, comfortable vehicle and the two paramedics looking after me spoke perfect English. They were gentle in their manoeuvres, efficiently reconnecting my IV lines (my last link to the Mitera) and the transfer was smooth and painless. Once settled we set off at speed for the airport, a journey that took less than an hour. As I lay back on my stretcher and closed my eyes, I visualised the people I had just left behind. Suddenly, I felt exhausted – not surprising given I'd had very little sleep the previous night due to my anxiety about the journey home.

I dozed off but was woken abruptly when we arrived at the airport. I could feel my heart beating at breakneck speed. Even though the paramedics were reassuring me at every moment, I found the transfer from the ambulance to the plane quite frightening. This was the first time I had been out in the open air since the fire. The August heat, the searing sun on my face and the sharp light piercing my eyes were unbearable, especially as I was accustomed to gentle hospital lighting and cool air-conditioning. One of the medics noted my discomfort and kindly tried his best to shade my face from the sun with his body while I closed my eyes tightly and imagined being elsewhere.

In minutes I was on the plane and safely strapped into my new stretcher, where I was introduced to two new paramedics who would be my travel companions. The plane was compact and comfortable and while I was lying strapped to a gurney for my own safety, I was relieved to find it cooler and darker than outside. Beyond that, I can't remember much else about the journey, other than the fact that I was thirsty, really thirsty. The paramedic gave me cold water through a straw and eventually I closed my eyes again and fell asleep.

Fast asleep at last. Off to the land of nod, as my mum used to say.

Off to nothingness ...

PART TWO

You're gone but you'll never disappear
You are silent but your voice I can still hear
Your kindness will live on in future years
Your laughter will still ring out in my ears
Your love I will carry till my end
My knight, my true love, my best friend.
(ZH)

18

A BATTLE ANEW

arrived in Dublin later that evening and was transported to St James' Hospital burns unit. By then I was dipping in and out of consciousness and was in the grip of a severe fever so I can't really recollect anything. My memories are sketchy at best. Somewhere between my departure from Greece and arrival in Ireland, I had become delirious and my homecoming was definitely not what I had envisaged it would be.

I would later learn that I had contracted a rare condition called toxic epidermal necrolysis, or TEN to you and me. Put in simple terms – although even simply put TEN still scares the living daylights out of me – this condition starts as a skin reaction and heightened temperature that induces a blistering and lifting of the skin. The skin tissue effectively dies and starts to detach, resulting in sepsis, dehydration, pneumonia and multiple organ failure. More than fifty percent of those who contract TEN die from it. One in a million people are affected by this condition each year. I was that not-so-lucky one-in-a-million this time around. Unbeknown to me, my life was under a greater threat than ever. This was a whole new battle for survival.

TEN is a very severe form of sepsis and can be difficult to diagnose but the rash and blisters that had broken out all over my body put the team in the burns unit on red alert. The cause of this condition is difficult to ascertain, but it can sometimes be connected to an allergic reaction to certain antibiotics and it generally attacks patients who are already in a vulnerable state. Treatment can therefore be difficult and dangerous to apply because the wrong meds can be lethal. I will never know when exactly I contracted TEN, but certainly the symptoms took hold on the plane when I was unconscious. It could possibly explain why my appetite was so poor in Greece, but again, the timing can never be certain. My poor darling mother, who had so eagerly awaited my return, was not even allowed see me when I arrived at the hospital. She was there with my brother Stephen, arms filled with flowers and gifts, awaiting an emotional reunion. We'd spoken on the phone the night before so she was expecting, if nothing else, a responsive daughter, but she wasn't allowed anywhere near me as I was rushed straight into intensive care and the fight to save my life began in earnest.

What happened next was fresh torture for my mum, brothers and whole family. They had been through so much already. It was merely days after my father's funeral and I was supposed to be on the road to recovery, yet all of a sudden I was once again in real danger of dying. My condition worsened rapidly. I developed horrific blisters all over my body, inside and out, including my mouth and eyes. In a cruel twist of fate, the areas that had been clear of burns from the fire, like my 'good' right arm, hand, entire back and chest, were now being ferociously attacked by this infection. In septic shock, my body was effectively savaging itself. The blisters became rock-hard, crusted growths and my chest bore the brunt of long, deep slash marks where no scars had been before. All over my body, skin began to burst open and peel off in areas that had previously healed or had been entirely unaffected. Within 24 hours I was seriously ill and pivotally, over the next few days, my organs began to fail one by one. My heart was showing signs of duress and I developed pneumonia. Eventually, I went into renal failure and had to be put on dialysis.

The day after I was admitted my family was called to an emergency meeting with the consultant plastic surgeon and director of the burns unit, Mr Odhran Shelley. Months later, John recollected their shell shock as he broke the news to them. Mr Shelley explained that my condition was critical and the next 48 hours were crucial. They had tried numerous antibiotics but my body had rejected three combinations of medication. The TEN was getting stronger. It was killing me. He explained that I'd gone into shock and that with every attempt to save me using antibiotics, the symptoms had become more severe. My fate rested in Mr Shelley's hands. If he didn't find the right combination of drugs to get this infection under control, I would not survive. It was like playing Russian roulette with antibiotics – without them, I couldn't beat this thing, yet the wrong combination would prove fatal.

After the meeting with Mr Shelley, my mum turned to my brothers and asked them if this was it, if they were going to lose me too. Having lost both Brian and Dad in such a short space of time, what was once unthinkable in our family was now entirely conceivable. I could be the next on the list. My brothers made the impossible promise that I would rally through, but neither they nor the best medical experts knew if this was true. All they could do was sit and pray. My sister in-law, Fiona, began the thankless duty of informing my close friends of what had occurred. Everybody was in shock and the bad news travelled fast.

To give my organs the best fighting chance, Mr Shelley placed me in an induced coma, though I believe I was already unconscious. My body started to bloat and fill with water. I could no longer breathe and went into acute respiratory distress, so I was put on a ventilator to assist my breathing. I have no memory of any of these occurrences. I was blissfully unaware of what was going on. Sadly, the same couldn't be said for my family. They knew everything that was happening, minute by minute.

The first sign of hope was when, after several long days and nights, my temperature finally stabilised. It seemed that Mr Shelley and his team, who had been working around the clock, had finally cracked it. The right combination of antibiotics seemed to have been found and for the first time it looked as though I might have a chance. Unfortunately, there was no magic wand and this didn't mean I was cured by any means. Many organs were still under considerable strain, but at last there was that first glimmer on the horizon.

Over the next few weeks, while I was still in the coma, numerous surgical procedures took place to save my life. I lost approximately 90 per cent of my epidermis and 10 per cent of my dermis. Using donor skin, a form of grafting was performed on my back, buttocks and legs where the TEN had been particularly aggressive and several other operations were performed to stop my skin lifting and splitting across my chest and arms. Still, there were complications. I had difficulty breathing, so twelve days after I had been admitted it was found necessary to perform a tracheostomy to insert a breathing tube through my windpipe and aid delivery of oxygen to my lungs.

What happened during my sleeping hours, and what eventually led to my recovery, is a testament to the phenomenal skill and determination of Mr Shelley and the expert burns team at St James' Hospital. It would be a long time before I'd hear about all the surgeries, prayers and tears that saved my life, but by week three I was out of the critical zone. I was still on dialysis, breathing through the tracheostomy, or 'trach', and linked up to half-a-dozen tubes doing numerous essential tasks to keep my organs functioning, but it looked like I was going to make it.

Through all of this, over a period of fourteen days, I was still in the land of nod.

For any of you who have ever wondered whether or not people in a coma can hear what's going on around them, well, my answer is a firm yes ... a firm yes and a confused no.

I was there, but I was locked away in a strange parallel universe. While the doctors and nurses were battling to save my life, I was trapped in a dream (or nightmare) state, away from my family, desperate to communicate with them. I knew they were there, I could hear the voices of Mum, John and Stephen, but of course there were other voices that were unfamiliar to me. I had a strong sense of foreboding, as if there was danger looming and felt terribly frustrated that nobody was listening to my warnings. I could hear all of them, but no one could hear me.

Inside the coma I was living my dreams, vividly and without end. In a sense, I knew that I had come back home, knew that I was in a hospital setting once more, but this was not the homecoming I had expected. This was a confusing mirror world, filled with some familiar sounds (namely the voices of my family) and many frightening, unfamiliar ones. It was a disturbing place and my overriding impression was one of fear: I was constantly on high alert. It was also intensely hot, as though I was once again burning but this time the flames were invisible. In my imagination the hospital was under siege; in reality, it was my own life that was once again under threat.

That threat took several forms. Bizarrely, the lead character in my mind-play was an overgrown, anthropomorphic snack food, Captain Peanut (to give him his official title), who had set up camp in a castle opposite the hospital. He had captured my mother-in-law, Rosemary, who happened to be wearing a dress remarkably similar to my own wedding gown, and she was his prisoner of war, though thankfully she seemed oblivious to the fact. This villain had gathered an army, adorned in striking flowing garments of red, and was readying them to destroy all that was in their way. I was desperate to protect my family and did all I could to warn them, but nobody would listen, no one could hear my cries of caution. No one, that is, but my cat, Meow. Wearing her ears pinned up in pigtails (much like my Pippi Longstocking hair in Greece), she set up shop in the basement of the hospital, where in a custom-made breeding facility she created our own army of monkeys, sworn to protect and serve me and all that sheltered in the hospital grounds.

The monkeys, beautiful, pale-mink creatures, wore red berets and carried machine guns on their backs. Some had moustaches and looked like miniature versions of Che Guevara. They were my little band of revolutionaries, experts in guerrilla warfare and monkey mayhem, and were my source of comfort and protection. As reassuring and amusing as my fluffy army was, I still couldn't shake that feeling of impending doom, that we could all die at any moment. I searched fruitlessly for Brian, wondering where he was, why he hadn't come to my rescue. He was never late for anything and I had the terrible sense that time was running out.

The nightmarish scenarios that followed were as real as the flashbacks I had experienced in Greece. I watched in horror as a gang of hooded terrorists captured my father and my younger brother, Stephen, after their car crashed in the basement of the hospital. I was in the back seat, trying desperately to reach them both, but frustratingly they were just beyond my grasp. The leader of the gang was terrifying, with six eyes of a glaring, yellowish hue. His partner, a woman, was dressed in long black shrouds that reeked of death. She grimaced and revealed rows and rows of filed, pointed teeth – an unnatural amount of teeth. The pair grabbed my father and brother, dragging them from the car and, ignoring my pleas for mercy, brutally slit their throats before my eyes. The terror, the agony of watching my father die once more was unbearable, and this time, to add to the torture, Stephen was also taken. Echoing from somewhere behind me I could hear a male voice shouting, 'Go in through the throat!' I could hear him, was aware of his presence, but couldn't see him, as though he was very far away. I screamed a silent scream as I felt a cold blade slice across my own neck. And yet still I knew I was not dead, although I was mystified as to why I had survived while those I loved continued to be taken from me.

I recall seeing red everywhere – the crimson shade of blood, or perhaps the colour that served as a warning of danger. And yet there were moments in my strange, solitary world when I also experienced calm and comfort. The sweet reunion with my mother was one: her voice I heard clearly, the touch of her hand I felt on my face. She reached me from the other side. Sadly, no matter how hard I tried, she didn't seem able to hear me, as if I were on mute.

Aware of constant movement around me in the hospital, of the doctors and nurses tending to my wounds, that sense of urgency never disappeared. Try as I might to talk to the nurses, who were continually by my side, my requests fell on deaf ears. Trapped behind a glass wall, silenced and very alone, I couldn't shake the feeling that the worst was yet to come.

19

STRANGE AWAKENINGS

On 7 September, two weeks after I arrived in St James', I was brought out of my induced coma. I awoke in a confused state to unfamiliar surroundings. Unaware that I'd had a tracheostomy, I couldn't understand why I had no voice and why, when I attempted to speak, only a muffled gurgling sound came out. My room was quite dark, with tinted windows (almost blackened out), as opposed to the larger, brighter suite I'd occupied in my coma dreams. Nurses and doctors were talking to me. I didn't recognise any of their faces, but their voices were familiar. I knew they were there to take care of me, but I still felt uneasy, under threat, though from what I couldn't possibly say. As a nurse asked me a question, I saw a couple of Meow's monkeys shuffle past behind her and out the door. I noticed a monkey lieutenant pitched up in the corner of the windowsill, keeping guard. He saluted me in deference, for I was his captain, and had I been able to move my arm I would have returned the favour. I was glad that my faithful monkeys remained by my side. As I slowly regained consciousness from my coma fog, they were pretty much the only thing around me that was familiar. I found their company comforting.

Otherwise I felt utterly bewildered, and it wasn't just the alien surroundings, it was that I felt terribly unwell. The nurse gently explained that I'd been asleep for quite a while, so it was natural that I was groggy, but that soon I would feel a lot better. I had no concept of just how long I'd been out for the count but presumed it was the day after my arrival, that is 24 August. I was focused on the exact date because I was eager to talk to Mum about Dad's birthday, which was coming up on 27 August. I knew we had lost Dad, believing then that he and Stephen had been brutally murdered, but I thought we should still celebrate his birthday in his honour. We always made a fuss on birthdays and I didn't want the first one after Dad's death to be any different.

The nurse introduced herself as Trish and explained that I'd been very ill and had had a throat procedure, which was why I was having difficulty speaking. Apparently, it would take some time before my voice would come back completely. There was a tube inserted into my windpipe to help me breathe and some sort of valve that she could adjust if my voice was too weak to communicate. A speaking valve in my throat ... it sounded like something out of a science fiction or horror movie to me. I immediately concluded that Trish was insane and that everything she said was absurd. How could I possibly be unaware of this contraption stuck in my neck and, if it was true, then who the hell put it there in the first place? I became agitated and quite angry. Trish became evasive and stopped answering my questions. When I asked her what day it was, she totally brushed over the topic, wittering on about pain relief instead. From the depths of my morphine-addled brain, I couldn't quite fathom if she was being purposely deceptive or was simply too stupid to know the answer. Trish, like many of the other nurses tending to me, displayed what could only be described as the patience of a saint.

Further fuelling my irritation, I seemed to be tangled up in a spaghetti junction of tubes appearing from virtually every orifice, each one connected to a different machine. This was strange because when I was in Greece there weren't so many tubes. It was so cumbersome that I found it difficult to move, like I was chained to the bedframe. Trish told me they were all necessary to help me recover, that the monitors were keeping an eye on my heart and lungs, the catheter was in place should I need to relieve myself, I was on dialysis to help my kidneys work properly and the feeding tube up my nose was to ensure I was sufficiently nourished. Next to the gizmo wedged in my throat, the tube up my nose was the worst. It didn't hurt exactly, but it felt really uncomfortable. At least I wasn't in pain and the beeps and boops I could hear were familiar sounds, so they didn't distress me. The unsettling issue was that niggling feeling I couldn't shake, that I wasn't being given the full picture. It was that uneasy suspicion of being kept out of a joke that had everybody around you amused. I couldn't help feeling that I was the butt of that joke.

I can't remember exactly when I saw my family – or what remained of it – but it must have been within hours of my waking. How wonderful it was to see Mum at last and though she looked frail, tired and oh so tiny, I had never seen her so beautiful. It was disappointing though that we couldn't embrace or even touch each other. Mum had to wear a protective yellow overall, mask and gloves, as would any visitor who came into my room. I was used to those shrouds in Greece, to prevent me catching infections, but my little mother looked swamped in that get-up, her petite frame dwarfed by this huge yellow gown. She had shrunk since my wedding day and looked like a tiny, delicate flower. One thing left me baffled: Mum seemed to know every nurse by name and they likewise were familiar with her. Everyone was acting as though they'd all known each other for a long time, but sure, I'd only just arrived in the place.

After Mum, I saw John briefly. I was only allowed one visitor at a time. I was surprised to see him fending off tears. It wasn't that long since I'd seen him in Athens, yet he was acting as though I was the prodigal daughter returned. When John left, I had the biggest shock yet. Wearing the requisite yellow garbs and mask, in walked my younger brother, Stephen. I hate mentioning this now and hope he will forgive me for ever imagining such a horrific thing, but I truly believed he'd been murdered and I was utterly mystified to see him there. I closed my eyes and opened them again, but still he stood, right in front of me, beaming his beautiful smile. The only explanation, in my morphine-addled mind, was that Stephen was a ghost who had come to comfort me in my hour of need. We were always so close and I convinced myself that this remarkable apparition, my ghost-brother Stephen, was there to look out for me from the next world. As I lay there staring, sure he'd vanish in front of my eyes at any second, I even winked at him to let him know that I could see him. I'm pretty sure he winked back. Who knew ghosts could wink!

Needless to say, that first family visit was a memorable one.

Clearly this all sounds utterly insane now, but in that post-coma moment my conclusions seemed perfectly logical. Given that monkeys were hanging around in the background and Meow put in the odd appearance wearing pigtails and shuffling across the floor, nothing was too out there in the realms of my new reality. My brain was a drug-muddled mess. I'd awoken to the world's worst hangover and the morphine was providing more than just pain relief, it was keeping my parallel universe alive. I was still living in my dreams, still convinced that an attack on the hospital was brewing and that we were the prime target, but no one else was aware of that. Some days later I even spoke to Mum about one of the scenarios we'd played out together in my alternate reality and was utterly perplexed that she clearly hadn't an iota what I was talking about. I deduced that the shock and grief of losing Dad had impacted her mentally.

My reality and fantasy worlds were overlapping and clashing, allowing paranoia to rule the day. Increasingly, I became suspicious of who I could trust. I started to test people, and poor Nurse Trish came top of the list. Convinced that she was working with my sworn enemy, Captain Peanut, I attempted to winkle the truth out of her, but she continued to hold back information from me and cunningly avoided answering my interrogations. Obviously, the less I knew, the stronger they grew. I decided not to share my suspicions with my family, who visited every night without fail. I looked forward to seeing them all day and didn't want to concern them with my burdens.

One evening Mum and Stephen were allowed in together. I believed that ghost Stephen had slipped in with her unnoticed. I got some fright when Mum turned to my younger brother and asked him to fetch something from her handbag, which had to be kept outside my room for infection control. Stephen nodded and left to do as he was bid.

Shocked, I quickly exclaimed, 'You can see him too?'

Baffled by the question, Mum responded, 'Of course I can.'

She looked so upset and confused that when Stephen came back into the room, I swiftly changed the subject. I again reached a 'logical' conclusion: my brother was also haunting Mum and due to her delicate state of mind, she hadn't yet worked out that he was just a mirage. Bless her, she actually thought this Stephen was real!

I explained my ghost theory to a nurse later that evening, after my visitors had left. I wanted advice on how to break the sad truth to my mother. The nurse looked alarmed momentarily, then quickly responded that both my brothers, John and Stephen, were very much alive and there was no such thing as ghosts. She looked so earnest, but it didn't add up. I tried to explain how I'd been a witness to his murder, but she was having none of it, so I concluded that she was either lying, ill-informed or simply working for the enemy. The suspicion that I was being kept in the dark about something was getting stronger by the minute.

The following evening Stephen came to visit me alone. He sat next to my bed and for the first time since I'd woken up, I got the chance to really inspect him closely. Sporting a deep tan, he looked so handsome and smiled sweetly as he patiently listened to my whispered words. No doubt I was staring at him intently, waiting for him to disappear into a puff of thin air. Suddenly, the nurse that I had confided in walked into the room, looked directly at my brother and said, 'Hello Stephen.'

Stephen responded politely by asking her how she was. That threw me, I have to say. They were actually conversing back and forth! I rolled it over in my head. First, Mum had claimed that she could see him and now the nurse was actually talking to him. Had I got this all wrong?

In that instant, I saw it all clearly. What a fool I'd been. Stephen, this Stephen sitting by my bed, was no ghost. This man, who admittedly looked identical to my brother, was in fact an exact replica, a cloned substitute sent to look after me while I was trapped in hospital. Introducing Robot Stephen!

It seemed ridiculous that I hadn't worked it out before then. The guy sitting by my bed was much too young-looking, had perfectly tanned skin and a dazzling smile. (For the record, my brother carries all these physical attributes.) I looked closer and convinced myself I could just make out the shadows of 'robotic' nuts and bolts by his hairline. Whoever had created Robot Stephen had done an exemplary job. There were no obvious glitches, no loose wires or faulty craftsmanship to be seen. Only somebody really close to him, who'd known him all his life, somebody like his sister, could tell the difference. Deciding to go along with the charade I told the robot that I finally understood and gave him a knowing wink. Across Stephen's face flashed a look that was becoming all too familiar to me – one of utter befuddlement. He shrugged his shoulders, smiled that patient smile and continued talking.

After that visit, it was clear to everyone that I wasn't quite firing on all cylinders and was still floating in a parallel universe. It was time to introduce me to Mr Shelley, the man who I would eventually learn had saved my life when I was struck down with the TEN infection. In fact, I would later find out that Mr Shelley had contacted Mr Moutoglis, who sent all my medical files (mountains of them) over to Dublin. My team in Greece had no idea I had contracted TEN and were no doubt deeply shocked to hear it. Poor Mr Moutoglis didn't hear back for weeks after that and was unsure if I had lived or died. People with severe burns are vulnerable to these types of sepsis infections, but even so my form of TEN was extremely rare, so Mr Shelley had to wade into unchartered territory. Within five days my skin was bursting and shedding all over the place. I was extremely lucky to have survived. The odds were most definitely stacked against me and it is to Mr Shelley I owe thanks for having saved my life against those odds.

I was impressed by Mr Shelley straight away and thought to myself that he seemed to be a clued-in character. At last, here was somebody who could answer my questions honestly.

Cautiously, he began by explaining that I had been very ill when I arrived and had been in a coma for quite some time. When I asked the date – I was still obsessed with Dad's birthday – he disclosed that it wasn't in fact August anymore, that we were well into the second week of September. That shocked me. I started to count the days that I'd been out for the count, but Mr Shelley stopped me before the conversation totally derailed. He asked me how many people were in my family. I answered that there were just three of us, where once, not so long ago, there had been five. I explained that both Dad and my brother Stephen had been murdered by terrorists in the car park under that very hospital, adding that I had been a witness to their murder. I asked Mr Shelley if he'd seen the incident on the news and did he think we were still under attack. He looked at me seriously and said he was terribly sorry to hear that I'd lost my father, but that he was under the impression Dad had died of natural causes while I was in Greece. He added that there had been no terrorist activity in the hospital and, in fact, it didn't have an underground car park. By way of explanation, he suggested that perhaps I had just had a very bad nightmare, a common symptom experienced during comas. He told me gently that I had imagined the whole horrific event.

A little mist began to clear in my brain. There was a vague echo, a recollection of Dad passing away while I was convalescing in Athens. The cogs slowly began to turn. To press home his point, Mr Shelley then posed a query: 'How could it be possible for one man to die twice in a lifetime, in two separate incidents at two different locations? That's not logical, is it?'

I thought it over and had to agree, it didn't make sense. His account of my father's death certainly seemed more realistic. I had another flashback then, a painful memory of a long night crying over Dad, looking out at the stadium. If I had to choose one of the two scenarios, Mr Shelley's seemed the more likely. He pushed it a little further, mentioning a nice conversation he'd had with Stephen earlier that day. Surely, he proposed, if he could see and speak to Stephen, then that must mean that he's alive. Again, he used the word 'logical' and I had little choice but to agree. Everything he said made sense, so slowly I nodded in agreement. Mr Shelley asked me if there was anything else bothering me. I shook my head and thanked him for clarifying matters. He smiled and told me I was very lucky to have survived and promised that he and his team would take excellent care of me. Then he left.

I lay in bed and thought it through. Dad had died while I was in Greece, that was a tragic truth, but it was a comfort to know he hadn't met the gruesome end that I'd conjured up in the dark recesses of my mind. If that was the case, then it was likely that Stephen hadn't been murdered by the terrorists either. That was phenomenal news – my brother was alive! For the first time in a long time I allowed joy to enter my heart. I hadn't lost my gorgeous little bro, my pal. The Holohans weren't a posse of five anymore, but likewise we weren't just three. Finally, I could sense hope on the horizon.

Alas, my delusions didn't end there. I was still convinced that the bloke I'd met in the hospital wasn't my sibling. My wonky brain concocted a brand-new scenario: my real brother was, in fact, an international spy and this guy, this Robot Steve, had been sent in his place as his cover. While my bro was off on a secret mission, jetting to exotic locations, probably doing something terribly important for the war effort, the robot was sent as a decoy. I knew I had to keep this to myself, not wanting to blow his cover, and I still didn't know who I could trust. It was enough to know that somewhere out there my brother was alive and well, protecting the world. For the meantime, this replacement seemed terribly nice anyway.

As for Mr Shelley, I decided he was one of the good guys. It was a pity that he wasn't fully aware of the extensive threats still surrounding us, but perhaps that information was above his clearance. Some instinct had told me not to confide in him about Captain Peanut and his army – best to keep that under my hat for now. As I closed my eyes to take a nap, blessing my secret-agent brother, one of my monkeys skipped across the floor, saluting me as he exited the room via the door.

I fell asleep, knowing I was safe ... for the moment.

20

I'M A LITTLE TIED UP
RIGHT NOW

Eventually the brain fog that had been muddling my thoughts began to clear. The monkeys deserted me and I came to realise that I'd lost over a fortnight in time. The paranoia still persisted, mind you, as did the instinct that there were more surprises yet to come. Given that I still had no comprehension of what a close brush with death I'd just had, that suspicion wasn't without warrant. Mr Shelley and his team were taking the softly-softly approach, giving me titbits of information each day.

Confusion doesn't even come close to describing how I was feeling back in those first few 'conscious' days in St James'. In my mind, I had just left Greece after taking those precious thirteen steps and was chomping at the bit to take my next lap. I had no idea that my recovery had taken a huge step backwards, that my condition had, in fact, worsened considerably. Still in a mild state of delirium, I asked the nurses on numerous occasions when I'd be allowed to take a shower. I was unaware that my muscle capacity had weakened dramatically and that I could barely lift my head off the pillow, let alone take one step on the floor. Nothing was working as it should: my arms, legs, heart, lungs, kidneys, my vocal cords, all were out of action to some degree. And I still didn't get it! Even when my voice wasn't working because I needed a particular valve inserted to talk, I'd lie in bed shouting ludicrous demands that nobody could hear.

The medics didn't want to shock me by revealing how grave the situation was all at once, but there were some scenarios that required tough love. For instance, I have a vague recollection of asking one nurse, in the early hours of the morning, to take me to the bathroom and wash my hair. She was busy checking my monitors and gently explained that 3 a.m. wasn't the best time to take a shower. She told me to relax and go back to sleep. I was having none of it, became irritable and obnoxiously demanded that she either did as I asked or at the very least tell me where my bags were so I could get my own shampoo and do it myself. Again, she responded patiently, although this time a little more firmly, that it wasn't shower time and to go back to sleep. Totally exasperated and even more disagreeable (I'm sure she might have a more colourful word to describe my behaviour), I persisted with yet more ridiculous demands until eventually I pushed the poor woman to her limits.

'Fine,' she said. 'If you really want to a shower, it's just over there. Off you go.'

I tried to get up. I tried to move my upper torso, legs and arms … nothing budged. The nurse quickly explained that my body was still asleep, that it needed time to recover and wake up. She promised that if I rested and recovered, there would be plenty of time for showers later. That was a wake-up call – reality began to sink in.

I would like it noted that most of my less cooperative moments in hospital should be attributed to heavy medication which, combined with confusion and paranoia, created a rather objectionable Zoe. The lovely nurses who worked tirelessly, tending to my every need during this period, would definitely agree that I was a smidgeon cantankerous at the beginning (again, probably not the word they'd use). We laughed about this period many months later, discussing my difficult mood swings and some of my more creative conspiracy theories:

Conspiracy Theory No. 1: somebody stole my twelve ruby rings. One afternoon I demanded that my occupational therapist, a lovely bloke called Shane, search my room from top to bottom to find my missing ruby rings. At the time I had no idea who Shane was or why he was in my room, but I decided that if anybody was going to find my missing treasure, it was him. If he proved unsuccessful in his mission, I wanted him to call the police. Shane, being the top-notch guy he is, played along to appease my paranoia. A phony search took place and the mystery remains unsolved to this day. Naturally, nobody called the police and within 24 hours I realised that I couldn't have lost the rings or had them stolen, because I never owned any in the first place.

Conspiracy Theory No. 2: there was a water shortage in the hospital because nobody would get me a drink. Water had become my obsession. I'd gladly beg or bribe anyone who came into my room to smuggle me in a glass. Totally unaware that I had a great big hole in my throat and was unable to swallow my own saliva let alone drink fluid, I even resorted to offering monetary rewards in certain instances. Poor Mum, not knowing how to respond to my requests, told me one evening that the hospital had temporarily run out. As far as I was concerned, it was a rotten conspiracy and that while I was withering with the thirst, they were keeping all the water to themselves. Eventually Mr Shelley explained that I'd had a tracheostomy and that even a sip of water would be extremely dangerous, as it would go straight into my lungs. To sate me, I was offered a cotton-wool lolly to quench my dry mouth. Well, that was the biggest booby prize ever! Cotton buds are for cleaning your ears and do not make a refreshing treat.

It goes without saying that the most ludicrous conspiracy theory was my Robot Steve idea. Once I'd understood that this gentle creature was indeed my own real, true brother and not a metallic imposter, reality finally started to come into focus. I apologised to all those who had suffered from my mad morphine behaviour, particularly those I'd unjustly accused or offended.

Unfortunately, I also came to understand that there was a whole new set of challenges to face. The trach tube that ran from my throat to my windpipe was one: it felt really uncomfortable and alien to my body. To keep the tube clear, so I could breathe, I had to endure a frequent suctioning process throughout day and night. This was a deeply unpleasant procedure – and I'm sure it wasn't a bed of roses for the nurse who had to perform it either. The suction pipes were long, bendy wands and looked like they belonged in Harry Potter's pocket. I dubbed them my Dementors on account of the high-pitched squealing noise they made when clearing my throat. It really was the most unpleasant, invasive process – and that's from a gal who's had an enema.

Finding my voice was also proving difficult. There were several valves on the trach to work with: some to help me breathe and sleep but through which I couldn't make a sound (my silencers); and some to strengthen the vocal cords when I wanted to talk my head off. I have a sneaky suspicion that the silencer valve was used a little more frequently than required, especially when I was in crazy conspiracy mode. It was effectively a mute button (Brian would have loved one of those). At no stage did I ask for a mirror to look at the contraption in my throat. The idea of this foreign object wedged in my neck frightened me, so I thought it best to pretend, as much as I could, that it simply wasn't there. I couldn't even raise my head off the pillow, so there was no chance of an accidental glimpse of my reflection in the window, which was perhaps the only benefit of being in such a weakened state.

There were other tubes in places where tubes should never go. The feeder, inserted up my nose, provided a constant stream of nutritious green gunk from a drip bag behind my head. I swear the stuff in there looked like horse feed. While I couldn't really taste anything, I imagined a faint scent of hay every now and then. As for the other terrible tubes embedded into equally terrible places, well, I don't think I need to spell out the obvious. What finally became clear was that I was back at square one and that the road ahead was going to be ever more difficult to navigate. What I didn't know was that the TEN infection had brought with it a whole new batch of serious health problems, beyond the injuries I had already incurred in the fire.

Ignorance is bliss, as they say, but it wouldn't be long before that spell was shattered entirely.

21

THAT'S A LOT TO SWALLOW

Slowly, things began to improve. My kidneys were finally behaving themselves and about a month after I was admitted, I was taken off dialysis. My blood pressure was a trickier little so-and-so, however, with a tendency to bounce up, down and all over the place, so I now had my own Pac-Man machine to keep me entertained. It made me think about the elderly man in Greece. I hoped he was OK and still bee-booping away. I was hydrated intravenously, but I still felt thirsty all the time. Cotton-wool lollipops are a poor replacement for good old-fashioned water. My tongue felt like sandpaper and I often indulged in water-related fantasies, my favourite being swimming in a pool of ice-cold water, gulping away indulgently as I splashed around.

The TV mounted on the wall was set on one station and mostly on mute. Its silent advertisements would tantalise me with merchandise to sate my every desire. My obsession for water was replaced with a desire for Pepsi Max. I stared at the Pepsi goddess on the screen, whirling around on a skateboard, glugging back bottle after bottle of this heavenly liquid. McDonald's ads were just as enticing. I'd have given my right arm, or better still, my wonky left one, for a Big Mac and fries. These ads were my call of the sirens and even though I was never a huge fan of Big Macs or Pepsi before my hospital stint, they became the topic of many a delirious dream. It wasn't that I was hungry exactly, the tube up my nose saw to that, it was that I desired the physical act of eating. After my total disinterest in food in Greece, now I was haunted by thoughts of it. The irony wasn't lost on me. There, I couldn't abide the thought of food, whereas here, I was totally obsessed with it. I kept asking when I'd be able to drink and eat properly again and was informed not until the tracheostomy tube was removed and the wound sufficiently healed – that is, some time away.

First up, however, there was the most crucial operation yet, the one I'd been waiting for since Mr Moutoglis had given me my parting instructions at the Mitera. Mr Shelley and his team were going to perform the grafting procedure on my legs, arms and hands. In the midst of all the TEN drama, I'd almost forgotten what had brought me to St James' in the first place. All my hopes rested on this. I was ready to go back under the knife.

As in Greece, it was decided to get me back on my feet again before surgery. TEN had left my muscle mass so badly depleted that I'd lost all the strength in my core, legs and feet. I basically had all the stamina of a rag doll. Those beautiful strides I'd taken in Athens were a distant memory. I was going to have to learn how to walk all over again. Now virtually back at square one, I was pretty damn depressed about the whole situation.

One afternoon, I was introduced to a couple of young guys who were to become my interim physios. I think they were residents, as they looked very young to me, certainly no more than early twenties. I'm embarrassed to admit that for several weeks I didn't clock their names, although in my defence back then my brain was mostly made of fudge. While I was present in body, my mental state was somewhat adrift elsewhere and in that frame of mind I christened my physiotherapists Bill and Ben.

Bill and Ben were eager, I'll give them that. They got straight down to work on my legs and feet, pushing me to get those muscles working again. My movement was badly restricted because I was chained to half-a-dozen machines, so it was much tougher this time around. As with Yiannis, we began with the simple stuff, moving my feet and legs in the bed and I guess Bill and Ben were pretty good at their job because I quickly improved. It was no time at all before I was standing on the ground, with each physio propping me up on either side. No delicate blue socks this time around, however. They placed on my feet some shockingly ugly black corrective shoes – visualise clumpy clogs with steel-capped toes that no fashion-conscious woman would be seen dead in. Bill told me that they were men's shoes but were the only ones he could find that would fit over my heavily bandaged feet. He laughed and said nobody would know. But I knew. I was only too aware that I was wearing ugly, oversized men's shoes and in my contrary state of mind I was not happy, not happy at all.

This time around, learning to walk was a much quicker process and with their support I was soon able to take a few steps, but I still found it exhausting and painful. Thanks to the trach tube it was difficult to breathe and any manoeuvres out of the bed were cumbersome due to the plethora of monitors I was attached to. Throw in the fact that I was particularly belligerent to Bill and Ben, which I put down to them forcing me into the ugly footwear, and you could say every physio session was damn hard work. In retrospect, I feel sorry for the poor blokes, who were just trying to do their job.

The operation took place on 18 September and as I'd been through well over a dozen surgeries by then, this was almost familiar territory. Given that Mr Shelley had already saved my life, I knew I was in the best hands, and the night before the procedure I was strangely calm and devoid of nerves. I pondered on this life-and-death question and concluded that it was much like the throw of a dice. Though it may seem morbid now, I reckoned that it wouldn't be the worst thing if I didn't make it through. Twice already I'd narrowly escaped death, and twice in that same short period of time I'd lost two of my favourite people on this planet. Why I'd been left behind I couldn't quite fathom and I wondered if perhaps my time should be up, too, if perhaps my expiry date was overdue. Death wasn't as frightening a prospect as it had once been – in fact getting it over and done with under anaesthesia had its appeal. I didn't expect a gossamer-clouded nirvana on the other side, but I was content knowing that if I died on the table, at least I'd had a decent innings. What would be, would be.

For the operation Mr Shelley would use my own skin and tissue, a process known as autografting. He had already performed allografting, using donor skin and tissue, on my back, legs and buttocks when I was under assault from TEN and my own skin and tissue were effectively attacking my body. As I mentioned before that caused me to lose 90 per cent of my epidermis and 10 per cent of my dermis. This time he'd remove sections from my own skin and redistribute it to the most damaged areas. I reckoned Mr Shelley would do well in the old loaves-and-fishes brigade because he had to make my own donor skin stretch magically over a rather large area. My right leg and thigh provided the donor material, and it needed to cover the lower part of my inner right leg, the better part of my entire left leg and thigh, my right lower and left lower arms and my entire left hand. You do the maths. I still haven't figured out how he made it stretch so far, but he did. It was nothing short of a miracle – or the mastery of a bloody good plastic surgeon more likely.

It was a long and gruelling procedure, but it was ultimately successful. Hazily, as I regained consciousness, I recall Mr Shelley saying he was happy with the outcome. So far, so good. The grafts had taken, but there was, as yet, no guarantee that they would stay that way. If the skin shifted, it would be straight back to surgery to redo the whole process. Still, I felt positive. Perhaps my cards weren't up just yet ... my expiry date extended. There was little time for celebration, though, as just minutes later my post-operative checks identified a haematoma, or pesky little blood clot, and I was raced swiftly back up to surgery. It was close on midnight when they wheeled me back into theatre and I thought I'd have to finally succumb to my fate. 'Death by haematoma,' they'd say. 'Unfortunate, but not surprising, her time was up long ago.'

As the anaesthetist gave me more of the good stuff for the second time in twelve hours, I was reminded of the song Mum used to sing in her best Doris Day voice when we were kids: '*Que sera sera, whatever will be, will be* ...' And I was out for the count.

The following morning I awoke, back in my room once more. The haematoma evacuation had been successful. Doris would have her day, but today was not it. I was still alive.

Mr Shelley and his surgeons had completed their task with tremendous skill and if it sounds like I've taken all of this for granted, well, nothing could be further from the truth. I'm very much aware of how much I owe Mr Shelley. He gave me the chance of a somewhat normal life, recreating a fully functional hand, not to mention two grafted, reconstructed legs. In time I would learn this surgery was more than just healing the terrible scars, many of which I'm stuck with, and as much about improving function and minimising pain and tissue and nerve damage.

Nearly a year later I requested to see the photo diary of my injuries and surgeries. Due to the rarity of my case, it was a test study, so I had access to images of my entire treatment. It was a revelation. I saw how Mr Shelley had performed the grafts, put my limbs back together and effectively recreated my hand from scratch. His work was nothing short of genius. My last memory of that left hand from the day of the fire was gruesome: I had watched the skin and flesh from my fingers melt and erode. When Mr Shelley eventually began working with something that barely resembled a hand at all, I understood that I was truly in the presence of greatness. I was grateful to him on that September day, but it wasn't really until a year later that I truly understood what a mammoth task he had faced in the first place.

Back in recovery, I decided it was my turn to step up to the plate and focus all my energy into healing. I considered Mr Shelley and Mr Moutoglis, thought about all the effort they had put into meshing me back together again, so the least I could do was put equal effort into meeting the same endgame. One thing I could do to play my part was to stay really still to ensure I didn't damage the grafts or cause them to shift. If they did mosey, it was back to surgery for me, and for now I'd had enough of theatre. Sometimes, and through no one's fault, grafts simply don't take, but to give this surgery the best chance, I knew I had to stay immobile in bed, superglued to its base. Nothing and nobody was going to make me budge. Not even a well-intentioned, enthusiastic young physio team.

Less than 48 hours after my full-body graft operation, Bill and Ben bounded into my room filled with enthusiasm, ready to seize the day. They announced that it was time for me to get up and walk again. To say we weren't quite on the same page is no exaggeration. Hell, we weren't even in the same book, or library for that matter. The pain all over my body, after the grafting, was excruciating. Not to put too fine a point on it, I had been skinned and patched back together. The donor side on my right leg, where skin and tissue had been sliced and removed, was phenomenally painful every time I flinched. In fact, the pain was on a par with the day of the fire. Thankfully, we live in a civilised society and I was given a handy morphine distribution system: all I had to do was press a little button to release the magic elixir. Oh, how I loved that button of joy! I would have happily pressed it every five minutes, if I could. Of course, I didn't know it was on a timer, so even if I did push it more frequently than I should, it would only release the medicine at set intervals. Anyway, the magic button certainly took the edge off, but if I moved my limbs suddenly the pain would rip through me like I was being skinned alive. Staying very still was the only option.

I think I've made it clear that there were occasions on this path when I didn't behave like a model patient. This was one of those times.

Bill and Ben belted into my room like a pair of exuberant puppies and told me it was time to put my feet on the ground again. I couldn't believe my ears. I explained that I was recovering from major surgery and was under Mr Shelley's orders, no less, to stay perfectly still. I would not be standing that day, there would be no pushing and pulling my legs and feet and definitely no walking. The club-foot shoes would have to stay in the corner where they had been banished for the time being and nobody, absolutely *nobody*, would be touching me at all. End of story!

Bill and Ben were undaunted, however, and I began to feel alarmed. I wondered if, as residents, they had some mighty bucket list that had to be ticked off daily to get them the A grade.

Bill and Ben's Bucket List
Get patient walking in miraculous time-frame ... tick!
Ignore obstinate patient's refusal to move and proceed with goal ... tick!
Place hilarious clown shoes on difficult patient's feet for a laugh ... tick!

They were moving towards me with slow determination and Ben, the younger of the two, smiled and said something along the lines of, 'Ah now, Zoe, come on, you were doing so well. Don't you want to walk again?'

He was talking to me as though I were a senile old bat. They had the dreaded shoes in hand and were moving stealthily towards the edge of the bed. Alarm bells were now ringing loudly in my ears: these guys weren't taking no for an answer. I raised my voice and told them that if they moved my legs, it could shift the grafts. I asked them to find Mr Shelley so he could explain, reiterating that this was not the time for physio. The response I heard was that my surgery had been two days before, I was only being difficult and sure, a little walk around the room wouldn't do any harm.

That was the last straw, and I have to confess that my reaction at that moment was somewhat less than ladylike. I told the two lads, in no uncertain terms, that they could take their 'ugly shoes and their little walk' and shove them up their ... well, I believe the medical term is rectum. To emphasise my point, I also told them to 'f**k off out of my room' and come back when they'd 'graduated from school'. The message had landed, if the gasps of laughter outside my room were anything to go by. A couple of nurses walking past had heard the whole exchange and were evidently highly amused. Swiftly, the two physios exited my room and left me alone for several days after. Not my finest hour, perhaps, but it felt good to know I had some fight left in me yet!

22

FINDING MY VOICE

A few days later I underwent a decannulation, meaning the tube was removed from my throat, and other tubes and devices soon followed suit. With them gone, I slowly began to feel less like a machine connected by intertwining cables and more like a human being. The only downside to the trach removal was the gaping hole it left in my throat, which required some clever concealment with a bandage. I still hadn't seen my reflection since waking from the coma because I was afraid of the valve contraption embedded in my neck. I had frequent dreams of transforming into Frankenstein, with patched-up skin, cogs and wheels poking out of my neck and head – even with my wild imagination, it wasn't far from the truth. So while I was delighted to be freed from the breathing apparatus, I still refused to look in a mirror and replaced one nightmare for another: scared to see what I looked like with a hole in my throat.

Without the magic trach valves, I now had to get my vocal cords in shape and learn how to talk again, all before the opening in my throat had fully healed. Learning how to control my breath and using it to form speech in a voice that was familiar was expected to take up to a couple of weeks. This was an utterly bizarre experience – and that's coming from somebody who was fast collecting a lifetime's supply of utterly bizarre experiences.

It was like playing with an old transistor. I had to tune in my voice and locate my sound, as one would attempt to find a favourite radio station. But instead of finding Radio Nova, for instance, my favourite station, I kept hitting some squeaky bandwidths that were agonising to the ear and certainly not what I was looking for. Normally my voice has quite a husky tone to it, due in part to all those cigar-smoking years, but that Zoe voice was nowhere to be found and try as I might to locate her, I could not. Instead, I emitted sounds that no human should ever make, nor have to listen to for that matter. One minute I'd transmit a high-pitched, dolphin-like squeak (think Mariah Carey on a really off day), the next I'd give Barry White a run for his money, so low could I go. Sometimes my voicebox gave up the ghost entirely and those silent days were the most distressing.

I wondered if I'd ever sound like the old me again, if I'd be able to sing my blues tunes or even work in sales. How could I sell without a voice? For nearly 25 years I'd worked in advertising, jokingly describing my number-one job skill as 'nagging'. If I sniffed the chance of a sale, I wouldn't let go until the deal was closed. That was something I excelled at. Although it goes without saying that I never nagged outside the workplace, even if Brian may have disagreed on that note.

To help me find my voice I was assigned a speech therapist. She taught me how to breathe, speak and even to swallow again.

Swallowing was something I was most excited about because the pot of gold at the end of that rainbow was being allowed to drink and eat by myself. The fantasies emerged once more. That refreshing, cool glass of water (or Pepsi) I'd been lusting after for so long was within touching distance. I was coming for it … could almost taste it.

If I'd felt childlike in Greece, now I truly felt like an infant, being taught how to talk and swallow properly. You'd think I'd be used to it, having taken my 'first steps' numerous times by now, but that feeling of terrible vulnerability and of starting back at square one again left me bewildered and exhausted. How many times would I have to start this process again? I couldn't help wondering why, with every step forward I had taken, I seemed to take at least three steps back. However, I followed all of the therapist's instructions and did my exercises as I was desperate to speak normally again. In fact, some days I was desperate to speak at all. The irony of this situation will not be lost on anyone who knows me well. I've never been accused of being too quiet for my own good. Usually it's a challenge to get me to shut up for any length of time. Ornaith used to joke that I had the unique talent of making any short story long as opposed to a long story short. Now all I could hope for was the odd squeaky sound that mildly resembled a human voice. Soft or loud, long story or short, I didn't care so long as something came out of my mouth.

Then there was the simple act of swallowing, something we don't think about at all because it's as natural as breathing or blinking. If I drank fluids before the tracheostomy had fully healed, the post-operative risk of flooding my lungs was very real and dangerous. Precautions had to be taken and patience had to be learned, given that it was most certainly not one of my virtues. I was told to be realistic with my expectations and warned that I wouldn't be able to drink until much further down the line. Water was too fine a liquid to commence with and was strictly off limits. Instead, I started with a thicker, unpalatable concoction known as 'heavy water'. It had a weighty, gooey consistency, a taste that resembled boiled cardboard and was like swallowing cold, thick, flavourless soup. It was even less appealing than that vile protein drink I'd had to consume in Greece. But once I'd mastered the heavy water with ease, I could eventually move onto the real McCoy, the good stuff – agua, aqua, plain old light, not heavy, water!

Eleven days after the tube was removed, a time that felt like an eternity, I was finally permitted to swallow three teaspoons of cool, clear water. I cannot tell you how thirst-quenchingly delightful those first cold drops felt as they trickled down my throat. I swore never again to take water for granted, for as long as I lived.

Eventually, I said *sayonara* to nearly all of the tubes, including the ones that were inserted into unmentionable places: the less said about those, the better. The last one to hang in there was the feeding tube, which was still firmly shoved up my schnoz. While I was hooked up to my 'horse feed' I hadn't a hope of eating and drinking freely and though I couldn't taste its wholesome goodness (thank the gods) and wasn't ever hungry because it was so filling, I found myself increasingly craving and virtually hallucinating about real food. It was time to open up negotiations with the nutrition team to persuade them to let me take the next step. And so we began my next lesson: how to chew and swallow, how to sip, not greedily gulp, slowly, over and over. Eventually, Mr Shelley agreed that it was time to release me from the confines of that last shackle.

There was little pomp and ceremony when the time came and I was a bit shocked, if I'm honest. Nurse Josette whipped out the tube in seconds, with virtually no warning. She just got me to lean back my head, look at the ceiling, and before I knew what was happening, she'd yanked it straight out. Of course, Josette was quite right not to warn me what she was about to do because had I known, I would have totally freaked out. I thought it was going to be surgically removed under sedation, but actually it was a quick, painless, but yet again utterly bizarre process.

At last it was bye-bye, horse feed and hello, human cuisine.

Those first few mouthfuls of real food were some teaspoons of smooth peach yoghurt. If that was delectable, the Solero ice-cream John brought me some days later was just sublime. In no time at all I was introduced to the very finest selection of 'slurpy', non-solid foodstuffs that would form the staples of my diet for several weeks. No wonder I keep making baby comparisons – think shepherd's pie puree and other such soupy delights and you'll get the picture. Gooey or not, I cannot remember ever enjoying food as much as I did in those first days after my feeding tube was removed. These are the things I sometimes remind myself that we too easily take for granted in life. So every now and then I raise a toast to a refreshing, cool glass of water, or perhaps an equally refreshing cold glass of wine, and some very basic fare. I thank my blessings for the simplest of pleasures.

23

LOSING ME

U p to this point I had avoided mirrors and reflective surfaces at all costs, but I knew it was time to face my demons head on. 'Head on' was exactly the problem, though. I had a suspicion that something had gone awry with my noggin. Truthfully, I caught a glance of my reflection in the window of my room the first time I met Bill and Ben. As they were lifting me off the bed, they turned me towards the window and before I had a chance to close my eyes, which I did pretty damn swiftly, I spotted this spectre in the darkened glass before me. It was a brief flash, no more than a split second, but it was enough. At first, I wasn't entirely sure if my mind was playing tricks on me or if I'd simply imagined it because the image I saw bore no resemblance to my face. I saw an emaciated, deathly pale creature with wide black eyes set in hollows staring back at me. This ghoul appeared, as far as I could tell, to have no hair on her head. It was like looking at Edvard Munch's *The Scream* – a gaunt, tormented creature.

The shock was so great I told the physios that I was feeling dizzy and begged them to put me back to bed. I lay back and closed my eyes and tried to erase that image from my mind.

Sadly, that incident was not born of delirium and, like it or not, it was indeed my own face staring back at me. It took weeks before I mustered up the courage to ask one of the nurses, Maya, to bring me a mirror so I could inspect the truth for myself.

The topic came up late one afternoon, while she was bandaging my throat. Maya asked me if I was sure that I was ready to see my reflection. I gulped and nodded, knowing I couldn't avoid it any longer. She did as I asked, but almost immediately I regretted it. The results from the TEN infection were there for the world to see. I had lost all my hair, bar a couple of wispy, shocking white strands that mysteriously sprouted up here and there. As a result of the toxic shock I had lost pretty much all my bodily hair too, including my eyelashes and eyebrows. I was skeletal thin and the burns down the side of my face were all the more prominent and reddened when compared with my deathly white pallor. I didn't recognise myself. Another piece of the Zoe I had once known had disappeared, another part of my identity annihilated. I was devastated but held back my tears, not wanting Maya to see my distress.

The great efforts of Anna and Maria and the supreme styling work of Paulina had gone to waste. All their hard work amounted to nothing. Though I had far greater health concerns, the loss of my hair was symbolic. I felt like I'd lost yet another battle, had failed once more. Maya was prepared for this reaction and tried to comfort me. She reminded me that I'd been seriously ill and was lucky to be alive at all. I'd had multiple organ failure and symptomatically, from the shock, my hair had fallen out. There was nothing they could do to prevent it from happening. I was only half listening as I stared at this stranger in the mirror. Maya gently took my hand and promised me that it would be alright, that my hair would regrow. I wasn't sure she was telling the truth. I wasn't sure of anything anymore.

Anyone who has suffered hair loss as a result of serious illness will know how distressing an experience it can be. All the more so if you are a woman. To me, it represented the final desertion of my femininity and that dramatic alteration of my appearance affected me more than I thought possible. I waited until Maya left me alone before I allowed my tears to flow and try as I might not to cry – I thought if anyone saw me weep, they'd think I was weak or ungrateful – I couldn't help myself. Seeing my true reflection pushed me over the edge. Beyond crying for Brian and Dad, I bawled for the loss of my womanhood, for the last vestiges of the girl I once knew and no longer recognised. She was gone now, she too was dead. I sobbed all evening, unable to stop.

For a long time after this night I truly felt that Zoe was dead, so much so that I experienced a disconnect from my own name. I imagined perhaps I should choose a new name as Zoe belonged to the person who was now long gone, the woman I used to be. There are plenty of days I still feel that way. Certainly there are two of us, and we are very different creatures: pre-fire Zoe and post-fire Zoe. I live with both of them – one in my head, one in my body. It's a very strange dichotomy.

The following day, Maya was on night shift. Originally from India, she was blessed with many of the natural attributes women from that country possess, certainly those I've encountered anyway. She had huge dark eyes and the clearest sallow skin. Her beauty glowed from the inside out. Astonishingly, Maya displayed no egotism and initially seemed shy and gentle. As we got to know each, however, especially during the night shifts when the ward was quieter, she opened up about her life, her birth country and family, and especially about her little daughter, the apple of her eye. As before with the nurses in Greece, I enjoyed those late-night chats with Maya, curious to learn as much as I could about her world and traditions. This was a way to transport me far away, even if only in my mind. We'd exchange anecdotes about our lives as two ordinary women may do anywhere in the world.

On the evening that followed my bald discovery, it wasn't long before the topic of hair raised its head. I suspected Maya was hiding sheaths of long, lustrous black hair, though it was always neatly pinned up, and as we talked I found myself staring enviously at her head. Using a reverent tone, considering the sensitive nature of the subject, Maya asked me how I was feeling about my hair loss. I joked that I still hadn't quite got my head around it, but then quickly confessed that I had shed some tears. I suspect she already knew that. A sucker for punishment, I asked her if she would bring me a mirror once more, so I could properly inspect the sorry state of affairs. She did as I asked and together we gazed at my reflection in the subdued lighting of my room.

Now that I could no longer avoid it, I looked closely at my image. I wasn't entirely bald: there were about half-a-dozen thick tufts of hair stubbornly hanging in there, against all odds.

They were the sepsis survivors, little warriors clinging on for dear life, that had gone snowy white from the toxic shock. Their texture did not resemble any hair I'd ever seen – it was a little like cotton wool. These tufts made me look deranged, so I decided the fluffy follicles had to go. Maya interjected that I wasn't stuck with that look, that there were things we could do to rectify the situation. The best way, she said, to invigorate a new healthy head of hair was to shave off those strays and start anew. I readily agreed. After all, who better than a woman with a long, beautiful mane, to give advice on hair care. We made a secret pact: Maya promised that she would take care of it asap.

The following night, Maya returned to my room with an electric shaver that she used on her own little girl. She explained that in India it was customary to shave babies' heads until their hair grew in thick and lustrous. This was an insider tip that fascinated me. I'd always been curious how women from India all had luxuriant locks. Now I knew – and hopefully I could benefit from their wisdom. Solemnly, shaver in hand, Maya asked me if I was ready to say goodbye to the remaining strands. I promptly answered 'yes' before I could change my mind. She went to work. In less than a minute, the job was done. I looked in the mirror: I was now as bald as bald can be.

There, in the darkened room, staring at my reflection, we two embraced the silence. There was a reverent atmosphere that is difficult to describe. She had done for me what, I imagine, many women have done for their friends in similar situations the world over. My heart filled with unexpected warmth for this seemingly simple task, although we both knew it was more than that. I was incredibly grateful. It wasn't just the swift manner in which she carried it out, but also her kind and gentle way of doing it. Maya smiled sweetly and whispered that soon I would welcome new hair. In that moment of rebirth, I was indebted to her for gifting me a fresh start.

24

HOISTS AHOY

Mr Shelley was anxious that I start welcoming some new faces to visit me. I was reluctant, now that I was aware of my dramatically changed appearance, to see anybody outside my direct family. Mr Shelley wanted to break that pattern as early as possible. The first on my list was John's wife, Fiona. I had always got on well with my sister-in-law; we had a laugh together and I considered her family for sure, but she had two 'real' sisters of her own, so our relationship rarely strayed outside family occasions, which were mostly related to my two nephews. From that day on, the situation changed.

When Fiona arrived, I could see she was doing all she could not to cry. As ridiculous as it sounds, I hadn't yet fully registered that everything that stemmed from the fire had a shattering butterfly effect on many more outside my immediate family. I wasn't so self-absorbed that I didn't realise many had been devastated by the tragedy – Rosemary, Adey, Lisa, Caroline, to name but a few – but there were certain people I'd forgotten to count in the emotional mix. It hit me that afternoon. As Fiona stood by my bed, I could see signs of grief and strain etched all over her face. She had loved my dad and was no doubt missing him terribly. All the while she was having to prop up her husband John, wearing a brave face as the tragic events unfolded. It all played out when I looked into Fiona's eyes. Relief was there, too, but there was something changed about her. Sadness and fear had touched her and that altered our sister-in-law relationship into something closer. We were no longer just family through marriage.

Funnily enough, it had never occurred to me that certain relatives and friends would be so concerned for my well-being. I was totally focused on how everybody was affected by the death of Brian and my dad. Initially, I found their reaction to me surprising. I certainly didn't expect such raw emotion when they visited my bedside. I guess I was unaware of all the prayers and tears that had happened when I was fighting for survival from TEN in the coma. My family didn't think I was going to make it; they were told the odds were stacked against me. From my perspective, I definitely felt removed from everybody. It was like I was fighting my own battle, on my own little island, alien to anybody outside my immediate family. I didn't realise it then, but I'd lost certain emotional connects.

Blinking away her tears, Fiona was soon beaming from ear to ear, evidently excited to show me what booty she'd brought with her. I could see that she was laden down with bags and the gifts she bore couldn't have been more thoughtfully chosen or better timed. Fiona presented me with a vast selection of hats and scarves, in every colour and style imaginable. They were the best present anyone could have given me and I was overjoyed. Only a fellow girl knew the perfect remedy for my bald quandary.

We laughed as I rummaged with glee through the bags, like a child at Christmas, and I was truly appreciative, not merely for the head gear but for all that she had done for me and my family over those last few, terrible months. I found a neat little red felt cap, red being my favourite colour, and plonked it straight on my head. In my new chapeau, which covered my skinhead, somehow Fiona helped me restore just a little of my lost femininity that day. Perhaps there was still a chance that the lady in red would rise again!

And rise again I did – for soon I would be back up on my not-so-steady feet.

The good news: now that I was released from all those IV lines, I finally had greater freedom of movement. The not-so good news: Bill and Ben were back with renewed vigour, and this time they weren't taking no for an answer. To herald the new phase in my physio, they came equipped with their latest implement of torture – the dreaded hoist.

One morning, once my grafts had properly settled and my grumpiness had abated, the lads wheeled in an enormous machine with straps and pulleys a-plenty. The hoist was supposed to help me out of bed and, if not quite onto my feet just yet, given that it was too soon after surgery, it would be utilised to transport me across the room and plonk me, sitting upright, into a chair. The red leather chair was the other new, unwelcome addition to my quarters. It was wheeled into the corner and I was told in no uncertain terms that, by hook or by crook, I'd be sitting in that chair every day. A sign bearing my name, ZOE, was even taped to the back of the chair, in case there was any doubt as to where I should be. That less-than-subtle hint made me laugh, I have to say. Bill and Ben claimed it was labelled so that nobody would remove the chair. That made me laugh even more, because who in their right mind would want a clunky orthopaedic chair? Plus the thing looked like it weighed a tonne. Clearly, the physios were hoping that by plonking my name on the chair, eventually my derrière would be plonked there too.

Before that could happen, they had to get me out of the bed and into the hoist. No easy task. I was dead-weight heavy and as malleable as a lump of wasted muscle goo. It would be fair to say that I was also less than enthusiastic to move. I really didn't want to leave my comfortable bed. But Bill and Ben were on a mission and not to be dissuaded. They had even gathered a couple of soldiers (nurses) to assist and slowly I was manoeuvred into position. First, I had to be lifted into the contraption's seat – that took four people to achieve – and then strapped in for safety. Holding on for dear life with my good hand, I was slowly and very carefully hoisted up in the air.

It was hilarious and horrible in equal measure. I felt like an enormous load being winched up to the ceiling, a giant bald baby in a sling with its useless legs dangling in mid-air. The machine, moving at a snail's pace, then lugged its cargo all of two metres across the room to where the dreaded chair patiently waited. With a heavy sigh, the hoist lowered me down and cautiously dumped me on target, much to the delight of the victorious Bill and Ben, the machine's manipulators, who were having great fun playing with their new toy.

Mission completed. They had won: I was out of the bed and sitting upright. To add insult to injury, the grotesque safety shoes were placed on my feet. I wasn't exactly looking my best anyway, so how much worse could clumpy clogs make me feel? I gave in gracefully(ish) and before long was diligently doing my exercises to get those legs moving in the direction they needed to go.

Each day after that I was hoisted back and forth to the dreaded red chair. I've often wondered if that machine was part of a cunning plan to get me on my feet because I hated it so much, I found myself begging the physios to let me walk instead. Even that agony was preferable to my hoist humiliation. And with those first steps, my muscle memory clicked in with gusto. It was no time before I was introduced to my new friend – the walking frame. Clopping around in my clown shoes, I had fulfilled my own prophecy. Now I actually was Zimmer Zoe, the slowest walker in town.

These achievements didn't give me hope exactly – that would be too strong a word. I was amused by the irony of becoming Zimmer Zoe, but it's also the sort of moronic joke that I vowed to never make again outside the hospital walls. So if not quite hopeful, I would say I was definitely focused. Every day was a battle to make little parts of my body work and I was totally zoned in on that. It soaked up all of my physical and emotional energy. It took me back to those daily victories I needed to achieve in the Mitera. Once again, the small, incremental achievements were all I thought about. In its most literal sense, my whole life was about putting one foot in front of the other.

25

SKIN DEEP

Bed baths are not an enjoyable activity – well, perhaps they are for individuals with a particular proclivity but definitely not for me. They are necessary when one is bed-bound, but a little embarrassing. So when I was finally given the chance to have an actual bath, alone, in a proper bath tub, I was terribly excited. I imagined soothing warm water mixed with luxurious lotions covering my entire body and I could hardly wait. This was to be a much desired, long-awaited relaxing experience. And it was at first ... and then it was anything but.

On the morning it was scheduled, I was wheeled to the bathing room by Nurse Marie. I wasn't allowed to Zimmer-walk my own way there for safety reasons. It took two strong women, Marie and Maria, to help me into the deep steel receptacle.

It was no easy task. We all laughed as I not so gracefully plopped into the water, making a loud splash. I thanked the nurses for not making it a mortifying experience. I knew they'd seen it all before, but I was still a bit bashful and the laughter eased my embarrassment. I had virtually no core strength, so to stop me from going under I was propped up with a special stool at my feet and an inflatable cushion by my head. I was perfectly safe and comfortable, but should I feel panicky, my nurses explained, there was an alarm button within easy reach. With that, I asked for a few blessed moments of privacy and the nurses left me to it. I lay back and began to relax. The warmth of the water, swirling with emollients, soothed my pains as the moisturisers seeped into my skin.

Within a couple of minutes, the fogginess of the water cleared and it was then I caught a glimpse of my body beneath. It was the first time since the fire and the grafting operation that I'd had the chance to properly inspect the damage. Now that I was alone and naked, there was no avoiding it any more. Skimming beneath the water's surface was a horrifying sight. I had dark red raised tram-track scars running up and down both of my legs, from my toes to my thighs. There were elongated patches of raw sliced skin in strange cut-out shapes all over me. One resembled a map of Italy, another looked like a hammerhead shark. I had expected to see scars, of course, but nothing could have prepared me for this sight. My grafts were pinned with staples all over. I was literally stapled together, barely human. I couldn't look at myself a moment longer and started to thrash about in the water, trying to cover myself up. That didn't work, so I tried to haul myself up out of the bath but my useless arms weren't strong enough to lift the load. Desperate to escape I pressed the buzzer attached to the side of the bath and in a split second the nurses were back.

My pride wouldn't allow me to reveal the real reason I'd buzzed, so I pretended the water had gone cold. I'd been in there for such a short time, I've no doubt they guessed what the actual problem was. They immediately agreed to lift me out. Tenderly, they carried me from the bath to a chair in the corner and gently began to pat dry my skin, treat and dress my wounds. All the while I was struck dumb, just sitting and staring down at my legs. There was nowhere else to look but at those horribly marred limbs of mine. The nurses, as quickly as they could, covered me from head to toe in ointments and bandages. The laughter from just moments before was a distant memory and I started to shake and shiver with shock. I started to hold my breath for long periods of time to prevent myself from crying. After what felt like forever, Marie eventually wheeled me back to my room and gently helped me back into bed. It was once she left me entirely alone that I turned my face into my pillow and screamed a long, muffled scream. My skin, my beautiful unblemished skin, was destroyed. I knew it would never be the same again.

After that day, each time I took a bath I closed my eyes. I tried to imagine my body as it once had been, although that was a dangerous game because it led to thoughts of what my life had once been, too, and then loss mounted upon loss. So my new strategy became voiding my mind of any thoughts during those bathing moments. I became adept at focusing on the nothingness.

Eventually I progressed to the shower in my own room. The biggest benefit of the shower was privacy, of course. I didn't need several nurses to lug me in and out, just one to manoeuvre me onto my special plastic chair. Even with the nurse showering me as I sat, it felt like it was quite an achievement. Three helpers had become one, and I'd always preferred showers to baths, so this could be counted as one more step towards normality. Closing my eyes, I almost fooled myself into believing I was a regular human being.

My daily routine began to take form. Each morning a doctor would wake me early to do blood tests and monitor checks and I'd take my medications before breakfast arrived. Though I was still a bad sleeper, I always endeavoured to greet the doctor with a smile on my face. Indeed, often I was truly grateful to be woken up from my nightmares. No matter how bad the night before had been, I tried to embrace each new day with positivity. Some mornings this was simply not possible.

One morning Nurse Josette was assisting me in my routine. She was a lovely woman and usually we had great chats to pass the time, but I'd had a bad start to the day and was in subdued form. All night I'd suffered particularly gruesome dreams involving fire and torture, and that morning I couldn't quite shake them off. Josette read the mood and silently unwrapped my bandages to prepare me for the shower. With echoes of those macabre images still whirling around my mind, I found myself fixated on my own cooked flesh. The view I was now presented with was just as repulsive as the visions from my nightmares. Worse still, as I looked at my limp, scarred body, I couldn't help thinking that Brian, were he still alive, could not possibly love me as I now looked. How could anyone desire such a disfigured creature?

I immediately admonished myself for thinking such a thing and guilt shot through me like an arrow. Brian was the kindest man I had ever met and he was not a shallow creature, interested only in the skin-deep. He loved me then and surely he would have loved me still. We would have coped together with whatever challenges life threw at us. The problem was that Brian was not alive to reassure me that I was still lovable. He would never again hold my hand, would never again tell me I was beautiful, because he could no longer speak. He was gone for eternity.

From my little plastic shower seat, with water cascading down my face and body, I let out a loud primitive wail, a sound that surprised even me. It sounded as though it had been released from the core of my very soul. No choice this time, no power to hold it back, I wailed and wept and my tears flowed as fast as the water gushed from the shower-head. I no longer cared who heard me. I lost control and couldn't stop.

Josette did in that moment what only somebody with true life experience and a tremendous ability for compassion and love would do. She stepped into the shower fully clothed, as the water flowed around me, and took me in her arms. Josette held me tightly in a hug and allowed the healing water to cascade over both of us. I let her hold me, and I let it all go. I cried my heart out for my lost love and for the loss of our future. She gently began to rock me to and fro, as a mother would a small child, and started to sing in a low, soothing tone. It may have been a hymn that she sang, or it may have been a lullaby. It didn't matter what the song was, it mattered only that she held me and sang its soothing melody over and over, as the water continued to wash away the flood of my tears.

She could have been my own mother in that moment, such was the power of her tenderness.

Eventually, Josette helped me out of the shower and dried me off. Gently, she bandaged my wounds, still humming rhythmically while I continued to cry, though more quietly now. I cried all that afternoon until I was so exhausted, I fell asleep.

When I think back on that day now, I remember this. At that moment of my greatest sadness, one that I shall never erase, I could still feel the warmth of human kindness and the comfort that was selflessly given by a virtual stranger. She was my saving grace that day. Up until then, Josette was a nurse I didn't know very well, but in my moment of great distress she reached out to me, not as a nurse but as one woman to another. Her blessing stays with me for ever.

26

MUTINOUS MOMENTS

n no time at all we were halfway through autumn and I was at last well enough to say goodbye to my intensive care unit and move down the corridor to a huge blue room. My new quarters were kitted out with everything I'd need to get my body back in good working order. The challenge was set, and it was time for me to do my part. Amongst some of the exercise apparatus to assist me in my mission were a special stationary bike, to help me strengthen my leg muscles and core, and a set of portable steps with a variety of sizes, to help me learn how to ascend and descend staircases. The red chair also followed me to my new abode, with my name tag still hanging on for dear life. My blue room was so expansive that I dubbed it the West Wing. It was a bedroom, sitting room, gym and private bathroom combined. It was clear that Mr Shelley had invested a lot of thought into my recovery and together with my new home this compelled me to strive that much harder to succeed.

I was introduced to the head physio, Joanne, and we quickly gelled. I liked her immediately and that made me feel a little guilty about being so obstinate with her colleagues, Bill and Ben. Although I'm willing to bet they had a better word than obstinate to describe me! Now that my brain was wide awake, I promised her I'd do everything required to get me moving again. Flashbacks sparked in my mind of Yiannis and Dimitra cheering me on: it was time for a new victory. Perhaps the reason Joanne and I started on a good footing was that we were a similar age and it made communication easier. No doubt her colleagues had warned her about me, so she started by telling me that she expected my cooperation with her plan. That was fine by me because I was beginning to apply more pressure on myself than anybody else could apply. I was enthused about working with her and Bill and Ben on the common goal of waking my slumbering legs.

Each morning after breakfast I'd spend at least half an hour on the bike, beginning with a gentle setting then quickly increasing the level to reach tougher targets. This was a medical device as opposed to a regular bike, specifically designed for people with physical challenges like mine. So while I wasn't quite Tour de France or Lance Armstrong standard (although I probably had less medicinal assistance than he did), I quickly began to see the benefits when it came to leg strength.

Zimmer Zoe mostly came out at night when I needed the bathroom in the early hours. The frame was always close to hand. It became a multipurpose accessory, functioning as a part walking aid, part clothes-horse. Certainly, it was the perfect place to hang the numerous dressing gowns Mum had bought me. Even with my walker's multifunctionality, I eventually had to bid it farewell when Bill and Ben called time and moved me on to a more independent mode of transport: crutches. I have to say that it was quite the feat of persuasion on their part as I was convinced I'd fall flat on my face without the support of the frame. My buckled Bambi legs and puny upper arms hardly looked strong enough to manage crutches, but it took just days to adapt to them and soon I enjoyed the taste of freedom they gave me. It was incredible the difference standing upright made. I immediately felt stronger. While the frame was wonderful in the early days, and certainly a step up from the wheelchair, I was hardly moving at an Olympic pace and eventually it made me feel weak and infirmed. If I was a shoulder-hunched prehistoric woman on the walking frame, I became an upright, homo-sapien girl-about-town on the crutches … well, girl-about-hospital at any rate.

Even with all those breakthrough moments, I still demonstrated the odd childish rebellion. One day, for example, Ben gave me some new exercises during my afternoon physio session. While I was demonstrating my best hobble on two crutches, weaving my way around the blue room at what I thought was rocket speed – I could have given any snail a run for his money – my physio observed that I was really only using a single crutch, leaning mostly on the right one. In fact, for the most part I was dragging the left crutch, not using it for support as it was designed, but more as a forgotten accessory. Furthermore, Ben believed that I was more than capable of taking a few steps without either crutch. Like an expectant father awaiting his baby's first steps, he smiled encouragingly and said it was time to give it a go. I was not convinced and thought he was asking me to run before I could walk. Digging my heels in, refusing to hand over one stick, let alone two, I whined and objected. The poor bloke was back on familiar territory.

'My legs aren't strong enough … you're pushing me too fast' and so on.

Clearly, my whingeing did the trick as he swiftly gave in. I must have worn him down over time because he looked as though he was ready to give up entirely. Truthfully, I can't say why I was so bloody-minded when it came to dealing with Bill and Ben, and yet welcomed Joanne with open arms. I often wondered if it had anything to do with the fact that the first time I met the two lads coincided with the night I caught my reflection in the window and was appalled to my core. Perhaps somewhere in the back of my psyche I associated them with that feeling of shock. On the day Joanne assessed me, on the other hand, I was particularly vulnerable. I'd been crying all morning long and, try as I might, couldn't stem the tide. She was comforting and tender. Perhaps it was as simple as that – I associated the lads with a negative emotion, and Joanne with something more comforting. Mind you, my stubbornness with Bill and Ben could also have been connected to the hideous shoes, the horrible hoisting moments and the fact that they sometimes spoke to me like I was a belligerent child. Either way, my cantankerous behaviour must have been wearing. However, good things come to those who wait and Ben would have his day very soon.

While alone in my blue room, I liked to take a lap around my kingdom, stretching my legs or, better still, doing a little tidy-up. I really missed my favourite pastime: cleaning. Even though the cleaning staff were impeccable in their duties and left my room immaculate, I had managed to gather quite a lot of stuff during my stay. There were the piles of PJs and dressing gowns, leggings and hoodies, hats and scarves and mountains of cards, gifts and treats. My favourite afternoon distraction was to tidy these piles of items into some semblance of order.

It happened later that afternoon, just a short time after my awkward refusal to hand Ben the crutches. I was doing one of these tidying sessions in my West Wing. As I moved around, I found both crutches were superfluous to my needs, so I put one aside and continued my spree. For over half an hour I busied myself cleaning, sorting laundry, walking to the far side of the room to adjust the dodgy TV aerial. All these tasks I performed leaning on either a crutch or against the wall as I manoeuvred my way around. At times, even the one crutch was chucked to the side, but I was so distracted by my duties that I was totally unaware I was walking unassisted.

Unknown to me, there was a spy in my midst. Ben had spotted me through the glass door happily going about my business unencumbered. It was just hours since my little temper tantrum, refusing to hand over a single crutch. Revenge is best served cold, so he saved his 'Aha!' moment until the following morning when, with a triumphant grin, he revealed what he had covertly witnessed. He ceremoniously confiscated one crutch, promising the other would soon follow suit. I knew there was nothing for it. I'd been caught red-handed. Taking a bow, I gave in graciously.

Incidentally, during one of my tidying sessions I 'accidentally' binned the ugly black clogs. That most offensive-looking footwear was finally sent where it belonged: to the trash. It was a definitive moment of fashion glory and as a far more pleasing replacement, Fiona purchased an adorable pair of light-blue runners. They were a size larger than my usual, as my feet were severely swollen from the burns, but no matter, I was thrilled to finally have something stylish on my feet. Anything would have been an epic improvement on their predecessors. It's funny, the little things that mean so much when you're in hospital. The new runners were just the pick-me-up I needed. Though not exactly moving at the speed of light, I could now walk two full laps around the room unassisted, using the walls to lean against if ever there was a wobble. Ben was clearly right: not only were two crutches superfluous to my needs for short jaunts, there were times I could manage without any at all.

In addition to daily physio sessions, occupational therapists (OT) worked continually on my upper-body strength and, in particular, on my left hand, which from a functional perspective was my most damaged limb. Shane was my regular OT, famous for his role in the Mystery of the Twelve Ruby Rings during my post-coma morphine craziness. I must confess, his visits were my favourite, even though they came with considerable physical pain. He became a daily fixture, focusing mostly on my left hand and fingers. I had major difficulties with movement. Post-graft, my bandaged hand was frozen solid. It was basically an immovable object stuck on the bottom of my arm. My wrist was inflexible, my fingers couldn't bend and I was unable to grip. It was a sorry state of affairs.

Working intensely with Shane on my hand meant the inevitable would soon happen: the bandages would have to be removed to offer me more scope of movement. As yet, even when I bathed, I had not seen my left hand. It had been protected, sealed away in bandages and plastic coverings at all times. In fact, I hadn't caught a glimpse since that first time Mr Moutoglis had examined it, the day after the fire. Eventually, Shane gently told me it was time to see what was hidden underneath. It was time for the big reveal.

What emerged from under my bindings was not at all what I expected. Quite the opposite, in fact. The first time I saw that hand up close and unbandaged, I was astonished. Unlike my previous experience in the bath, seeing my legs for the first time, this great reveal was uplifting. I marvelled at my fingers, each one covered with skin, at the framework of my hand and arm. It wasn't the prettiest thing I'd ever seen, with its dark red snake-print skin, but to me it was remarkably beautiful. In my nightmares I still saw my hand as it was on the night of the fire, but now, as Shane unwrapped the post-graft results many months later, that horror-movie vision was replaced by something wondrous. Mr Shelley had given me the ultimate gift and even if it had some way to go to make it function, it was still the most stunning creation I'd ever seen – a true work of art.

Considerable effort was required to get that work of art functioning properly. The ligaments and tendons were immobile: they had effectively been cooked. Shane explained that the tissues and muscles had hardened or gelled into a solid mass and then glued like cement over the months since the injury. My fingers were like stiff pegs, stubbornly refusing to bend and grip – except for my ring finger, which had no strength at all and constantly flopped downwards. My wrist was rock solid and wouldn't flex a millimetre, let alone an inch. Shane and Michelle, the head clinical occupational therapist, worked with me tirelessly every day, manipulating and exercising the joints to thaw my wrist and flex my fingers. They gave me hours of hand exercises daily and applied custom-made splints, with weights and pulleys, to improve movement.

This wasn't a pain-free process, especially during the intense hand-manipulation sessions. However, Shane's sense of humour and clever diversion tactics always distracted me, temporarily, from the pain. Mind you, there was the odd yelp and curse when it got really painful. He soon learned that my potty-mouth moments were a clear indicator that I had reached my pain threshold. Every day without fail, Shane or Michelle would spend an hour in the morning and again in the evening determinedly massaging, stretching, plying and exercising my hand and wrist. For my part, I diligently continued my exercises throughout the day to get my hand and digits performing to par.

The mutineer in our midst at that stage was, for once, not of my doing. My little finger was the new rebel: she just wasn't playing ball. When all the others were doing their damnedest to bend and flex, when even my floppy ring finger started to stand to attention, my pinky would show me up and refuse to cooperate. So insubordinate was she that I – and eventually everyone else – named her 'my little f**ker'. I'm afraid to say that to this day, my little f**ker is still acting up. She maintains her contrary outlook, straightening when the others bend, sticking out from the crowd and frankly behaving like a right pain in my ... well, hand!

My finger wasn't the only black sheep to report. Another part of my body was behaving badly and was determined to cause me great embarrassment. My throat, or rather the hole in my throat, which had yet to close over completely, was the cause of many a red-face scenario. Carefully bandaged daily by the nurses, the wound across my neck had a habit of releasing air at the most inopportune moments and in a most impolite fashion. On numerous occasions, when I was laughing with Shane while he mangled, I mean 'stretched', my hand, or when I'd be entertaining a visitor, my trach hole would, without warning, exhale a gasp of air and emit a long, loud farting noise. Out of nowhere, it would parp away to its own content, not caring a jot who heard. It was mortifying and entirely out of my control. I found myself frequently excusing my throat farts, explaining that while these sounds did originate from my body, they were not of my doing and weren't to be confused with the traditional variety of derrière farts. Thankfully they also came minus the accompanying scent. They were still bloody embarrassing, though, and continued to occur for weeks, until the trach hole finally sealed over. During this period my friends kindly dubbed me 'Fart Throat'. I'm glad to say that it is a nickname that hasn't stuck – or, if it has, they don't say it to my face.

Mum and son,
Rosemary O'Callaghan
Westropp and baby
Brian at Lahinch
beach, Co. Clare. How
adorable was he in his
mustard jumper?

My big brother John, aged about three years old, and me as a young baby posing old style in black and white (well, it was the '70s).

Brothers Colin and Brian O'Callaghan Westropp at Brian's graduation. This was the first of many educational accolades for Brian; eventually he went on to earn an MBA, awarded to him posthumously several months after his death.

My graduation day in UCD when I was awarded an honours BA in English and Classics. This was taken during my boho/hippy phase, long before hair straighteners were invented.

My dad and I, snapped at a family gathering. Dad had won a golf tournament that afternoon and was in a true celebratory mood.

The Holohan siblings: Stephen, me and John. I reckon this was taken on John's birthday, possibly when he turned 25/26. While I busied myself shovelling cake into John's face (methinks drink was taken), Stephen was off in his own world – nothing new there!

Brian and I at his friend's wedding. This picture was taken about a month after we met and was the first night I met Adey and Lisa. I confided in Lisa that night that I was already thoroughly smitten.

A quick smooch between sets at a Rolling Stones gig. (The gig was epic, incidentally. Jagger was a total legend and had us dancing our socks off for the whole concert.)

Table Mountain, Cape Town. This was taken during our South African expedition. It was the holiday of a lifetime and the spectacular views from the top were worth the petrifying cable-car ride up the mountain (not a fan of lifts, cable cars or trams of any description).

My first biker rally in Arklow, Co. Wicklow, organised by Brian and Adey. I plonked myself down on the first red bike I could find as it matched my new red leather jacket. I soon discovered that while I was lousy on motorbikes (terrifying things), I excelled at the after-party festivities. It was a cracking weekend!

Brian and I decked out in our glad rags at the Q Ball, an annual event to raise funds for spinal injuries. Dad donated a beautiful painting to the auction, which raised several thousand that night. We had a ball, literally! (*Courtesy of Jerry McCarthy*)

A quick selfie taken by a cliff-top restaurant in the sunny town of Cascais, Portugal. This picture was taken moments before Brian proposed (2 April 2017).

There were lots of celebrations after we got engaged. This photo was taken at a party in our friends' house (Brendan and David, not pictured here).

We had a fun Easter (the bubbly gives it away). No idea where the Minnie Mouse ears came from!

Respectable shots of my hen party in Dublin, taken early in the evening before it all got a little messy. Celebrating with me here (well, just getting warmed up) are pals Ornaith, Gill and Caroline.

Stephen had to be part of my hen party gaggle – Brian wanted him to join the lads at the other side of town for his stag, but I pulled the big sister card and won that battle. Much later in the night, both parties – boys and girls – merged for a real blast of an evening.

Bridal bubbles. Getting ready in the bridal suite with my bridesmaids, Ornaith and Caroline. Here we attempted our finest Charlie's Angels pose (it's a tradition, don't ask me why – we've been playacting like this for years). Minutes after this photo was taken, I galloped down the aisle to marry Brian.

Brian and Adey. This picture was taken on the morning of our wedding. No signs of pre-wedding jitters, I'm happy to say. This is one of my favourite pictures of these two brothers-in-arms.

Just wed in the pretty floral gardens of Clonabreany House. I think our smiles say it all; my heart was bursting with joy in that moment. I had just married the man I loved with all my heart (19 July 2018). (*Courtesy of Jim Gallagher*)

Beaming bride and groom – we smiled and laughed all day and night. (*Courtesy of Jim Gallagher*)

Posing with our pantomime pals Karl Broderick and his husband Alan Hughes (aka Sammy Sausages) in the scorching sunshine. Brian and I loved our annual visit to their outrageously funny Christmas show with Adey and Lisa's children. (*Courtesy of Jim Gallagher*)

The wildfires in Mati, Greece, where 102 lives were lost, including my gorgeous husband Brian. My life changed forever on 23 July 2018. (*Above:* © *Valerie Gache/AFP via Getty Images; below:* © *Angelos Tzortzinis/AFP via Getty Images*)

Manos Tsaliagos, a true hero. Manos rescued me from the boot of a burning car, just seconds from death. He is a civil volunteer, who risked his life to save many on that fateful day in Mati.

Dimitra Andrianoy, one of my numerous angels who worked in the Mitera hospital. Dimitra demonstrated immense kindness during my stay there. She had the gentle nature of a true healer and, like many nurses I encountered that year, went far above the call of duty.

Yiannis Kentarchos, the best-looking physio in town! Yiannis not only taught me how to breathe properly (courtesy of ping-pong therapy) and restore my physical strength, but also, crucially, gave me back the ability to walk. With every agonising step, Yiannis kept me smiling too. A true gentleman.

Mr Georgios Moutoglis, the only person who managed to make me feel truly safe after the terrible events that brought me to the Mitera hospital. He's not only a tremendously skilled surgeon, but one of the most compassionate people I've ever met. Mr Moutoglis showed me tenderness and empathy, and his round-the-clock care was unlike anything I'd ever experienced in my life.

Shane O'Carroll and Michelle O'Donnell (occupational therapy department, St James' Hospital) happily posing with one of their chosen 'implements of torture'. In truth, this device helped restore strength and flexibility to my wonky left hand. This pair of phenomenal therapists not only gave me back a functioning hand, but always managed to keep me laughing through the process. Apologies for all the cursing! (*Courtesy of Anthony Edwards/St James' Hospital*)

Mr Odhran Shelley, Consultant Plastic Surgeon at the burns unit in St James' Hospital. A kind, patient and tremendously skilled surgeon, Mr Shelley rebuilt my hand from the flimsiest of structures, grafted both of my legs and arms and, crucially, saved my life when I contracted the often-lethal Toxic Epidermal Necrolysis. Without his expertise, I simply would not have survived. (*Courtesy of Anthony Edwards/St James' Hospital*)

Adey and I (I'm the one in the fuzzy blonde wig) at the Blood Bikes East memorial rally in honour of Brian. Here we are posing by Brian's bike, which Adey rode from Dublin to Tipperary, accompanied by a huge posse of BBE riders. The rally raised considerable funds for BBE and was a wonderful way to celebrate all the work that Brian did with the charity through the years. It was quite an emotional day. Brian would have loved it; I could feel his spirit with us every inch of the journey.

Katharine (Lady C) and I snapped at the top of Howth Hill. This picture was taken in March 2020, just days before the whole country went into lockdown due to the coronavirus pandemic. Little did we know what lay ahead when her husband Robbie took this photo. It was a beautiful, sunny spring day and I was grateful that my knees managed the steep climb to the summit, though I paid for it later that evening.

Ringing in the changes – time to step out of the shadows! 2020 was the year I finally decided to go back to my natural dark hair colour (well, some of it's my hair; some is borrowed from elsewhere) and stop covering up my body from top to toe. A wonderful tattoo artist, Fran Hartnett, designed and created the perfect camouflage to cover scars on my chest, upper arm and shoulder, which gave me a new lease of life (no more wandering silicone strips for a start). I could finally re-introduce my old wardrobe (though little lace dresses aren't really *de rigueur* during a pandemic) and get back some long-lost confidence and sense of self. Each piece of body art has some personal significance, and I am finally proud of my canvas. My close friend Marian Slevin kindly took this photo, which shows me burns, bandages and all. (*Courtesy of Marian Slevin*)

HERE COME THE GIRLS

Nurse Marie was great craic and someone I immediately got on with. Under different circumstances, she'd have fitted in well with my gang of pals: same sense of humour, same insatiable desire for gossip and yet, like my girls, sincere and sensitive when that was called for. Also, much like them, Marie was direct and straight to the point. One evening, while dressing my burns, she brought up the subject of visitors and, not being one to beat around the bush, she suggested that it was high time I invited my troupe to come visit. By then I'd been in the blue room for a few weeks and, apart from seeing my family, had become a little reclusive. My friends were no doubt surprised by this because I'd welcomed them with open arms in Greece, yet had refused all pleas to visit me since I'd returned to Ireland. I craved seclusion from the outside world and, with the exception of my family and medical team, I wanted to be left alone.

It was a strange reaction, especially considering the fact that I spoke about my friends constantly, telling the nurses funny stories of our antics, hoping to add colour to those long days and nights in the confines of the ward. I trusted my friends with my life, knew they had been my constant support in Athens, offering me comfort, love and practical help. I was blessed with some truly wonderful allies. Why then, Marie probed, was I so reluctant to see them now that I was back on home turf?

The truth was that the more my physical health improved, the weaker my mental state became. I felt vulnerable and deeply reluctant to step outside the comfortable family circle. There had also been a major shift emotionally since I'd left Athens, and much of that was to do with my damaged appearance. Since I'd awoken from my coma, I'd not only lost all my bodily hair but also acquired a fresh batch of physical injuries. I now had a greater understanding of the true damage to my body and my sense of self and confidence had been destroyed. While I attempted to smile outwardly each day in the safety of my blue room, inside my spirit had evaporated. I believed that whatever beauty I had possessed was gone forever.

The realisation had dawned that I would never look like the old Zoe again. I didn't recognise myself in the mirror and I certainly wasn't ready to embrace my baldness. My face was scarred, though it could have been so much worse, and I was concerned about keeping hidden the ugly secrets that lived beneath my bandages. I was different now, changed from the person my pals had once known, and I wasn't yet ready to reveal those changes. My problem was beyond vanity. My issues lay in that vast distance I now perceived between me and the friends I had known for decades. I felt un-human and separate from everyone I had ever known. All that I'd taken for granted had disappeared and I didn't know how to express my feelings without displaying pain or resentment. My barring order on my friends was my way of keeping these emotions under wraps. In letting them in, I was terrified of what I would let out.

My body image wasn't the only topic closed for discussion. I didn't want to distress my family, so I worked hard on keeping conversation neutral and never strayed into emotive subjects, like grief or loss. This was my way of establishing control – it seemed to be the only area where I could. I knew that as soon as my friends arrived, there was a risk my self-imposed rules would go out the window.

Nonetheless, Marie persevered, insisting it was time. She said there were things that I couldn't talk about with family, things only girlfriends knew, and was convinced that by keeping my walls up I was only damaging myself further in the long run. She also hinted at another benefit to welcoming outsiders. I had become, shall we say, more than a little bit lazy with my appearance. I could barely be bothered to change out of my hospital gown most days, even though I had a selection of respectable PJs, dressing gowns, etc. Outside the daily medical activities like physio and occupational therapy, when pyjama bottoms were essential, I would happily lounge around in my pale blue hospital gown that gaped at the back, propped up on my red leather chair, watching TV morning, noon and night. Well, I would have been happy to do so if the nurses let me get away with it.

There was one decent excuse for staying in my hospital gown, other than sheer slovenliness. Getting dressed without assistance, even into PJs, was no easy feat. In fact, it was a bloody nightmare.

I was wrapped in layers of bandages all over, was stiff as a board, had extreme difficulty bending my knees and only had use of my right hand, so even putting on underwear was an endurance test. Mortifyingly, I usually required help to get it done. Next to bed baths and enemas, needing assistance putting on knickers was my biggest pet hate. One morning, on one of those rare occasions when I wanted to seize the day fully clothed, I decided to pull the curtain around my bed to get some privacy. I was determined to dress myself from head to toe, including the complicated stuff, like knickers and a bra. I waved at Helen, the nurse on duty, through the window as I pulled the curtain, indicating my request for some time alone. She nodded approvingly and left me to it.

My mission wasn't what you'd call a great success. It took me twenty minutes to put my knickers on and virtually the same time again wrestling with my bloody pyjama bottoms. Well, you try it without bending your knees! Eventually, Helen came into the room, concerned that I was hiding behind the curtain for so long, only to discover me rolling around on the bed cursing my bald head off, with one leg in the PJ bottoms and one leg dangling over the edge of the bed and stubbornly refusing to cooperate. Forty minutes, and I'd only managed to dress one bloody leg! As you may imagine, my potty mouth came out to play with gusto that morning. So now that dressing was no longer fun, I had an excellent excuse for my lackadaisical attitude to sartorial elegance.

Next, there was my beaming bald noggin to contend with. Even though Fiona had given me a range of elegant headscarves to disguise my skinhead, actually putting them on was a challenge. With one wonky hand to contend with, featuring my uncooperative little f***er, wrapping a scarf around my head in a fetching manner and securing it in place wasn't an easy thing to do. This time Deirdre, a lovely young Dublin nurse, came to the rescue. She fashioned the scarves into nifty turbans, tying them in such a way that even this one-handed bandit could manage. They never ceased to surprise me, these nurses, with the skills they possessed far beyond their medical prowess.

And then there was my face …

Marie encouraged me to wear make-up again, convinced it would boost my confidence. She had me there, must have known me in my past life, as I'd always referred to make-up as my battle armour and would never have been seen outside my front door without it. With unsightly raised burns on my face, it would be a true test of my skill to cover them up. While I couldn't erase my scars, they could be disguised with cleverly applied foundation and concealer. This happens to be my area of expertise.

I had always been quite good with cosmetics, often comparing the application process to a work of art. One layers coverage on the face as one paints on a canvas. Marie wore me down – I've learned that resistance is futile with nurses – and eventually I gave it a try. Initially, this work of art was like painting a stranger's portrait; bizarre, given that the stranger's face was attached to my body. Again, that sense of alienation crept through and no amount of concealer could airbrush that feeling away. But I persevered and started practising each day. Something within me knew that if I got it right, maybe I would feel a little better … a little bit closer to my old self.

Back in the good old days, I was rather a fan of the bronzed goddess look. I loved my Fake Bake and often emerged wearing, if not quite tangerine dream, certainly not the most subtle of tans either. Mum brought my old make-up bag from home and with paintbrushes in hand, I set to work. Given that my skin hadn't seen sunshine, or daylight, for nearly three months, and that my face had been surgically peeled on numerous occasions since the fire, I quickly discovered that I was working with a mismatched palate. While my foundation was a deep biscuit shade, my skin paled in comparison. This mismatch wouldn't have been a problem for an old pro like me, I could blend the make-up and hide my pale skin beneath, except for one glaring problem: my stupid white bald head! Next to my cappuccino-coloured face, my scalp glowed like a neon moon: not a visually appealing combo. I wasn't about to start painting my head (my pillowcase would end up looking like the shroud of Turin), so I asked Deirdre to create an extra-smart turban to cover my entire head.

It was quite the exotic ensemble in the end. With my heavily bronzed face (seriously, was my face always that orange?), my turban-clad head and my brand-new pyjamas, with both legs where they needed to be, my dress rehearsal was complete. It was as good as it was going to get and I realised that I couldn't hide away, partially dressed, for the rest of my days, avoiding all my friends. It was time to greet the outside world, or at least a part of it, cappuccino features forward. So I agreed. Marie put out the word and my first non-family member came that very evening, before I had a chance to change my mind.

Adey was first through the doors, and I didn't realise how eager I was to see him until that very moment. His eyes filled with tears the instant he walked into the room and the first thing that occurred to me was how proud Brian would have been of his best friend for all that he had done. It all flashed through my mind: how he'd identified Brian's body, organised his best friend's last journey home, looked after Rosemary in her hour of need. He was even there to hold my hand when my dad died, something I'd be eternally indebted to him for. I knew Adey had done all of this and much more for the love of his chosen brother, Brian. The pain he was enduring from that loss was palpable and it was something he would carry for the rest of his life. Selfishly, I took solace in knowing that we could share that burden of grief. Looking at Adey that evening, I had no doubt Brian's death had cut him to the very core. His hurt was visible.

Yet that night we both did our best to be cheery. Adey admired my deluxe blue room, marvelling at the sheer size of it. I discovered the reason I had such a huge ward all to myself was due to the TEN infection. I had to be isolated from other vulnerable burns patients. That's not the spin I gave Adey, of course, teasing him that I had VIP status, hence the luxury suite with my own private gym (exercise bike), stylish red leather lounger chair (which I still detested), executive bathroom fully decked out with seated showering facilities, etc. I even joked that the portable staircase in the corner was part of stage one in my plan to build a second floor, where I could entertain guests for dinner parties.

It wasn't long before the conversation turned to Brian, but with Adey it felt perfectly normal to talk about him, as though, just for a moment, he'd just slipped out of the room. Sometimes, to this day, when we share stories of Brian's antics, I forget for a split second that he's no longer with us, as though nothing has changed at all.

Once Adey had been and gone, it was open-door policy for my friends in the blue room. Ornaith (she of bride-slave and chief cake-maker renown) was next up. She had not made it to Greece, had been in Spain with her family when the tragedy occurred and was actually due to arrive in Greece on the day I was urgently flown back to Dublin. She was disappointed not to have made it to Athens and was anxious to see me as soon as possible. Foolishly, her visit was one I'd been avoiding for the simplest of reasons.

The plain truth was that I knew I wouldn't have a hope in hell of hiding my true emotions from her. Ornaith and I had been friends for over two decades and together had been through all the highs and lows that life can bring: love, marriage, miscarriages, divorce … and all the bits in between. It wasn't just the risk of floodgates opening, that was a given – even for a covert crier like me. It was the fact that she could always read me and, beyond my grief, I was afraid she'd uncover my true feelings of alienation and despair. I was lousy when it came to pretending around her and didn't want her, or any of my gang, to know how removed from their world I had become.

The following night I finally saw Ornaith for the first time since my wedding day. Thankfully, Nurse Marie was on duty and she was prepared for the emotional outcome of this meeting, with tissues at the ready, because I'd explained to her that we hadn't seen each other since my big day. The very second Ornaith stepped into my room, we both burst into tears. She couldn't hug me as I still couldn't be touched by outsiders, but just seeing her was as close to a monster hug as one could get.

We covered a lot of ground that evening. Marie let Ornaith stay well beyond official visiting hours, and I think she was secretly thrilled that we'd finally reconnected. There were lots of tears shed, but like the previous evening with Adey, there was laughter too. I knew the one thing that was guaranteed to make her chortle: my tanned face next to my ghostly, pale scalp. I couldn't resist revealing a tiny patch of my neon scalp from under the turban. The contrast between whiter-than-white head and bronzer-than-bronze face was just the ticket and try as she might, Ornaith couldn't help but burst out laughing. I wasn't embarrassed – it was my intention to make her giggle – and that moment was a blessing, dispersing our sadness and bringing hilarity into what would otherwise have been a totally sombre evening. I needed the chance to laugh with my friend, to behave, just for a moment, as we would have done in any other setting.

Incidentally, Ornaith quickly resolved the make-up issue by delivering new foundation the next day that actually matched my new skin tone. Now that's a good girlfriend! After that, every evening other members of my little posse dropped by to my room and, little by little, managed to break down at least some of my barriers.

I still felt different, for sure, but at least in their eyes I saw a glimpse of the person I once knew. I wondered what Brian would have thought as I caught my reflection that evening, a smiling reflection at that. I hoped he understood that even in those brief moments of laughter with my old friend, the tragedy of losing my true love was never far from my mind. Every time I thought of him, a stabbing pain shot through my heart – a very real physical pain of absolute loss. I wondered how it would feel as time went on, as I attempted to re-enter some form of 'real life' without Brian by my side. Would he approve of the choices I made? Meeting my friends again, taking tentative steps towards my old life opened a can of worms and brought up an abundance of questions I couldn't yet answer. One thing I did know, even with the finest of friends in my corner and the greatest support: without Brian in my life I felt very much alone.

28

DON'T WIG OUT!

My girlfriends decided to resolve my bald head problem and Katharine (Lady C) was designated as the best person for the job. Every group of friends, no matter their age group, is made up of individuals who play different roles. The more diverse those roles are, in my opinion, the better the group functions together. If each character has a distinct part to perform, combined they can achieve great things. My gang is like that: we have a chatty one, a sensitive soul, an adventurer and a practical problem-solver. Lady C falls into the latter category. She's so good at solving problems, sometimes she sees one before it actually exists. Immediately, she set her plan in motion and contacted a wig company that specialises in helping cancer patients. Katharine was determined to find me a new head of hair. She'd already been through this process with her own mum, so she was quite the expert.

Within a couple of days, she showed me several images on her phone and asked me to select a style I liked. Such temptation! I didn't really know where to begin: short or long, dark or fair, the choices were endless. As I'd become rather attached to the bob style that Paulina had created in Greece, I eventually decided to replicate that look. Katharine immediately purchased for me a beautiful brown, silky, bobbed-style wig and gifted it the following evening. Her generosity blew me away and her lavish present was a crucial step in making me feel more feminine – or, as I referred to it, helped to humanise the alien.

The wig made a vast difference to my appearance and was a huge boost to morale. There was a way to go yet: I was a pale, hairless, gaunt creature with facial scars, an open wound across my throat and no eyebrows or eyelashes. I looked like a mangled, scraggly Sphynx cat. But the make-up and wig improved the aesthetic dramatically. I even learned how to fashion eyebrows using a pencil. That didn't always go to plan, though. Sometimes I ended up looking permanently surprised (a hastily applied arch line), while at other times I resembled Mrs Potato Head (caterpillar brows coloured in a little over-enthusiastically). However, my friends always knew what to say to make me feel better, even if it meant laughing at my make-up faux pas.

Caroline was determined to get me into some comfy, functional clothes – anything but the blue hospital-issue gown. I told her to grab my old leggings from home, but instead she went shopping and purchased half the leisurewear in Dublin. Okay, that's a slight exaggeration, but it's not far off. It was a nice change from the oversized jammies I'd been living in, some of which had become impractical now I'd started to walk more. Loose clothing was fine when I was bed-ridden or lounging in my red chair all day, but now that I was attempting to walk around my spacious room I found those stretchy PJ bottoms a risky choice at best. In fact, during one physio session with Bill and Ben I found those bottoms let me down badly – by which I mean they actually fell right down around my ankles. I'm not sure what was worse: the incident itself, or the fact that I couldn't bend my knees far enough to pull them back up. I had to ask one of the lads to do that on my behalf. Oh, the shame! Later, when I described my utter mortification to Caroline, she resolved to sort the issue and brought me sturdy, elasticated leggings, guaranteed not to fall down, in an effort to protect what was left of my modesty.

As embarrassing as these mishaps may have been, it felt good to laugh about them with Caroline. I've always been slightly accident-prone, the clumsy one, and I was happy to play that role once again. It was a nice change from the weeping widow. Caroline did her utmost to treat me as she'd always done and always wore a brave face around me. She put a huge amount of energy into helping me in any way possible, as did all of my friends. They tried to help me heal, each in their own unique way, taking my broken shell and gluing the pieces back together into something more presentable. Visualise Humpty Dumpty ... with a wig, surprised eyebrows and a lot of make-up, and you'll get the picture. As Nurse Marie used to say: 'Never underestimate the power of your girlfriends!'

Neither, apparently, should you underestimate the determination of hospital staff. Take the senior intern doctor, Dr Owen, for instance. He was the one blessed with the thankless task of waking me each morning to take bloods, check my blood pressure and perform various different tests to ensure all my organs were playing ball. I said before that I tried to greet each day smiling, but anybody who knows me will tell you that even at the best of times, I am not a morning person. Back then I hardly slept at all, usually conking out at about 4 a.m., so waking me three hours later at 7 a.m. was the very epitome of pulling the short straw.

Every night it was the same old thing: an hour here, an hour there, punctuated by horrific dreams and physical pain. When it got really bad, the nurse would bring me something extra to knock me out, but I was still afraid of strong sleeping tablets after some frightening experiences in Greece. I was terrified of getting trapped in that nightmare world, unable to wake up. So with very little sleep under my belt, my waking mood was often less than delightful. However, Dr Owen had the nicest bedside manner, both patient and polite, as he woke the bear from her slumber. I'd like to say I was never rude in the mornings, but no doubt there were times when I was unresponsive, whiney or just plain grumpy. No matter my mood, Owen would greet me with a warm 'Good morning' as he gently turned on the lights – only the little ones mind you, not the big, ultra-bright spotlight – and, as efficiently as was humanly possible, did the tests that were required. He'd smile and apologise as he withdrew my blood (he got an A+ for blood extraction, never hurting me at all) and would then follow up with the same routine checks, day in, day out.

Of all those checks, the only question that was guaranteed to make me giggle was the one Dr Owen dreaded asking the most. As pathetic as it sounds for a woman in her forties – I can be ludicrously immature – I'd crack up every time the young doc asked me about my bowel movements. I could always tell that he was working his way up to this topic by his ever-increasing blush, and naturally I'd do my best to come up with a suitably absurd or inappropriate response. I thought I was being terribly witty but, in retrospect, I was just being a bit of an arse. I'd admonish him for his soopa-poopa obsession, reply that 'a lady never tells' or that my 'lips were sealed'. Basically, I'd say anything to make that moment less mortifying than it had to be. Although, looking back, I think my juvenile responses might have had the opposite effect. One thing I know for sure is that with the patience of a saint, Owen was already showing signs of making a wonderful physician. I never told him, but his gentlemanly manner reminded me a lot of my husband's own demeanour.

Those who spend prolonged stints in hospital, be they patient or medic, will tell you that having a sense of humour or the ability to laugh at oneself is sometimes the only thing that will get you through a difficult day. I wasn't the only person who tried to make light of embarrassing or awkward situations. Filipina, a senior nurse who often worked the night shift, had a lightness of spirit and a special ability to make me laugh. She told great stories of her life well-travelled, including some fascinating anecdotes of when she'd worked as a young nurse in Dubai. It was the animated way she could tell a tale that introduced colour into what otherwise would have been a mundane evening.

One occasion demonstrates Filipina's sense of fun to perfection. It was shortly after Katharine had dropped off the new wig and I was prepping for bed. Filipina was tending to a bad wound on my leg where the graft join had opened. She bound it tightly so as not to disrupt the graft site. For the record, it hurt like hell. As always, however, the nurse was quite the expert at distraction and turned the conversation to the hot topic of the day … the wig. We discussed how best to care for my new hair and agreed that perhaps I should get it trimmed, to better suit the shape of my face. Once my bandages were complete, I settled back onto the bed to watch a little TV before dozing off. Filipina disappeared out to the main ward and I didn't even notice that she had left my room with my wig hidden under the boxes of bandages.

About half an hour later, just as I was about to switch off the TV, the mischievous Filipina reappeared. Wearing the widest of grins, she presented me with what can only be described as the most hilarious wig-stand I had ever seen. Attached to the neck of a long, slim vase, borrowed from the staff room, was a blue medical glove balloon, fully blown up and firmly fixed in place with approximately half a roll of medical tape. On top of this 'nouveau art' creation rested my beautiful new wig in all its glory. Filipina had not only fashioned me the most creative of wig-stands, she had also taken the weave itself, brushed it, styled it and set it so that it was ready to be worn at a second's notice. I still laugh at the memory of my wig being ceremoniously planted on top of what looked like a bloated blue cow's udder each evening, happy to bob there until I was ready to wear it again. Filipina: what a talent, what a laugh! Beyond her impeccable nursing credentials, I wondered if she may have missed her true creative calling. Like many on the burns ward, she displayed great talents beyond medical skills, with her power of invention and sheer whimsy. One thing was for sure: she always managed to put a smile on my face.

29

BURRITOS, BIRTHDAYS AND BREAKOUTS

The pieces of the makeover jigsaw were beginning to come together. I had the make-up, the wig, the adult clothing that didn't fall down and the presentable footwear all finally sorted. Hell, I was even wearing bras again: onwards and upwards (literally)! The next step was to get me out of the ward and into the real world. It was now October and I'd been effectively hiding behind hospital walls for nearly three months, although it felt closer to three years. Now that my legs were beginning to do my bidding, albeit still with the help of my trusted crutches, for longer distances, it was time to get back out there.

In my mind there was a clear divide between two very different worlds. I existed in the safe hospital zone, where I'd come to no harm and where everybody was kind and caring. The outside world, by comparison, was a terrifying place where danger lurked around every corner. Nobody stared at my alien appearance on the burns ward because the doctors and nurses had seen it all before, but it was anybody's guess how outsiders would react when they saw me.

I liked my sterile surroundings, was accustomed to the familiar schedule of medical procedures and therapies. Mind you, it wasn't all wine and roses – for a start, both wine and roses were barred in the hospital – and many procedures were unpleasant and painful. I had constant blood tests and injections into my stomach. Frequently, I hid the syringe from the nurse, hoping she'd forget my nightly clot jab, but sadly my ploy was always foiled. I detested the skin peeling off my grafts: I now have a permanent aversion to tweezers. However, I endured those minor trials because I knew they came with good intentions. I was cared for by the very best. Nurses had become my favourite people and the doctors and specialists were my confidants. I found it difficult to contemplate ever existing outside those four walls. Some would say I was institutionalised … I would simply say I was petrified.

Bizarrely, it turns out that greed proved to be the key in helping me overcome my fear. Though I never went hungry because the kitchen produced delicious food and the portions were more than generous, I just couldn't get enough. Haunted by the memory of that horse-feed nasal tube, I was half convinced that at any second I'd be placed on nil-by-mouth again. I started to eat all around me. Mr Moutoglis would have been so proud. Even so, I was over a stone underweight. My body was making up for lost time. It was just a few weeks since I had been hooked up to a ventilator, dialysis and all the rest, so my appetite was justified. The irony of this situation wasn't lost on me. I had spent the first half of 2018 on a die-hard diet in an effort to squeeze me into the wedding dress of my dreams, and the second half desperately consuming everything in sight so that I'd pile on the pounds. This was yo-yo dieting on a whole new level, and I certainly wouldn't recommend it as the optimal nutrition plan. I had the perfect excuse to put away the calories, but it was the enticement of something different from my usual fare that persuaded me to step outside my safe zone. The nurses, Trisha and Marie in particular, cottoned on that food was going to be the perfect carrot to dangle and finally get me out of the ward. Cunningly, they introduced me to the St James' street food market.

Every Tuesday, in front of the hospital, there was a gathering of food-sellers offering an array of dishes from all over the world. I'd heard the nurses and doctors discussing, conveniently within my earshot, the selection of food available, everything from sushi to steak, fish and chips to fajitas. Eventually, curiosity got the better of me and one Tuesday morning, while Trisha was wrapping my legs, I asked if I could check out the market that lunchtime. In hindsight, I can almost visualise her rubbing her hands in glee, like George Peppard in true *A-Team* style, declaring, 'I love it when a plan comes together.'

Needless to say, she enthusiastically agreed to my request and offered to accompany me on my foodie adventure. I couldn't walk very far alone – anything further than a few metres left me totally wrecked – so I knew I'd need her help. This was a truly momentous moment. It was a puny task for regular humans, but a vast expedition for me: my first breakout into the open air.

Marie decided to join our little expedition, while a couple of others on the ward stood by and waved me off. It was really quite sweet: they looked like proud mums sending me off on my first day at school. Hobbling cautiously on my crutches, the journey along several corridors and out the front entrance was the longest I had walked since the day of the fire. It was exhausting, but my hunger goaded me on. Trisha and Marie were like my bodyguards, one pitched on either side, and they made it quite the happy occasion. Excitedly, we discussed which stalls we'd visit, who had the tastiest offerings, etc. As always, these nurses made every task that little bit easier.

When we finally reached the revolving door and stepped outside, I was hit by the bright midday heat. That year, 2018, was the hottest for decades in Ireland and sun like this, in October, was unheard of. It took me by surprise. I was used to softer lighting and couldn't help but be reminded of that glaring sunshine that had blinded me on the day I flew home from Athens. I quickly filed that thought away. I wanted this to be a positive experience and couldn't risk slipping back into an unhappy memory. Trisha and Marie stayed close and I knew with them I'd be alright. My feet were a little unsteady, so I leaned heavily on my crutches and walked at a snail's pace out the front door.

It was then I saw the food market, and what a sight it was to behold. Colours and smells, music, chatter and positive energy everywhere. It was a little overwhelming, like a sensory overload. My eyes had to adjust to the glare of the sharp light and my skin to the midday heat. I was uncomfortably hot, but the aromas of the street food compelled me to keep moving. There was food from all over the world, with crowds of people either queueing at stands or sitting at picnic tables, enjoying their al fresco lunches. Trisha recommended the Mexican/Thai fusion and had filled my head with stories of their legendary burritos, so that was where I was heading.

I started to enjoy myself. I was outdoors, purchasing food and laughing with the two girls like a regular human. Internally, I knew I didn't exactly look 'normal' with my lopsided wig and hastily applied camouflage, but so far, so good. Nobody had stopped to point and stare, no one seemed to notice or to care, for that matter. They were too preoccupied with getting fed. So was I. Minutes later I couldn't believe my luck when I was handed the biggest burrito I had ever seen, bulging with enough filling to feed a family of five.

Suddenly, it all became too much – the stalls, the smells, the light, the heat and so many people. The world began to spin on its axis and out of nowhere my legs gave way. Thankfully, Marie and Trisha were there to catch me before I hit the grass and swiftly helped me to a nearby bench. I'd blacked out, but only for a second or two, and was embarrassed and annoyed with myself, hoping I hadn't made a scene. All I wanted was to merge in with the other humans and I couldn't even get that right. On the plus side, the nurses caught me before I face-planted the ground, minimising the drama. On the extra plus side, I was still grasping the intact burrito in my hand, hanging onto it for dear life. Now that made me laugh. Perhaps I wasn't a lost cause after all. Once I regained my strength, we slowly made our way back inside. Even taking the minor wobble into account, I was still proud of myself. Nothing ventured, nothing gained, and my reward for stepping out of my comfort zone was the best darn burrito I'd ever eaten, washed down with a can of ice-cold Diet Coke. A feast fit for a queen!

Now that I had taken my first steps to freedom, there was no going back. Pandora's box was open and it wasn't for closing again. My birthday was looming, on 6 October, and Mum was eager to mark the occasion. She had spoken to Mr Shelley about options and was very excited. I was the opposite of excited. I didn't want to celebrate it or register a new year without Brian or Dad and would have been happier forgetting about the entire thing. However, my family and Mr Shelley colluded and came up with a master plan – to send me home for a few hours. It would be the first time I'd returned to my apartment since I had left, two days after our wedding. I felt physically sick at the very thought of this idea. Logically, I'd known this day would come, but emotionally I had put it on the back-burner, so when the plan to release me for a few hours was announced, it really took me by surprise. The deal was that my family could take me home for a sedate celebration (no bumps or shots of tequila this birthday, I guess) and return me back to the ward later that evening. Damn you, burrito, I thought. It wasn't the first time my stomach had got me into trouble. If it hadn't been for my greedy gut, I may have escaped the outside world for weeks, or possibly even months, yet.

The truth was, of course, that Mr Shelley and his team had been prepping me for this event for weeks. I had been in training *Rocky* style: climbing up and down the steps, sitting down on chairs unassisted (still couldn't get up without help, mind you), walking longer stretches on the corridor, attempting (and mostly failing) to grip with my left hand … the list went on and on. I was put through a series of examinations and once he was happy with the results, Mr Shelley sent me off on my (not so merry) way for the birthday celebration. At least he promised that if I became overwhelmed, I could come straight back to the hospital. I agreed to do this on one proviso – that I needed some time alone in my home to acclimatise before my family invaded en masse. It was agreed that Fiona would bring me there first, giving me some solitary time to adjust. I didn't want to upset Mum if I became hysterical as soon as I turned the key, so this plan bought me time to compose myself should the worst happen.

On the morning of my birthday, Nurse Dolly (cute name for a cute lady) wheeled me out the side entrance to the loading bay, where Fiona's car was parked. I laughed as Dolly carted me to the door. I was perfectly capable of walking the short distance myself, but either hospital policy didn't allow it or the staff wanted to make sure I really did leave the building. Fiona, my chauffeur for the day, was eagerly waiting outside and off we went.

It was a sunny afternoon and I stared out the window, watching the world go by as Fiona drove the short journey to my home. She was full of stories about my nephews' latest escapades and I was grateful for the chatter. My heart pummelled like an electric drill when we pulled up to my apartment block, and I felt so anxious that I actually wondered if I could persuade Fiona to turn around and head back to the hospital. I knew that wasn't an option. I had to see this through. I prayed that I wouldn't bump into any neighbours as we made our way inside and by some stroke of luck the place was mysteriously deserted. That was a relief. I wasn't ready to handle any chance encounters right now. Getting through the front door was going to be a big enough challenge as it was. My sister-in-law was fantastic, just the right mix of helpful without being intrusive. She stepped back as I turned the key in my front door and pushed it open.

I can't describe how strange it felt, entering the apartment for the first time since I'd left on our honeymoon – back when I was happy and in love, oblivious that my whole world was about to be turned upside down. I'd lived in this duplex apartment for over thirteen years, four with Brian, and it had been my citadel when I first went to live there, but it truly became my home when he joined me. Now I was scared it may have transformed into some strange, foreboding place in our absence.

The first thing I noticed was the smell. Every home has its own unique scent and mine is a mishmash of lemon, fresh linen and something else I can't quite describe, perhaps the essence of the two people who used to live there. The fragrance brought me comfort, it was familiar and reassuring. The next thing I spotted, as I stepped into the hallway, took my breath away. Hanging at the bottom of the staircase was Brian's biker jacket, waiting patiently for its owner to return. It looked just the same as always and I took it in my arms and felt its rugged weight. My eyes welled. I felt sad for this jacket. It had taken on the shape of its owner, moulded itself around his body, and was now, like me, lost without him. I pulled the garment up to my face and breathed it in, trying to locate Brian's individual scent. But I couldn't find it.

I asked Fiona to give me a few minutes and she went upstairs in the duplex to the living area, leaving me alone with some much-needed space. My mission was to find something that held Brian's fragrance. If it wasn't on his jacket, it had to be somewhere else. While Fiona started to organise the food for the birthday upstairs, I searched the bedrooms, like a pathetic sniffer dog, rummaging through Brian's clothes in the wardrobe and the drawers. I examined all his jackets on the coat-stand, the bedsheets, even the towels in the bathroom, even though I had replaced them all before we left on honeymoon. Nowhere could I capture his scent and the panic started to rise in my throat, the tears stabbing behind my eyes.

My last attempt, before I gave up and gave in, was successful. There, hanging on the bathroom door, silently waiting, was Brian's deep-blue dressing gown. Embedded in the soft towelling fabric was my love's own unique essence. I could finally breathe him in, smell that fragrance nobody else on this planet possessed. Enveloping my face in the gown, I inhaled his scent like I was inhaling oxygen for the first time. My panic abated. I allowed my tears to be absorbed into the fabric. Brian was still there. I could feel him close to me. He would give me the strength I needed to get through the next few hours. I was home and so was he, by my side once more.

It wasn't long before my strength was tested. There, in the spare room, hanging in full view outside the wardrobe, was my wedding dress and veil, where I'd left them so many months before. The sight of my shimmering dress, which had brought me such joy, now only brought intense pain. Yet I couldn't seem to look away. I started to daydream about wearing it again someday, indulging in a morbid Miss Havisham moment. I quickly binned that idea. It was sadistic to even look at the gown, let alone contemplate ever wearing it again. Swiftly, I zipped up the dress and veil in its garment bag and shoved it in the wardrobe, out of sight. The suitcases that contained our honeymoon clothes were close by, still carrying the stench of smoke and death. Those I left untouched. I could barely look at them. That was a chore I would have to address another day.

Eventually, I joined Fiona upstairs where yet more challenges waited. I was ambushed by dozens of wedding cards and presents, which we had hastily opened before heading to Greece. There was wedding paraphernalia displayed on every inch of shelf space available. As I'd requested, they had remained untouched. How tragic that the joyful messages on show would soon be replaced by those of condolence; words of love and happiness to be usurped by sadness and woe.

Before I could dwell on that thought, Mum and my brothers arrived in ebullient form. I'm sure they were just as nervous as I was, but they put on the best show they could. Fiona presented a birthday feast of all my favourite dishes, and Mum revealed a variety of cakes and deserts, enough to feed an army as she'd say. We all ate way more than we needed to. My Oscar-winning moment was when I managed to smile and swallow my tears as everybody sang 'Happy Birthday' over a candlelit cake. The lyrics fell on deaf ears. As lovely as their intentions were, this was not a happy birthday. There would be no more of those. Birthdays I couldn't prevent, nor could I control the passing of time, but the marking of it with joy I could never see happening again.

That evening I returned to the hospital with box-loads of cakes and treats for the nurses. Dolly was certainly well rewarded for wheeling me around for the second time that day. As I climbed back into bed and awaited my injections and medications, I felt a sense of dread in my gut. I was near the end of my stay. It was only a matter of time before I was discharged for good. How was I going to cope with the lonely life that awaited me outside my safe blue room? I wouldn't have to wait much longer to find out the answer. The countdown was well and truly on.

30

PUTTING IN THE PREP

The waters having been tested, over the next few weeks I would slowly spend more time at home – first for a few hours, then eventually overnight. I was conflicted about this. On one hand, I found my home turf comforting, surrounded by memories of Brian. On the other, I felt vulnerable and would miss the security the hospital offered.

Healthwise, the news was promising. The grafts had settled and for the time being there were no more major operations. However, there were still a couple of unpleasant procedures yet to endure. I hate that word, 'procedure'; you never really know what you're going to get. For a start, I had to be de-stapled: hundreds of little metal staples that were embedded in my flesh, all over my legs, thighs and arms, had to be removed. They had been used to hold my grafts in place and were no longer required. Cheekily, I gave it my best shot to try to persuade the team to perform this under general anaesthesia, but my powers of persuasion failed. Of course, the nurses gave me extra pain meds – I mean, we're not dealing with psychopaths here – but it was still a damn awful process. My potty-mouth went off the Richter scale. I even invented new curse words for the occasion. There are times in life when 'ow' just doesn't suffice!

Speaking of 'ow' moments, my nails finally withered and fell off, all twenty of them. That was extremely unpleasant and highly irritating. You'd be surprised how handy fingernails are for everyday tasks. I'd enough trouble trying to grip before, now without nails there were loads of simple tasks that proved impossible, like opening a yoghurt carton or scratching the itchy stubble on my head. Aesthetically, my fingers looked horrible without nails – another flaw to add to the list – so I decided to paint the tips bright red, to look like pretend fingernails. Applying paint onto bare skin felt yucky, but once completed my hands looked slightly less revolting.

To prep me for leaving, the nurses taught me how to bandage my burns. This could be tricky as certain graft sites had a tendency to open and bleed, like a zip splitting apart. I never knew what area might open or why, which is apparently a normal part of the graft healing process, but my right leg seemed to be the biggest culprit. Walking put increased pressure on the wound and caused it to open, but this was a catch-22 situation: I couldn't stop moving, so I had to suck it up and get used to it. I watched the nurses like a hawk and became quite adept at treating these sites.

My feet also required maintenance. They were so swollen I nicknamed them Miss Piggy's trotters. Some days they'd inflate to such a degree that my toes looked like little fat sausages, hence I still wore oversized runners, although anything was better than Bill and Ben's corrective shoes. What a turn-up for the books:

in the past I had boasted that I was born in high heels, such was my love for their vertiginous glory. Now I could wear only the flattest footwear. My impressive shoe collection of glorious, high-heeled creations was banished under my bed. I couldn't bear to gaze upon their beauty, and certainly couldn't manage to squeeze my trotters into their confined space. As frivolous a complaint as it might sound for one who was just learning to walk again, I was still a girl at heart and missed my heels dearly.

Once I had proved to Mr Shelley that I was capable of managing the basics, and even though dinner time was still like feeding at the zoo, my grip not being the best, an overnight stay at home was proposed. I had to be accompanied by somebody for the visit and while there, Michelle, the head occupational therapist, would drop by and assess my living quarters. She would examine me on everything from climbing the stairs to using the bathroom, from boiling a kettle without scalding myself to getting into and out of bed without tumbling onto the floor. Michelle would scrutinise my kitchen, bedroom and bathroom and see if any adaptations needed to be made to improve my living environment. She had to be sure the home I was returning to was safe and would suit my needs. I confided with Mr Shelley and Michelle that once I was fully discharged from St James', I wanted to live alone in my apartment. They were under the impression that I'd move in with a family member. I was quick to dispel that idea for two reasons. First, I couldn't risk any family member witnessing my burns, especially as my legs and arms looked particularly gruesome at that stage. I wanted to protect them from that for as long as possible. Secondly, I knew the only way I could cope with my new existence was to go it alone. I needed to find my feet without constant assistance or supervision. It was not open for negotiation.

A mule would be considered a less stubborn creature than I am and once Mr Shelley realised that I wasn't going to budge on the subject, he eventually agreed, on condition that I followed certain rules. I had to return to hospital several times a week for appointments and also register for home visits from a locum nurse. I needed to prove that I could not only treat my burns myself but also do everything else needed to survive. The hospital even offered me a domestic home-help service, which I politely yet promptly declined. I couldn't wait to unleash my inner OCD domestic goddess. Before Mr Shelley would green-light any of this, though, I'd have to build up my time at home, starting with an overnight stay, then a weekend, progressing eventually to my complete discharge.

For my first overnight stay, which was around mid-October, I asked Caroline to be my babysitter. I reckoned she was the perfect person to chill with and she's also a physiotherapist so if something went awry her skill was bound to come in useful. Ideally, I just wanted a relaxed evening with my buddy and that, it turned out, was easily achieved.

To kick off this special occasion in style, I decided that we would consume a shocking amount of junk food. The prisoner released, I was intent on guzzling all those guilty pleasures I'd been fantasising about for months. The McDonald's and Pepsi Max were collected from a drive-thru on the journey to the apartment, and that was devoured in two minutes flat. It wasn't quite the sumptuous feast I had dreamt of from those enticing adverts on TV that had taunted me for months – that's the thing with fantasies: they never quite keep their promise – but it was demolished nonetheless. I'd barely digested that meal before my next junk gorge commenced. All the things I couldn't get in hospital: pizza, chocolate, fizzy drinks. Poor Caroline couldn't keep up with my gluttony and looked on in mock horror as I made a total pig of myself. Well, I knew it would be back to healthy hospital food the following day. Together we fell into a comfortable old pattern as we watched silly movies, caught up on gossip and behaved as we had hundreds of times before. She gave me the normality I so badly craved that night.

The first night in my own bed wasn't quite so simple and was anything but normal. I took my medications, but even a horse tranquillizer wouldn't have conked me out that night. The last time I was in that bed was with Brian, on the day after our wedding, so there wasn't a hope in hell of closing off my mind or getting peaceful sleep. When I eventually did drift off, my nightmares were particularly vivid and it almost felt like punishment for enjoying the evening with Caroline, for forgetting my troubles for a few hours. Back home, as in the hospital, there was no escape from reality at night.

Caroline left early for work the following morning, sneaking quietly out the front door so as not to disturb me. She couldn't have known that I had been wide awake for hours. I waited until she left before I slowly got out of the bed and readied myself for the big inspection. I put all my energy into the mission at hand, bathed and dressed my wounds, deciding to prove that I was capable of doing it alone. Michelle turned up on my doorstep, as arranged, a couple of hours later. Her timing couldn't have been better as by then my enthusiasm was waning, exhausted from the lack of sleep and feeling terribly vulnerable at home alone. It was a relief to see her face. I had become very fond of Michelle in the hospital and was truly delighted that she was the first person who made the crossover between both of my worlds.

I welcomed her inside and we got straight down to the inspection. She thoroughly checked out every inch of my home and watched as I navigated around it. The stairs test, in particular, was quite the endurance workout. I was literally hauling ass, hanging on to the banister at times for dear life. She also checked the bathroom facilities, the kitchen and the bedroom and I demonstrated all those little functions we take for granted every day, like getting in and out of bed, showering or performing simple kitchen tasks without accidents (I'd had enough burns to last a lifetime). Thankfully, Michelle was blessed with patience, as every task took considerably longer than it would have done for a regular human.

Together we mapped out how I'd spend my days and what challenges I might face, working out ways to overcome any potential difficulties. This exercise was more than a day-planner, it was a way to visualise what my future would look like. The boost was that I could tell Michelle was impressed (minus the slow-coach bit on the stairs) that I had managed most tasks without falling on my face. There were still a few things to work on before I could move back home for good, but I was getting there.

Sadly, before that happened, I would have to contend with yet another loss in my world. While I was in recovery, Meow, my beloved cat, was being cared for in a delightful cattery called Bellinter, about half-an-hour's drive from where I lived. The owner, an incredibly kind and generous woman called Olive, had kept Meow for nigh-on three months, refusing payment after having learned of my unfortunate situation. Meow had been nurtured by Olive as if she were one of her own pets and I was truly indebted to her for that. I adored that moggy to an almost irrational level. She was the naughtiest little kitty, prone to scratching furniture, reorganising the contents of my wardrobe and even the odd bout of cat burglary. (Thankfully, my neighbours were blessed with tremendous patience and found it amusing when she climbed in their kitchen window to check out their abode.) Meow was my pet, my comfort, my partner in crime, and I couldn't wait to have her home with me. I knew the apartment would feel just a little less lonely with her there.

Tragically, as my extended stay in hospital continued, Meow became despondent. She started to refuse food and was evidently pining for her family. Perhaps she thought we'd abandoned her for good; maybe she too had a broken heart. After all, animals are far more intuitive than we give them credit for. Whatever ailed her, a couple of weeks after I was discharged from hospital, I received the news that Meow had died. It was clear that Olive had taken loving care of Meow, but nonetheless my little darling inexplicably passed away one night. I never had the chance to say goodbye and can't imagine ever giving my heart to another creature in the same way.

31

HOMEWARD-BOUND

I t was agreed that I would be discharged from hospital at the end of October, just in time for Hallowe'en. Finally, I felt ready to go.

A big part of my heart now belonged to the staff of St James'. They were my support network during the most difficult time of my life. I wondered how I would survive without the nurses who had hugged and held me, bandaged my wounds, put up with my bad moods and sometimes my utterly insane behaviour. I thought about the kindness shown to me by Shane, Michelle and Joanne, who had laughed with me when I needed to laugh and let me weep unashamedly when I needed to weep. They always allowed me to be who I needed to be in the moment. Without these amazing people, I wouldn't be able to walk, talk or breathe properly and I'd probably have an entirely useless left hand. I'd become accustomed to Dr Owen's gentle wake-up call and the night nurse's quiet 'Goodnight.' How would I cope without all these angels taking care of me, day in, day out?

The king of this castle was Mr Shelley, and to him I owe a debt I can never repay. He saved my life, refusing to give up even when the prognosis was at its bleakest. He restored my hand, a work of art and engineering built from the feeblest of structures, and of course he performed exquisite grafts all over my body. He and his team were my pockets of light and without them to prop me up, I was scared the darkness that lurked around in the shadows would finally catch up with me. While in James', the focus had been all about physical recovery and I was surrounded by people invested in that same goal. Now that I was homeward-bound, there would be a new focus and I would finally have to face reality. That reality was that I was going to have to start a whole new existence without Brian.

I knew there were huge physical and psychological challenges awaiting me and combined with the inevitable loneliness of living alone, I was terrified it would all become too much. I'd ignored a lot of my true feelings up until my homecoming ... now I had no choice but to face the truth. I would have to pull up my big-girl pants (this was my favourite expression since I had regained the actual ability to pull up my own pants) and start again, by myself.

I guess my biggest worry was that the ticking time bomb of grief, anger and confusion I had swallowed, which had been set on a delayed timer, would finally explode once I was removed from my safe hospital surroundings.

On my leaving day, I once again put on an Oscar-winning performance for the nurses, doctors and therapists who came to wave me off. I was determined to say goodbye to my precious blue room with dignity and a smile on my face, even if I was also leaving with a heavy, confused heart.

My heart, incidentally, wasn't the only thing that was heavy. Hilariously, I was vacating the burns ward with seven large suitcases of luggage. I couldn't believe how much stuff I had acquired during my stay. Apart from all the clothing, accessories and cosmetics, I had box-loads of cards, letters and drawings from well-wishers. One suitcase alone was filled with a hefty supply of bandages, dressings, lotions, potions and pills – enough to keep a small pharmacy going. John had the thankless task of wheeling bag after bag to the car as I said my emotional goodbyes. I tried to fight off the lump in my throat, but with every hug and handshake, the more pronounced it became. Eventually, once the tears started to flow, I knew it was time to get out of there before I changed my mind. The ridiculous part of this dramatic adieu was that I was due back in three days to start my new regime of appointments. I would be seeing Shane, Michelle, Joanne and Mr Shelley on a regular basis for a long time yet.

Hallowe'en was always one of my favourite celebrations: any excuse to dress up was fine by me. In years gone by I had rocked Xena: Warrior Princess, wore my pretzel-haired Princess Leia costume with pride (the force was with me that night) and on one occasion even carted around baskets of cake dressed in a voluminous Marie Antoinette gown. Given half the chance, I'd usually embrace any Hallowe'en frolic, but that year I'd forgotten all about it. As John drove me through suburbia, it dawned on me that I was totally out of sync with the rest of the world. We were surrounded by spooky decorations of neon skeletons, tombstones, pumpkins and crooked-nosed witches. There were children in costumes everywhere. Ironically, even though I hadn't realised what day it was, I pretty much blended in with all those celebrating. With my lopsided wig, mascara-streaked eyes and several inches of make-up plastered on my face, I could well have been in fancy dress. This year my 'costume' wasn't quite up to my usual standard, but had I been looking to achieve the drag-queen-gone-wrong look, I would have knocked it out of the park.

Eventually we reached my apartment block where, as usual, there were lots of young families and plenty of life and noise about the place. I confess, I had never managed to get properly acquainted with any of my neighbours and knew virtually none by name. Brian, on the other hand, was a dab hand at getting to know everybody. He'd only moved in a wet week and was already familiar with every person on our floor. He knew their names, jobs, spouse's or partner's name, favourite colour (slight exaggeration ... but not far off) and he put me to shame. I'd always been in the smile-and-nod camp whereas Brian was a master when it came to neighbourly relations. He was friendly and warm, and I was proud of how my neighbours warmed to him.

Hallowe'en, however, was the one time when I'd redeem myself, roll up my sleeves and get involved. I always stocked up with a plentiful supply of treats and looked forward to hearing the doorbell ring all night. Happy to hand out handfuls of goodies, this was my chance to wear a costume, embrace my inner child and mix with the parents and children alike. Forget the healthy fruit and nut option that we had to endure as kids,

Hallowe'en is what keeps dentists in the lifestyle to which they are accustomed.

I decided there was yet a chance to make something of the celebration and en route home stopped to purchase several tubs of teeth-busting treats, just in case any trick-or-treaters decided to drop by. Once John had lugged my luggage up to the apartment and I was settled in, I released him from his brotherly duties. I'd plenty of offers of company that evening, but had declined all. I stacked the tubs of sweets by my front door and as soon as I heard the sound of children laughing in the corridor outside, opened the door and peeked out to let them know I was ready for the trick-or-treat invasion.

What happened then was unexpected: a large group of neighbours started to gather on my doorstep. Word must have spread that I was back. The funny thing is, thanks to my hospital bubble, I still didn't understand how impactful the news coverage of the tragedy in Greece had been. I suspected that some of my neighbours might have wondered where Brian and I had been for four months, but I didn't think they'd know the reason for our absence. My main concern was that I looked so different they might not recognise me. I dreaded having to explain what had happened and hadn't worked out what to say. So I was unprepared when the doorbell rang and I opened the door expecting a gaggle of costume-clad kids and instead found about a dozen adults standing there. At first, I was taken aback, but when I clocked their concerned smiles, I quickly realised they were a welcoming party.

More parents joined the initial troupe and one of the dads spoke up and told me how much they had been looking forward to my homecoming. For the second time that day I found myself battling tears, although these were the good kind. It was a truly heart-warming moment. They didn't barge in or overwhelm me, just let me know that each and every one would be there for me in whatever way was required. They offered their condolences for my loss and also the hand of friendship. It was the gentlest, kindest welcome home.

Amusingly, the children who had gathered behind their parents started to push through the crowd. I was delighted to see that they had no interest in the serious stuff, nor were they concerned with my teary-eyed appearance, seeing me purely as a potential source of sweets. That made me laugh – kids are always the great leveller. The children lined up, hands out, and in my true family tradition, just as my grandmother Sally had always done when trick-or-treaters called, I insisted they had to either perform a magic trick, tell a joke, sing a song or do a dance to earn their reward. Only then would I hand over the sugary loot. Instantly, the mood changed from a sombre tone into one of great frivolity as my doorstep turned into a chaotic Cirque de Soleil stage with a highly amusing display of songs, bizarre breakdancing moves, dress-twirling and knock-knock jokes. We all laughed, adults and children alike, and I enthusiastically passed out their reward with handfuls of sweets.

My Hallowe'en homecoming was complete and when I eventually withdrew to my bed, much later that night, the sounds of laughter and song still rang out in my ears. I didn't get much sleep that night, but I couldn't help but smile at the friendly display that had greeted my arrival. If nothing else, I knew I wasn't totally alone after all.

THE MEMORIAL

had been planning Brian's memorial from the day his death was confirmed, as I lay in the ICU in Greece. It was the cruellest twist of fate that, having spent most of the previous year organising our wedding, now I was back in preparation mode, this time for my husband's funeral. I had begun composing his eulogy all the way back then in the Mitera and had rehearsed my speech repeatedly in my mind to the point of obsession. Sometimes I found myself making unwanted comparisons with my wedding speech, but soon realised that the pressure of getting this one just right was so much greater. It was my chance to honour Brian, to celebrate the great man that he was. I wanted Brian to be remembered for all that he had achieved in life and for the legacies he left in his wake.

At least when it came to planning his memorial, I knew exactly what Brian's wishes were. I touched briefly before on a portentous conversation we'd had just a few days prior to our wedding that covered the topic of our funerals. Initially, we were talking about my father's health. I was deeply concerned as Dad had become shockingly frail during his latest stint of chemotherapy and I was terrified of losing him. Somewhere along the line, the conversation led to when Brian had lost his father. Death was not as taboo a subject in the O'Callaghan-Westropp family as it was in ours, but then, it had not touched me as it had Brian, having lost his father, brother and stepfather too. And so, we ended up discussing our own funerals and last wishes. It was clear that Brian had put some consideration into how he envisaged his final send-off.

Brian wanted to be cremated and he even stipulated precisely where his ashes were to be scattered: a scenic spot at the tip of an island close to where he'd grown up in County Clare. He was not religious, I guess you'd call him agnostic, and he wanted a secular ceremony. Bizarrely, though, during this conversation he mentioned to me a particular fondness for an old family friend, Canon Brendan O'Donoghue, and said that he would make the perfect celebrant. My husband-to-be had lined it all up for me: the type of ceremony, his final resting place, the celebrant. The only sticking point was his choice of final lament. Brian's favourite song was 'Iris' by the Goo Goo Dolls, a supremely depressing ballad that I'd always hated. Brian was adamant, though, as it was apparently non-negotiable, and we actually mock-argued over his choice. Eventually, I conceded. I declared that it hardly mattered as I was convinced I'd be long gone before him, so this debate about his funeral swansong was probably wasted on me. I laughed and said, 'It's something I'll never have to worry about,' and with that we moved onto the happier topic of wedding music. Little did I know that everything we spoke about that day would soon become pivotal.

Nearly five months later, when I was finally strong enough, I was ready to give Brian the send-off he had carefully outlined. Thankfully, I had a lot of help at the time, with Adey and Lisa assisting and my girlfriends rallying around me in full organisational mode. Brian's mum, Rosemary, who'd planned too many funerals in her time, was fully involved as well. The venue was the much-debated topic as Brian's 'secular service' stipulation worried me. Rosemary wanted to use Kilnasoolagh church, a small Church of Ireland chapel where Brian's father and brother were buried. While it didn't strictly fit the bill, given the family connection it seemed to be the most appropriate option, not to mention the kindest for Rosemary. We tracked down Canon O'Donoghue and attained special permission to have him in attendance. This was necessary as he was Catholic and it was a Protestant church. Reverend Maurice Birr, Dean of the diocese, was extremely kind and cooperative and agreed that we could not only use his church but also that he and Canon O'Donoghue would celebrate the memorial together. With a little negotiation, they both agreed to abstain from a formal mass. We chose the date, 1 December 2018, and spread the word, placing announcements in the newspapers to let everybody know.

In the weeks running up to Brian's funeral, it became the impetus to get me walking properly. I was determined to step up on that altar, make that eulogy and afterwards walk out to the edge of that island to scatter his ashes. I knew that a wheelchair just wasn't going to cut it on the marshy land. This goal was the constant push that kept me going on the really difficult days. I confided in Adey that I needed to make Brian proud of me, which meant I had to walk unaided, head held high. Adey said that Brian would be proud of me regardless and that he'd carry me on his back, if needs be, to get me to the place his friend wanted to be laid to rest. He probably would have done so, too. In a sense, I often felt that Adey did carry me. He certainly was a constant shoulder I leaned upon.

There were a couple of other concerning factors before the memorial, the scar from my tracheostomy being one. Still healing, it was particularly unpleasant to look at, so I became a great fan of choker necklaces. Much more than a fashion accessory, they provided the perfect camouflage. I was also worried that my vocal cords wouldn't be strong enough to carry my voice for the speech. There were so many things I wanted to disclose about Brian: his kind deeds and generosity, his dedication to the Blood Bikes East charity, his warm, loving nature and light-hearted humour. I didn't want to paint him as a saint, though as I said on the day, he certainly had the patience of one. Brian loved juicy gossip, even more than any of my girlfriends, and he had a terrible habit of trying to match-make single friends, but invariably those plans ended in disaster. There were silly anecdotes to share of his travelling adventures and tales where he simply shone above all others. My voice had to be strong enough to carry all of this and more.

Finally, my last concern was related to the media. I hoped that we would be given the privacy we dearly desired for the ceremony. By then, stories had to come to me of 'friends' selling information and private photos from our wedding day and even though there were more important things to think of, I wanted his memorial to be just for the people who knew and loved Brian. I'd worked in the newspapers for over twenty years, and through contacts a formal request was placed to the ombudsman to leave us in peace on that day. Other than one unscrupulous reporter who ignored the request and sold details of the funeral to certain titles, we were thankfully left alone, something I truly appreciated.

On the sunny afternoon of 1 December 2018, several hundred people turned up to the pretty Kilnasoolagh church, County Clare, to celebrate the life of Brian O'Callaghan Westropp. In the graveyard behind the chapel, resting peacefully, were his father, Denis, and brother, Colin. It was quite a journey for many that day. The majority of the attendees travelled from Dublin, though many also came from further afield and a large proportion came from England, where Brian had spent many years studying and working. There were biker crews from all over the UK and Ireland, and a warm feeling flooded through me when I saw rows of his Blood Bikes East crew in the congregation, dressed in their motorbike gear (Brian's second skin). There were so many friends who made the journey to support me that day, many of whom I had last encountered at our wedding.

As the crowds gathered outside the church, I sat with Rosemary in her car opposite the church grounds. We watched as mourners gathered in lines outside the small chapel and I took her hand and promised her that we would get through this day together. Silently we hugged and slowly, mother and widow, we made our way into the church. We passed a sea of familiar faces. It was overpowering to see so many people in attendance and I found it difficult not to stumble over my crutch as we edged up to the top row. At last we made it and settled in the tiny pew by the altar: Rosemary, Adey and my mum by my side.

Amongst the throngs in attendance were representatives from the president's office and the government, there to show their respect to Brian. My brother John introduced me to Captain Eoin Troy, the aide-de-camp for the President of Ireland, Michael D. Higgins, and Captain Ciaran Woulfe, representing the Taoiseach, Leo Varadkar. I smiled, knowing full well that Brian would have loved having these important representatives of office at his funeral. He'd always been a fan of pomp and ceremony. Orla O'Hanrahan, the Irish ambassador to Greece, was also present at the top of the church. She needed no introduction, being a welcome, friendly face by then. Thanks to John, who'd filled me in just days before, I'd only just discovered all that she and the embassy team had done for me while in Greece, like taking care of a huge amount of red tape in processing Brian's journey home and organising accommodation for my family and friends. As much as I respected Orla's position, I still hugged her warmly, as one would greet an old friend rather than a visiting dignitary.

The church was soon packed to capacity and many people had to wait outside in the grounds. Much of the funeral passed in a blur, but some moments are vividly imprinted in my memory.

The time came for my eulogy, so clutching a small pile of notelets in my hand I tentatively walked up to the altar. I began to speak, but the words which I'd carefully rehearsed so many times before came out in strangled gasps. The moment I looked down at the congregation, at all those familiar faces, my voice deserted me and I started to weep. I hoped I could stem the tide long enough to get through my speech, but that hope quickly evaporated. Wiping my eyes as best I could, I continued to read, though entire parts of the eulogy were drowned out by the sound of my own sobs. The ink on my notes was so badly blurred from my tears that I could hardly read them, but I persevered, desperate to see it through to the end, hoping that Brian would forgive my lack of composure. After what felt like a lifetime, with tears still flowing, I finished. There was a split second of silence and then the entire congregation stood and started to clap. From outside I could hear echoes of cheers and clapping, too. Perhaps I hadn't let my darling husband down so badly after all.

Adey spoke next and unlike me did so with great composure. His eulogy was truly beautiful. He spoke of his best friend, of their lifelong brotherhood, sharing tales of Brian's fervent loyalty and affection for all those close to him. He painted a perfect picture of the great man we had all come to celebrate. 'Nothing was more important to Brian than those close to him, so let's keep close together,' he said, as I held tightly onto Rosemary's hand. My heart was shattered, but somewhere inside I registered that feeling of pride. As Adey demonstrated such deep respect and enduring love for his pal, I knew I was lucky to have had at least four wonderful years with Brian. I was honoured to have had his love and to have loved him completely.

When Adey finished and rejoined us in the pew, he breathed a sigh of relief. Next, it was the turn of his three children, Callum, Evan and Natasha, to remember their uncle. I'd asked Lisa if they would like to be involved and she said they were delighted to be included. I was astounded at their composure as they recited their poem with such clarity and strength. They looked so little when they took to the podium yet, side by side, they were a powerful trio. Brian had utterly adored them and saw them truly as his family. Callum and Evan wore cufflinks I had given them that morning, favourite pairs that Brian had owned. The cufflinks represented elements of Brian's personality: one set had a smiling face, to show his eternal good humour, while the other showed the tower of London, representing his love for travel. I could just about make out their shining symbolism from my seat and did my best to smile encouragingly at the children throughout their reading.

Rosemary sat quietly for most of the ceremony and we held hands throughout. Who knew what was running through her mind? I was aware of my own anger at the injustice of Brian and Dad being stolen from me, but she had lost so many loved ones in her lifetime – two husbands gone and now two sons. Her tears ran silent, her heartbreak evident as she gripped my hand as the ceremony continued.

Once the memorial came to a close and the church began to clear, Rosemary, Adey and I made our way to the front door. Standing outside the church, we readied ourselves to shake hands with all who had come to offer their condolences. So many came to say goodbye to Brian, and so many had stories to tell. There was the schoolteacher who shared cigarettes with Brian in his teenage years (I told you he was no saint), the childhood pals and former colleagues (brief tales of 'one too many' pints taken) and, of course, bikers from all over eager to relay their legendary rallies. Throngs of hand-shakers formed an orderly queue and I hugged friends and strangers alike for well over an hour. Faces began to merge, until one suddenly stood out from the crowd. My uncle Brendan, Dad's younger brother, stood before me and I nearly fainted with shock. For a fleeting moment, I thought it was my dad standing there in front of me. I stumbled and cried out as I came to the realisation that this wasn't my father after all. As my uncle shuffled away with my cousin, arm in arm, I wondered if that momentary vision was Dad's way of saying he was still close to me. Perhaps he was nearby, propping me up better than any crutch could.

The crowds dispersed back to the pub where I'd laid on plenty of food and drink and we private few went to scatter Brian's ashes. It was just Rosemary, Adey and Lisa, Caroline, Dinkey and Paddy (Brian's childhood pals). We made our way to the designated spot on the island and soon it was evident why Brian had chosen this serenely beautiful location to be his resting place. Carrying the small casket that held Brian's ashes, and grateful that the winter rain held off while we trekked our way through a small muddy wood, we eventually reached a clearing sheltered by trees near the water's edge. Along the way Adey, Dinkey and Paddy giggled and the mood lightened when they explained why they were so amused. Brian told me that he had chosen this scenic spot because it held fond memories of his childhood, so I'd envisaged Brian as a kid, with his pals, playing hide-and-seek or climbing trees. It seems he was somewhat economical with the truth. His fond memories of the island were not quite so virtuous. The childhood games were more like teenage antics. Paddy explained that their favourite spot was ideal for snogging girls, drinking cider and smoking ciggies without being caught by meddling parents. I laughed out loud, my rose-tinted glasses lifting just an inch. Little wonder he was so attached to this place, and God knows what else he'd got up to there.

Yet as I looked out to the glistening lake beyond, I knew this was a fitting resting place for the man I loved, and also, perhaps, for the teenage rebel that I was just beginning to learn about. I chose a spot by a large chestnut tree to sprinkle a handful of ashes and wished his soul eternal happiness. With that, each member of our little posse took a small handful of ashes and sprinkled them on the ground as we whispered our goodbyes.

Afterwards, we decided to join the throngs awaiting us back in the pub. Durty Nelly's had been Brian's favourite pub, he had worked there as a teenager, and his father had played traditional music there often, too. It was the ideal venue for his 'wake'.

At least a hundred people were still there when we finally arrived and the relief of having the ceremony over was palpable. What followed that evening was a true celebration of Brian's life and a proper dedication to his memory. We shared food and drink and opened our hearts until the early hours of the morning. All those who had known and loved Brian had tales of his exploits and adventures. We laughed and cried for him and it felt as though he truly was with us there in that room as we reminisced until the early hours of the morning. Finally, the last stragglers retired to a nearby hotel and by the time I'd completed my burns dressings, which took over an hour, dawn was breaking. At last I grabbed a couple of hours of deep, unhindered sleep, in part from sheer exhaustion but also due to the relief of knowing that the memorial had gone so well. There was so much love for Brian in that room that evening, my heart was truly warmed. He would have loved hearing all those stories. I could finally close my eyes and sleep.

On a side-note, while much of Brian's ashes were scattered on that island point, truth be told, he has many resting places. He stays with me in Dublin in a small wooden casket, is sometimes carried around in my pocket in a small plastic toy Adey made for me, rests with Rosemary at her house in Clare and has nourished three bountiful fruit trees planted by Callum, Evan and Natasha in their back garden. Even though I somewhat strayed from his instructions, I think I'd be forgiven for doing so. He was a well-travelled and much-loved man and his ashes, like his zeal for life, have touched many hearts and many places. This way, there's a little piece of Brian left behind to comfort each one of us who misses him the most.

PART THREE

Step forward one, step forward two
Where do you think you're going to?
Hang in there, kiddo, you'll be alright
You're not quite ready to give up the fight
(ZH)

33

LOTIONS, POTIONS AND
LOCKS, OH MY!

As life began to settle into a new norm, structured around a framework of regular medical appointments, I adapted to my new nine-to-five and living alone in my apartment. My old career in advertising, which I'd nurtured for over two decades, was fast becoming a distant memory, though my boss in the newspaper was still holding out hope for my return. Or was it me holding out hope? I couldn't yet tell. So much of my old life had been dedicated to work, now every ounce of energy I had was channelled into my recovery. That person, the old Zoe who'd thrived on the thrill of the chase and the landing of a client, belonged to the past. She was somebody I no longer identified with, but I hadn't yet worked out who this new Zoe was or where she would fit into the greater scheme of things. In the meantime, I would soon learn that progress towards that 'new life' was going to be frustratingly slow.

I often felt as if I were locked in a *Groundhog Day* scenario. In fact, I was constantly reminded of one of my favourite ancient

Greek tales: the legend of King Sisyphus. This fable was about a king's fall from grace. Sisyphus had been a man of great military glory but was also terribly boastful, and this was the flaw that led to his eventual downfall. In a moment of tremendous arrogance (and maybe I'm taking creative licence here, but perhaps Sisyphus had glugged one too many amphorae of wine), he compared his own achievements to those of the father of the gods, mighty Zeus. It was never a great idea to make conceited comparisons to the immortals, and Sisyphus had compared himself to the head honcho, so trouble was inevitable. Zeus was mightily pissed off (again, I'm paraphrasing). To punish Sisyphus for his egotism, the great god doled out a torture that was excruciating: he cursed Sisyphus to push a huge boulder up a hill for eternity. Every time the king approached the summit, the mammoth rock would slip from his grasp and roll back down to the bottom, and he was compelled to run after the slab and start the whole process all over again. This curse would be repeated over and over for infinity and Sisyphus would never reach the top of the hill, stuck in the repetitive cycle of torture forever.

Sisyphus, I can relate.

My boulder-pushing day goes something like this. I get up in the morning, take meds, bathe, apply lotions and dress my burns. I do physio to move and stretch my limbs and more often than not go to hospital, where my injuries are tended to. Bizarrely, the hospital days are my favourites. They give me a chance to catch up with the girls, who frequently offer lifts to and fro, and indeed see the gang in the hospital, who I've grown to rely on. These trips offer a structure to the week and without them I would probably go out of my tiny little mind at home. I take more pills, go home, eat tasteless food (eating alone is flavourless), try to relax, watch some TV. Then it's back to bathing and dressing my burns again before bed. I take yet more meds, try to grab an hour or two of sleep while fighting off gruesome nightmares. In the morning I get up, take meds and ... well, you see why it feels like a never-ending cycle. I can't help but wonder if this will ever change.

There were some improvements to report, though, too. My crutch was now banished to its new home under the spare bed, next to my heels, and I was walking unassisted. While most of the responsibility for my progress lies at the door of Joanne, Bill and Ben, much of my improvement could be put down to my enduring love of household chores. Cleaning was my home physio and probably got me back on my feet much quicker than expected. At first, even light dusting was exhausting, and I'd barely manage ten minutes of ironing before my legs would wobble and go on strike. Those sessions were frequently followed by a long siesta. However, I could feel myself getting stronger by the day, and soon found that I was hindered with the crutch in tow and finally became impatient with my prop. My legs straightened, my grip strengthened and I felt my body regain power when it had been limp and ineffective.

Walking solo was a big achievement, but there was still some way to go. Catching my reflection in the glass-framed hospital corridor one day, I was surprised by what I observed. Once I had carried myself with confidence, taking long, smooth strides in skyscraper heels. My friends used to tease me that I walked in a horsey, criss-cross fashion, as if on a catwalk ... though they were quick to add that's where the model comparisons ended. Now my stride resembled that of a drunken toddler: part stumble, part half-gallop, as if I had just tripped. Mind you, like any toddler I was terribly excited to be walking upright on my own two feet. Admittedly my gracefulness could use some work, but wonky, unsteady steps or not, they were mine and I was overjoyed to have mastered them.

In other news I continued progressing in occupational therapy with Michelle and Shane, though my uncooperative little f**ker was still giving me gyp. I sometimes thought of those sessions as half OT and half the other kind of therapy as I found Shane the easiest person to talk to. Although at least a decade younger than me – closer to two, if I'm honest – he continued to be the adult in the room, lecturing me on my shameful potty mouth, while I continued to excuse my cursing, calling it an involuntary response to pain. This is a medically proven fact (or maybe not) and, to be fair, nobody says 'Oops' when they stub a toe, so I reckoned I was well justified. Now that my trach was fully healed and my voice was restored to its former glory, my cursing had become more pronounced. I'd discovered a whole new vocabulary of gutter jargon, words I never would have dreamt of using before, and as a result I would get a frequent, deserved telling-off.

The odd twinge of pain aside, those sessions were really working: my grip was stronger, my wrist more flexible and use of all my digits (bar you-know-who) improved considerably. Even the electric-shock nerve pains that had plagued me through the night eased and while my hand may pose problems for the rest of my life, it's safe to say that Shane and Michelle have worked miracles with it. I'm sure they had a little fun along the way, mind you, especially when they took out their OT implements of torture, some of which wouldn't look out of place in the Spanish Inquisition. The giant solitaire board was one example. For those too young to remember, Solitaire was originally a board game with small pegs inserted in a variety of holes. The aim of the game was to move the pegs around, ultimately ending up with just one. Well, I didn't say it was a very exciting game. Anyway, this particular version was actually a medical device that just happened to look like a giant Solitaire board game. It had pulleys and straps attached to the pegs, around which my fingers were wound. The device then slowly pulled and stretched the fingers, ligaments and underlying tissue in the hand and wrist. The result is pretty amazing. Under the guidance of the experts, this gadget dramatically improved the function of my hand and fingers. The downside was that it hurt like a bugger – hence the many curses.

Other devices used by the OTs were custom-made splints. Michelle created the most remarkable contraptions to help strengthen my fingers and wrist. She's truly an artist, sculpting these devices by hand, and while they may have looked cumbersome, with straps and hooks attached to Velcro wraps around my hand, they also made a remarkable difference. I'm still a work in progress for sure and I'll never play piano again (was lousy at that) or tennis (was even worse at that), but you can't have it all.

I also attended Mr Shelley's burns and plastics clinic regularly. There, the nurses tended to any open graft sites and performed other medical procedures. The one I still objected to was the manual peeling of the upper layer of skin, which was, unfortunately, an essential process. Now, those tweezers really were an implement of torture. As my skin started to shed in areas on my legs in particular, the top layers had to be removed. The tissue and dermis underneath were both incredibly sensitive and the nerves would go crazy if the metal tool hit the wrong spot. I cannot stress how much I hated those damn tweezers.

I'm ashamed to say that I probably wasn't on my best behaviour during those sessions. In fact, once the nurse had to virtually pin me down while I squirmed and squealed. What can I say? It's not fun being peeled like a raw onion, although I did apologise for behaving like a big baby. When that process was complete and Mr Shelley entered the room, I was back to model patient again. Street-angel house-devil syndrome. We'd discuss my progress, the grafts and scars, how I was coping with the pain and medications, etc. Invariably, Mr Shelley would touch on my emotional well-being and I often got the impression he was as concerned about my mental health as my physical progress. He cared about every part of my recovery. Fixing my limbs and making them function was just one part of this journey. Helping me cope with life in my dramatically changed situation, well that was another kettle of fish altogether.

From an observer's point of view, I was coping well, with family and friends supporting me in any way they could. My girlfriends were a constant source of comfort and still included me in their normal lives, sharing work dilemmas, the trials of motherhood and family dramas. I needed that; needed a reminder that the world continued to spin. However, as much as I appreciated being kept in the loop, those normal conversations also reminded me how abnormal I now was. My world was so far removed from theirs. I could still laugh, gossip and offer the best advice I could muster, but I felt like a fake, pretending to be one of the crew. They were doing their best to treat me like the old Zoe, and I didn't have the heart to tell them that she was long gone. I was feeling increasingly separate from my pals, a true outsider. Overly conscious of not complaining or sharing my emotions, I was afraid that if I opened up about how removed I felt from our old, shared lives, I'd either cause offence or bore them to such a degree that they'd abandon me entirely. I was severely depressed at this stage but doing everything I could to hide that fact from pretty much everybody. I'd cut myself off from a lot of people, due to in part to my depression but also because of my appearance, and I was terrified that if I revealed how I really felt, I would lose my little gang too. Previously, my life had been extremely social and I was quite the butterfly long before I met Brian. Now, I was all but a recluse, save for my close friends and family.

I was also bitterly lonely, even when I wasn't physically alone. I was helped in every way imaginable and had constant support from my brothers, the gals, pals and neighbours who lived close by, like Marian and Rami. Adey made frequent treks from Clare to Dublin just to check on me. Simply put, everybody rallied around to make sure I felt safe and cared for.

In truth, though, there are still days when that crushing weight of solitude is unbearable. I don't believe I'll ever get used to the loss of Brian or be able to fully accept my solo role, relegated from the wonderful partnership I once belonged to. Something always stopped me from revealing those emotions to Mr Shelley, however. St James' was the one place I felt like I fitted in and with all the work he'd invested into saving my life, I didn't want to sound ungrateful. So when he asked me how I was coping, I would either focus purely on the physical elements of my recovery, or distract from the topic by cracking a stupid joke. The other stuff ... well, the time would come when I could no longer hold it in.

The best way to distract myself from despair was by keeping busy. That way, I'd less time to waste on self-pity. My daily regime of treating my burns didn't change much after leaving hospital and certainly filled up enough hours in the day. Moisture became my new best friend and I implemented a rigorous routine of massaging all my burns from head to toe for a couple of hours each morning and night, a time-consuming and often messy process. Incidentally, the moisturiser I still use, the one recommended in my hospital, is a natural oat-based product called Aveeno. (The nurses used to laugh about this – it was our little joke: if it's good enough for Jennifer Aniston, it's good enough for Zoe!) I use gallons of the stuff each week, practically bathe in it: the oats soothe and heal like no other. Massaging not only rehydrates the burnt skin but also invigorates solidified limbs and eases nerve damage. I purchased special physio instruments, otherwise known as my own home torture kits, to assist me and got great results in some of those difficult-to-reach areas.

My next step was to apply liquid silicone on my face to disguise my injuries. I learned the hard way that putting make-up directly on the burns was not a good idea, and I hoped this magic 'goo' would eventually make those scars fade. I used a more solid type of silicone in the form of long gelatinous plasters on my arms, chest and shoulders. Likewise, these strips helped with scarring, pain and itching. The only issue with my silicone patches is that they had a tendency to travel and often turned up in the most unexpected locations. (Don't ask!) When they went walkabout, I'd find myself having to retrieve the little darlings and do a quick re-patch job. God knows that in my past life, when I tossed around the idea of silicone enhancements in my chest area, this was not what I had in mind.

In the early days I had the added problem, one I've mentioned before, of grafts zipping open at the edge. Given the extra training the nurses provided, not to mention the suitcase full of special dressings, I became adept at dealing with these. A surprising addition to my medical kit was cling-film. I'd use up an entire roll in a week. It was a nifty way to seal bandages from moisture and keep them in place before my outer layer of burn garments could be worn on top. By the time I was done, I resembled a Michelin man, wrapped in layer upon layer of bandages and cling-film from head to toe. Adding an additional flair to the final result, I also rustled when I walked.

The outer layers of bandages, which I still wear today, are specially designed compression garments used to hold my grafts in place, reduce thickness of scars and protect the damaged nerve endings. These garments have been made to my exact measurements and cover my hand, both arms and the entire lower half of my body. Not necessarily the most attractive fashion statement, although that's the least of my problems, they must be worn approximately 22 hours a day – basically the only time they're off is when I'm showering or applying moisture. My hope is that they'll eventually help my scars to fade. There is an added benefit to these special garments in that they're sort of like a full-body Spanx, major sucker-inners, in other words. I will have to wear these garments for several years and each full-body set must be remeasured and remade every three months to ensure they are literally skin-tight. They come in a selection of colours but naturally, being a (former) fashion-conscious gal about town, my chosen colour is black.

Then there is the story that just kept giving: my hair, or lack thereof. The regrowth process was frustratingly slow. Nobody tells you that it takes up to a year before you get a decent short coverage –- although I've been told that after the toxic shock, I was lucky it grew back at all, so I mustn't complain. We've established by now that I'm not the most patient of creatures and I'd easily spend hours inspecting the spattering of stubble in the mirror, willing it to sprout forth. Word to the wise: staring at something doesn't help it grow (and I'm not just talking about hair!). Six months after it fell out, I had barely a centimetre of regrowth. The hair had grown back with a coarse, scouring-pad texture and was jet black. I hadn't had such dark hair since birth and though there may have been the odd grey intruder in the mix, the overall shade was unexpected. I'd been dying my hair for well over a decade with tints, hints and highlights and I'd forgotten my original, true hair colour. While the shade was a pleasant surprise, the texture and length were less so. It grew outward as opposed to downward and was about as silky as a briar hedge. There was no way in hell that was getting a public viewing, so the wig continued to be an essential accessory.

I had fun with wigs, actually, and amassed quite a collection in different colours and styles from various websites. A surprising result of using one particular site was that I started to receive unanticipated alerts, offering me not only different types of wigs but some other suggestions to complete my wardrobe. Evidently a computer algorithm had decided that I was a man in drag (must have been my choice of headgear: I do have a big head) and I was sent some highly amusing recommendations, such as: 'size 12 thigh-high red leather kinky boots' or 'fierce and fabulous leopard-print leotards with clever support panels'. As tempting as their offers were, I politely declined but kept purchasing wigs nonetheless.

I joked with Mr Shelley, during one of our appointments, that he could judge my mood by whatever shade hair I happened to be wearing: ginger on my more fiery days, black when I was feeling brooding and mysterious (my hit-woman for hire look) and when I wanted to appear normal, the brown bobbed wig that Katharine had given me.

Then, on a whim, I decided to go blonde. It began with Brian's memorial, when I knew a cheap wig wasn't going to fit the bill and the bobbed brown one didn't offer enough camouflage to cover my facial burns. An ex-colleague of mine called Aileen, who still worked with Ornaith, came to my rescue. The topic of hair loss raised its ugly head in their office one day and Ornaith, who was an immense help with Brian's memorial, mentioned that I was 'wigging out' over my hair. A few years before, Aileen's daughter, Julie, had also lost hers while battling cancer. During that time she wore a sleek, shoulder-length, real hair blonde wig. In an act of tremendous kindness, Julie, who had since beaten cancer and now had a full head of hair, offered it to me. It was an incredibly generous gift. (Have you seen the price of real-hair wigs? It's enough to make your hair fall out!) I'll never forget how excited Ornaith was when she handed it over just a few days before the funeral. It was totally different from my old hairstyle, but the old Zoe was long gone so I decided to go the whole hog and change my look accordingly. Time to embrace the blonde!

Eventually I loved being blonde so much that I purchased my own real wig specifically measured to fit my head. After considerable research, I selected a store called HairWeavon (the mecca for baldies) where in a private setting, I could view wigs in every style, length and colour imaginable. Ornaith, my wig buddy, inhaled with excitement as we entered the sacred rooms of hair-raising glory. There were so many options to choose from that I got a little carried away and began grabbing wigs in colours and styles that I had no intention of ultimately purchasing. Red ones, black ones, curly or straight ... I was like a child playing dress-up or, better still, like the goddess Cher on tour, each wig transforming me into some other character. I was in serious danger of forgetting the whole reason we were there in the first place. Thankfully, the assistant had seen this all before and patiently started to guide me back to my original mission. With her expertise, I managed to whittle down the choices to half-a-dozen blonde wigs of varying lengths and shades.

In the meantime, Ornaith was having a little fun of her own, the temptation proving too difficult to resist. Before long, she too was removing wigs from the stands and shoving them on her head. Well, who could blame her – why should I have all the fun? As my appointment drew to a close, I finally chose a lovely shoulder-length, straight blonde wig. This was the hair that I imagined would match my new identity, even though I hadn't quite worked out what that was yet. It felt good though to take back just a little control of my appearance.

34

THE INSANITY OF GRIEF

atrick Kavanagh's 'Memory of My Father' was a poem I treasured as a child. The sheer poignancy and raw emotion in those short verses spoke to me then and captured exactly how I felt in later life when my own dad died. Kavanagh describes frequent sightings of his father after he had passed away, whether travelling or at home. It felt to him like everywhere he went, so too did his father.

This was how it was with me for many months after I left hospital. It started shortly after I saw Uncle Brendan at Brian's memorial. I wonder was that the initial trigger? These happenings could occur anywhere: outside my front door, in the local shop, or often on the hospital campus. I'd spot him, just a few metres away – my father, Colm Holohan. The fact that the men in question bore no resemblance at all to my father didn't prevent the sudden certainty that it was him. I'd gasp with heartbroken recognition every time.

I imagine that sometimes these sightings came from a subconscious desperation to have my father back again, as though I had sent a message out into the ether calling for him and he'd responded by magically appearing in some form. Often, though, I wasn't thinking about him and he'd still appear, out of the blue, a happy surprise. Every time I'd glimpse him out of the corner of my eye, he was just far enough away to be out of reach, but close enough to let me know he was nearby. Nearby and watching over me.

My 'Dad vision' never looked at or spoke to me directly, but always carried certain physical traits that made him 'Colmesque'. He had thick grey hair (even after all that chemo, Dad's hair always battled to the fore) and a handsome, perma-tanned face. His walk was a giveaway: he'd saunter with a little skip in his step, and that would remind me of one of my favourite childhood memories.

Dad and I were on the main street, by some shops, and we were rushing to get somewhere, though I can't remember where exactly. I was probably five or six years old at the time and was having difficulty keeping up with his pace. I was lagging behind, dragging my feet whilst holding onto his hand. At some stage I must have let out a whine because he looked down and noticed that I was struggling to keep up. All at once he did a sort of backwards skip, a kind of mid-walk dance move that made me stop and giggle. I took two steps forward to catch up with him. He winked and did the same backwards jig once more. My tiredness was instantly forgotten and so was the urgent pace. I'm pretty sure we must have been late for our destination because we did this little back-and-forth skipping dance for the rest of our journey. We scampered and laughed together in the middle of the street without a care.

That was Dad: he could always make me smile, make a joke out of nothing at all. This special memory will stay with me forever and from that day, in my imagination, my dad didn't really walk anywhere, he skipped. So every time a 'phantom' Dad emerged into my peripheral vision, it was invariably a man who walked with a little skip in his step.

One odd note was that while these men always resembled my father in some way, there were often marked differences. Frequently, I'd wake from my trance only to discover that the man I was staring at in the street could not be my father because he was clearly Asian or African. Whatever the nationality, somehow that man would transform into my father and, for just an instant, I truly believed it was him.

Each time it happened I'd stop in my tracks. Then I'd blink. Dad would disappear and I'd find myself gawking at a total stranger. Sometimes it was like losing him all over again and I'd be reminded of the gaping chasm left in my world.

I worried that this constant Dad-spotting was not an entirely healthy phenomenon and mentioned it to Mum one evening. She smiled knowingly and told me that it was actually quite a common response to grief. Apparently, the same thing had happened to her when her own father, my grandfather, passed away. She promised that the phase, like many things, would pass in time.

I guess that must be true because I haven't come across a Dad vision for some time now. Secretly, I hope he comes back to visit again soon. Even the painful realisation of my mind playing tricks on me is worth that blissful nanosecond when he's back in this life again.

One thing that baffled me was that while I had frequent Dad-spottings, Brian remained stubbornly out of sight. I often wondered if it was simply because conjuring up my love would bring such intense pain that I may not be able to overcome it. Even thinking about the happy times with Brian tore through my heart with a savage force. My grief for him took on a very real, physical aspect. I now understood how somebody could truly die from a broken heart. I had never experienced agony on this scale before.

And then, of course, there was the guilt I carried, the guilt that I had survived and he had not. I understood that survivor's guilt was a common phenomenon, but nonetheless, night after night I would lie awake, trying to shake off that pit in my stomach. (Catholic guilt sticks like superglue: perhaps those biblical teachings from childhood have a lasting effect after all.)

I wondered what I had done to deserve such a fate, why Brian had to be taken from me in the worst of ways. Eventually, I whittled my 'sins' down to the big three:

1.   Greed: I'd wanted to have that perfect wedding day, with all the bells and whistles, and the loveliest of honeymoons in the luxurious villa.

2.   Pride: I'd boasted to all and sundry that I'd found the perfect man to share my life with. I was proud of Brian, madly in love, but was also bragging that I had found 'the one'.

3.   Vanity: I'd pretty much starved myself for the best part of six months to fit into *the dress*. I glued on the long hair, applied a glowing tan, fake eyelashes, nails – the whole kit and caboodle. (Hell, I'm in my mid-forties: I needed all the help I could get!)

Still, I couldn't help thinking that these 'sins' did not deserve such a punishment as I was now suffering – plenty have done much worse and live a life unscathed. I resigned myself to thinking that the guilt and the sense of injustice were things I would have to carry (like Sisyphus and his boulder) for the rest of my days.

As time passed, I became desperate to find meaning in the smallest of things, to connect me once more with Brian. If I didn't have visions, perhaps there were other signs that I'd missed. Certain occurrences could be put down to mere coincidence, but every now and then something would happen that was a little too out of the ordinary and I would convince myself that Brian was trying to reach me from the other side, wherever that may be. (So much for being an atheist!) These incidences I dubbed my moments of 'de-Brian intervention'.

Take my hubby's favourite 'man' biscuits, for instance, better known as digestives. Now, in my humble opinion these are an assault on the taste buds (dog treats have more flavour), yet every bloke I've ever known, including Brian and Dad, love them. Digestives were a constant cause of irritation to me as Brian would secretly stash packets of them all over the place – a couple in the bread bin, a few at the back of the cupboard behind the rice and pasta, emergency packs in the freezer. He'd buy in bulk and hide them everywhere. He could eat half a pack in one sitting, while I'd look on in disgust – not because he could eat so many (sure I'm capable of devouring plenty myself), but because his choice of biscuit was so rotten.

Anyway, on my birthday, that first time I came home from hospital, I discovered a half-eaten pack of those digestives in the bread bin. I'd been rummaging around the kitchen, checking to see what food in my cupboards was still in date, only to discover a bright red packet of those godforsaken yokes nestled in the corner. The bizarre thing was the expiry date on the pack happened to be that very day, my birthday, 6 October. An odd coincidence for sure. I decided that it was Brian's way of welcoming me home and wishing me a happy birthday rolled into one. To be fair, he knew I'd find them. I always did.

It took me months, long after the expiry date had come and gone, before I could bring myself to throw them away. The biscuits remained untouched, stale and sacred, in the bread bin. It took the hint of mould to get me to finally throw them away, but even at that I shed a tear as I discarded his precious, horrible snack.

Then there was the mystery of Brian's timepieces. He owned four watches and kept them pristine and safe in their own boxes. Over the years I gifted him one for his birthday, one for Christmas and eventually a really special one to wear on our wedding day. When I returned home from hospital, I decided to give a watch to each of Adey's sons, Callum and Evan, as they were the closest things to nephews that Brian had. However, I discovered that not one of the four watches worked any more. Not a tick between them, not a tock to be heard. Now I know perhaps batteries need to be replaced, but the fact that all four ceased to work at once I found most mysterious. Perhaps time really did stop once Brian left this world.

I have often wondered if others suffering from bereavement experience such moments of insanity as I have done. I call it insanity because there are times when I feel like I'm going out of my tiny mind. Are these coincidences really signs from the other side or, more likely, just symptomatic of my desperate need to keep Brian and my dad alive with me in this world? No matter how tenuous these links are, if only through a packet of biscuits or a brief hallucination of a man that loosely resembles my father, I have found great comfort in these connections to my past life. These are my memories reignited and they bring me solace in the starkest of times. If indeed grief can be described as a form of insanity, then this form of lunacy sits well with me. I have found the perfect rationale for my irrationality.

35

SHRINK MY BRAIN, DELETE MY PAIN

Despite my physical improvements, of which there were many, I began to feel as though my mental well-being was starting to spiral. There were mornings when I could hardly get out of bed, when I saw no reason why I should bother. I was suffering from an ailment I called my 'secret sickness' – a malady that only fellow grievers can understand. Some days it merely lingered in the background, like a dull headache I couldn't shake off. I'd put up with the thumping ache at the back of my brain and pretend to function like everybody else. But there were times when my sickness became overwhelming and I simply couldn't manage. Initially, I put all my energy into fooling myself and everybody else that I was coping just fine, but the more time passed, the more difficult it became. The sadness within me was growing stronger and I wasn't sure if I wanted to fight it any longer.

It was around January 2019, with all the pressures that a new year brings, that I found myself grappling with thoughts of what my future might look like. I had managed to survive Christmas, my first as a widow. 'Survive' was certainly the word to describe it: where once it had been my favourite time, that Christmas was a period of sheer torment. I spent the day with my family, trying my best to shield them from my true feelings, smiling, eating and drinking as though everything was perfectly normal while every moment of enforced joviality caused me to die just a bit more inside. I was in pain, heartbroken, but surrounded by people who were invested in making me happy. Though I appreciated their efforts, pretending to laugh and smile all the time was exhausting and it was an immense relief to get home, where I could finally vent my true feelings, even if it was just into my pillow.

My home reflected my true emotions. It, too, was in mourning. The walls and shelves remained bare and untouched by decorations. The tree that I so lovingly used to decorate each year remained in its box, unassembled, unadorned. I couldn't abide the joyous carols that I had once sung along to, and I found the tear-jerking, life-affirming seasonal movies offensive. Even the traditional foods I'd previously devoured with glee tasted foul in my mouth. For the most part, the TV remained off or on mute and there was no music playing in the background. In my private world the whole season was ignored or, better still, cancelled. No sooner had I waved December goodbye, realising that I had indeed survived that first landmark holiday, than another one popped up straight away to slap me in the face: New Year's Eve.

At least there I got my own way and spent New Year's Eve exactly as I wanted to, alone and wallowing, no performing, no pretend merriment. I lamented the year that had passed, that had cruelly taken Brian, the man I adored. I grieved for my funny, talented dad. And I grieved for the loss of my own identity – face, body, job and future plans. I wept for all that had been taken by the fire.

When I eventually crawled into January 2019, bleary-eyed and exhausted, I was so weakened it was as though I was waking up from a coma all over again. I knew then that I had a decision to make and I started pondering my options. Should I persevere and push through the next year and those that would follow, somehow find the strength to do it alone, or should I just give up and join Brian and Dad wherever they found themselves to be? The latter was a tempting thought, I have to confess. The chance for the great escape from it all. Ironically, it was the season of joy, peace and goodwill that pushed me to this teetering point of despair. The thought of never having to spend another December on this planet was oh so appealing. And so, on 1 January 2019 this was my coin-toss: heads, fight for survival and hang around, or tails, withdraw from the battle and end my life.

I carried my imaginary spinning coin around in my head for days, flipping and spinning, trying to decide which way to go. Eventually, I decided to seek some expert help, which I suppose means I chose heads. That was where Dr Collier, or Sonya, as I came to know her, came into the equation. Mr Shelley had spoken of Dr Sonya Collier on more than one occasion. She is the principal clinical psychologist in St James' and her areas of expertise cover treating those affected by trauma, grief and life-altering illness. I reckoned that if anybody could help me, she was my best bet. I requested an appointment. I wasn't looking for miracles, I knew she couldn't eradicate my secret sickness, but I hoped that she might at least be able to ease the symptoms.

For my first appointment with Sonya, I decided to be cautious in terms of exactly how much information I revealed. Honesty is not always the best policy and if I started by confessing suicidal thoughts, for instance, there was a distinct chance I'd be locked up in an institution. Given that I had finally escaped hospital, the mere prospect of entering another was frankly a step too far. I was also afraid that if I went there, I'd never be allowed to leave.

The other reason I was reticent to show the doc how low I felt was in case she decided to limit my supply of medications, should I be tempted to use them inappropriately. I was surviving on a steady diet of tablets to help ease my physical pain, severe nerve damage and the constant itch all over my body that comes with burns recovery. If I was deemed to be at risk of self-harm, they could reduce my meds or, worse still, take them away altogether. Needless to say, my thought process was not entirely rational at that time, but as I was just about managing my physical symptoms, I couldn't countenance the idea of reducing my meds.

So when I met Sonya for my first counselling session at the end of January, I decided to keep my live-or-die coin-toss to myself. We started with simple introductions. I was relieved that she already knew details of my case, so I didn't have to trawl through the whole tragic scenario straight off, even if I knew I'd have to eventually. Sonya explained her background and detailed her extensive experience dealing with trauma, anxiety, depression and, notably, the challenges facing cancer and terminally ill patients. With such weighty areas of expertise under her belt I felt a glimmer of hope that she might be the one to help me; in fact I thought myself lucky to have somebody of her calibre in my corner. We discussed cognitive behavioural therapy (CBT) as a course of treatment. In layperson's terms I would describe CBT as a form of brain training, enabling somebody with symptoms of depression and anxiety to think and act differently. The ultimate aim of this treatment would be to improve my state of mind and install coping mechanisms to deal with the problems I was yet to confront.

I confided to Sonya that I'd experienced CBT when I was younger, when I was suffering from depression and panic attacks, and had positive results from the therapy. CBT took me through those dark days and out to the other side. Even though I was a believer in its efficacy, I was worried that my current issues were a much bigger challenge than those I'd faced before. Instinctively, however, from the very start I warmed to Sonya and that gave me confidence in the process. If it was going to work, if I was going to reveal my soul, I needed to feel that I was in a safe, trustworthy place and she appeared to offer that. We seemed to have a good rapport and as she spoke about her background, it was almost as though she were interviewing for the job, which was amusing given how much I desperately needed her help. Having said that, had Sonya known then just how gruelling this 'job' would be at times, she might not have applied in the first place. From my perspective at least, I was sold. That was crucial because when it came to therapists, I'd previously experienced both the good and the bad varieties.

I'd briefly attended one not-so-good therapist a decade earlier, when I was suffering from frequent crippling panic attacks. To protect her privacy, let's just call her Anna. I found 'Anna' by doing an online search, which in hindsight is not the optimal way to find a reputable therapist. However, with my panic attacks increasing in frequency, I needed help urgently and locally. I arrived at Anna's door in a highly stressed state and I knew by my rapid heart rate that a panic attack was imminent. My legs felt limp. My panic attacks often took on a paralyzing effect, I'd either freeze where I stood or crumple to the floor. As I rang the bell, I prayed that she wouldn't find her new patient slumped in a heap on her doorstep. Thankfully, my legs did not give way and in a bizarre twist of fate I quickly found my emotions shifting from self-anxiety to concern for the young woman who answered the door. She appeared to be even more terrified than I was, literally shaking. It could have been my unhinged demeanour that caused her to shudder, maybe fear is contagious, but I reckoned it was more likely that she was out of her depth. She looked as if she was barely out of nappies, let alone college, and I wondered if I was her first ever patient. That session was beneficial because I spent much of the time worrying about her health and stopped focusing on my own – a new form of diversion therapy, perhaps? I left an hour later with no intention of ever returning and one resounding thought on my mind: Anna, the teenage therapist, was in dire need of therapy herself.

My other less-than-satisfactory experience was about six months after that. This time I went with a friend's recommendation, and therefore assumed I'd be in safe hands.

However, this therapist, we'll call him Bob, turned out to be less interested in my mental health and more interested in his sideline: drug-pushing. I've never encountered a shrink more eager to shove pills down my throat than Bob. He practically Xanaxed the living daylights out of me before I had even started to describe my problems. To be fair, the pills did dramatically lessen my symptoms, but the problem was they dramatically lessened everything. I found it difficult to formulate a sentence, stay conscious at work, pretty much function at all. I'm certainly not dissing anti-depressants, they are essential life-savers for many, but I felt that Bob prescribed strong sedating meds in the blink of an eye, just to get me out of his office as quickly as possible. I detested the sluggish, fudgy side-effects and ended up cutting the course short and that doctor free. It's worth noting that beyond those two scenarios I had, for the most part, excellent experiences with therapy and when I eventually found the right doctor, CBT helped me overcome my panic attacks and get to the root cause as well. I would not have been so eager to embrace the process again if I didn't believe it could work for me.

Sonya got down to the nitty-gritty, beginning with some tests to ascertain where I was on that big graph of anxiety, depression and all-out misery. This was not a fun exercise. Every memory, thought and emotion I had around the fire, Brian's death and my own physical appearance was examined. It was like picking all my wounds apart and then grading them in severity from one to ten. I was curious to know what my eventual score would represent: did a low number mean I was totally sane, while a high one gave me a fast-pass to the straitjacket? I answered every question as honestly as I could and while I seemed to score well on some (she'd nod approvingly), it was clear I didn't do so well on others (no nod).

Unsurprisingly, I learned that while I was coping extremely well in certain areas of life, I was pretty much hanging on by the skin of my teeth in others. That was not quite how Sonya phrased it, but you get the picture. It took two more of those deep-delving sessions for Sonya to come to her initial conclusions. She told me that I was suffering from post-traumatic stress disorder (PTSD), that I had severe body-image issues (as would anyone who had been flambéed all over) and was struggling in the depths of immense grief. She shared with me the test results compiled over those first few weeks and then set out a plan to show how we could reverse certain thoughts, change certain beliefs and create powerful coping skills to deal with the problems that weren't going to disappear.

Together we started the process by setting some realistic goals to achieve, and challenges to overcome. Each goal was to be completed over a short-, medium- or long-term period and the chart we crafted would become my map to the obstacle course of my life. Sonya promised that if I worked with her, I could overcome those PTSD symptoms that were overpowering me and learn to handle my grief and pain. The ultimate objective would be to accept my new existence and learn how to live a new, much-altered life.

We agreed to meet weekly and while some sessions were a little over an hour, most ran for well over two hours. Sonya was always gracious enough not to make me feel like I was on the clock. Slowly, she began to hone in on the most pressing issues, unpicking my brain and working out ways to improve how I approached, or more accurately avoided, things that I found difficult to face. Often those with PTSD relive their moments of greatest trauma through flashbacks. These can take different forms, and sometimes occur at the most unexpected moments, like while performing a simple day-to-day task. Everyday, ordinary activities suddenly became threatening or terrifying triggers. One such trigger that could transport me straight back to the fire was unpredictable weather and, in particular, strong gusts of howling wind terrified me. They opened up a window in my memory, one I desperately wanted to keep glued shut, to when Brian and I were running around in circles, our eyes weeping from smoke while the hot, fiery tornado whistled in our ears as it whipped up the burning embers that stuck to our clothes, our skin and hair. All these months later, it was stormy weather that brought on my first flashback.

One cold winter's evening, Caroline and I were walking home after an evening out. My friend was quite the persuader. In fact, I wondered if she was secretly on Sonya's payroll, so adept was she at getting me out into sociable settings, which was what the doctor had ordered. That night she coerced me into going for a bite in a local restaurant. I was deeply uncomfortable being out in public, so it was quite the challenge. Surprisingly, the other diners didn't stop and stare and after a pleasant meal and a good gossip, we started the short walk home.

On the way, we got caught up unexpectedly in a windy storm. It came from nowhere and instantly I found my mind hurtling back to 23 July. It could have been the high-pitched scream of the wind or the sensation of having no control – I was holding onto my wig with one hand and my crutch with the other – but suddenly I wasn't in Dublin anymore. I was back in Mati, back in the path of fire, danger and imminent death. I couldn't explain the terror I experienced in that moment, not even to Caroline who walked alongside me. She was oblivious to what was going on in my head, probably thought I was just my usual anxious self. Soon I hardly registered her presence anymore: it was just me, alone, battling the brutal gale that I was sure would bring certain death. The wind was in my ears and even though it was cold, I could already feel my skin begin to blister and burn from the heat of the flames. It's utterly amazing what tricks the brain can play. It was only when I got home and locked the door behind me that I finally allowed myself to breathe. Climbing under the duvet (my safe place), I hid from the 'blaze' outside. It took hours before my racing heart slowed down and there was no sleep that night.

Just when I thought I had those weather triggers under control, another one would catch me off guard. Some weeks later I was caught out in a particularly heavy rain shower. I was on my way to hospital when the friend who was driving me there had to cancel at the last moment. I started to panic, anxious to make it to St James' on time. I tried phoning several taxi firms, but had no luck. I began hobbling on my crutch up to the main road, to flag one down. This was not the wisest course of action. The heavier the rain lashed, the more difficult it was to walk and the more frightened I became. All at once I was no longer battling lashings of water against my body, but bolts of fire penetrating my skin. I huddled down on the footpath and covered my head with my arms to protect my face from the searing heat, which felt agonizingly real. Hunkered down in the torrential rain, with my crutch lying on the footpath beside me, I must have looked a strange sight to anybody driving past. By some miracle, Ornaith happened to phone me just then and hearing my hysterical sobs guessed that something was terribly wrong. Very gently she talked me down from the precipice, assuring me that I was safe, that it was just rain and that I needed to breathe slowly. Just hearing her calm voice on the end of the line was enough to shake me out of my waking nightmare. Switching off the tears was not so easy to do, however.

Ornaith organised a taxi to pick me up from that spot and within minutes the nicest driver in Dublin – part taxi-driver, part therapist – scooped me up and drove me quickly to the hospital. There, Shane from occupational therapy took one look at me and handed me a towel to dry off and a cup of hot tea for comfort. I must have looked a right sight after sitting in a puddle, and I'm sure my panda eyes gave away my hysteria. Back on the hospital campus where I was secure, with Shane my cheerer-upper, I felt strong enough to reveal what had just occurred. Flashbacks like these lingered for months, though they became far less frequent as therapy progressed.

Just as frightening were the nightmares I endured after dark. Peaceful sleep was something that belonged in the past and my nightly torture featured violent dreams that belonged in some kind of Dante's *Inferno*. Over and over through the night I'd wake just as these imaginings reached their macabre crescendo, drenched in sweat, in a state of utter terror. This became the norm. One evening, however, something shifted and I awoke from a particularly brutal nightmare to find myself in a bedroom thick with smoke. It was so heavy, I could hardly breathe. I pulled my legs over the edge of the bed, which took some time due to my injuries, and hauled myself into escape mode. The smoke told me that my home was on fire and I had to get to a safe place.

I didn't delay. I grabbed my handbag, just as I had that day in Greece, and moved as fast as my legs would allow. Coughing and spluttering, I waved the smoke with my arms, attempting to find a path in the darkness to the bedroom door. In seconds I made it out and up the stairs to the top floor of the apartment. There, I scrambled onto my balcony where I gasped in breaths of clean, cool air. Wondering momentarily how I was going to escape from the balcony, it took some time before I looked around and realised that there was no smoke at all upstairs, no burning smells or threatening flames, and I could hear no fire alarm. Cautiously, I edged back downstairs – still no smoke – to my bedroom, and after tentatively checking the handle to see if it was hot – it wasn't – I slowly opened the door once more. The light from the hallway flooded the room to reveal a perfectly untouched, smoke-free bedroom. The fog that was chokingly thick just a minute before had vanished into thin air. That was the one of the most vivid flashbacks I'd had since leaving hospital and it was one of the most alarming, because it encroached upon the safety of my own home.

I discussed each of these episodes with Sonya and together we worked to overcome them. I used breathing techniques to help stop the panic and to slow my brain down, enabling me to come back to the present reality as opposed to that horrific moment in the past to which I seemed to constantly travel back. We delved into the weather triggers to desensitise the power of the elements and I remember feeling really proud the first time I managed a walk in the park, reporting to Sonya how pleasant the cool breeze felt on my face. Up until that day any type of wind caused me to be fearful. It took quite some time to get there, though.

Three o'clock in the morning became my least favourite time, well, 3.25 a.m. to be precise. For some unfathomable reason I woke up, and sometimes still wake up, at exactly that hour virtually every night, for the most part drenched in sweat. When I awake the sheets are usually sopping and my face is pretty much glued to the pillowcase. No doubt there's a perfectly plausible explanation for my nightly wake-up call (flight overhead, car alarm, neighbours having sex), but whatever it is, it always coincides with me waking from a bad dream. My night terrors vary in format, the storylines change, but generally they carry one underlying theme, that of loss.

I can't find Brian. Panicking, I look everywhere for him and eventually realise that he's left me behind and I'm alone forever.

I'm sitting on the cold kerb as a child, waiting for Dad to bring me home, but he never turns up. Again, I'm abandoned.

I adopt a beautiful animal (usually a cat, but sometimes a small dog or rabbit), only to find that they die in my arms and I'm left with a limp ball of fur.

As soon as I close my eyes these ordeals begin. The more Sonya and I delved into my grief and PTSD, particularly once we started to unpick the events of 23 July, the more graphic and gruesome these dreams became and often, in the early days, they were gory in the extreme, with visions of dismembered bodies and graphic bloodied wounds. Little wonder I became addicted to late-night TV, anything to avoid the tormented inner crevices of my imagination.

One night I woke up abruptly at 3.25 a.m. and found myself in that strange part-conscious, part-unconscious state of mind, with a vivid memory of the dream I'd just had. It brought up an unsettling thought that I couldn't shake off: perhaps Brian's terrible end in this world had been predestined? It had all been outlined in the nightmare: we had been sent many signals down through the years, but foolishly had ignored every omen. In my nightmare, my body was being burned at the stake like Joan of Arc. My torso was pinned to a wooden post by sharp, narrow arrows that sliced through my breasts and stomach. Desperate to escape, I tried to remove the arrows but my hands were too injured to grip and my legs too weak to move. As I looked down upon my bleeding flesh, I could see smouldering flames creeping up, licking at my toes and feet. As the flames grew stronger and hotter, I heard a voice calling out, telling me over and over to 'follow the flames', as if that were the key, the answer to all my questions. When I woke with a start, I was muttering those same words, 'Follow the flames.'

As I tried to slow my breathing, waiting for my heartbeat to reduce to a normal rhythm, I began my nightly ritual of deep breaths: inhaling and exhaling, slowly sucking the air in and pushing it out. Eventually, the pounding in my chest calmed, but I still found myself repeating the words from my nightmare, and my mind began to wander back in time.

My first big holiday with Brian was to South Africa, about six months after we met. By then we'd been living together for some time (I wasn't one to hang around) and though we had taken some short breaks, this was to be our first of what I assumed would be a lifetime of big adventures together. Our journey would start in Cape Town and take us all around the renowned garden route of South Africa. It was a wonderful trip, truly one of the most incredible holidays I had ever been on. The fact that I was head over heels in love with my companion made it all the more thrilling.

We were hypnotised by the scenery of South Africa: one moment we'd come upon awe-inspiring mountains of red rock that seemed to sprout from nowhere, the next we'd encounter a quaint, 'ye olde' seaside village that was so pretty it could have belonged in a children's pop-up book. The only thing at odds with all this beauty was that virtually everywhere we went on this trip we came across fires: forest fires, to be precise. This shouldn't have come as a surprise. We were in South Africa and frankly it was bloody hot, so the odd blaze was to be expected. However, as our holiday continued, we couldn't help but notice just how many fires we encountered. In fact, at our very last pit stop, outside Stellenbosch, as we were checking out of the hotel we found the flames were getting just a little too close for comfort.

We noticed that the trees that lined the street to the entrance of the hotel had been burned: some were merely singed, others charred to a crisp. As we vacated the car park, smoke was billowing down from the nearby hills and I remarked to Brian that it was time to get out of there. I felt relieved to be leaving that particular town. We could see shimmering redness in our rear-view mirror, reflecting fires just a few hundred metres behind us, and we heard the sound of fire engines heralding our exit.

Back in my own bed, as I recalled that moment leaving Stellenbosch, I remembered how shocked we were that nobody seemed at all bothered by the proximity of the fires to the hotel and neighbouring village, or by the heavy smoke that was filling the air. We were surprised that all the other hotel guests weren't vacating the property. Surely they were tempting fate?

Follow the flames. Were the fires in South Africa our first warning?

Two years later, we visited Sorrento, Italy, for our summer holiday. It was incredibly hot, reaching the mid-forties most days, and we spent much of our time lounging by the pool. Well, I spent most of my time in the pool, while Brian hid under an umbrella in the shade because he wasn't a fan of the sunshine.

The hotel and its pretty floral gardens were set in a valley facing a heavily forested mountainous region. We spent the best part of the first week of our trip gazing at helicopters desperately dousing out forest fires in those hills opposite our hotel. I must admit, I watched on without fear for our safety. My curiosity was tinged with sadness as I observed the beautiful landscape go up in flames right before my eyes.

One day the hotel manager, a friendly bloke, warned us that if the fires came any closer, we would have to evacuate the premises. Still, I had an apathetic attitude, no alarm bells were ringing out in my mind, and with fascination I continued to watch the hypnotic show of floating helicopters fighting the blaze. I'm ashamed now to admit that with little sense of the seriousness of the situation, I shrugged off the manager's warning and went back to sunbathing by the pool. It was only later that evening I thought to ask him if there had been any casualties. He assured me no homes were built on the side of that hill, no injuries had been reported and no locals were affected. Now I realise that simply couldn't have been true. Even without casualties, I've no doubt some of the vast expanse of land demolished was probably farmland. Somebody always suffers in the end, and at very least someone's livelihood was affected. When we left Sorrento and drove through the beautiful countryside to the airport, we saw first-hand the destruction those fires had inflicted on the landscape.

As I lay shuddering in my bed, thinking back on those three holidays over the four years Brian and I were together, South Africa, Italy and Greece, I convinced myself that with every flaming omen we ignored, we overlooked the inevitable pre-destined fate that was mapped out for both of us. We had followed the flames, or perhaps they had followed us.

I confided in Sonya about the dream and my theory – that our fate had been pre-destined and the flames had been there, creeping in the background, all along. Sonya appealed to the logical self that was still nestled within me, explaining that Brian's death had less to do with destiny and more to do with a horrifically tragic event that was entirely out of our control. Try as I might, I still couldn't shake that guilty feeling that I'd ignored the signs and, like all the other things I couldn't face, including my constant fear and intense grief, I buried these dreams deep in my psyche.

MY PTSD

R ight from the beginning of our sessions, Sonya established that I was suffering from post-traumatic stress disorder (PTSD), which was a psychiatric response to the horrific events of 23 July. As well as feeling constantly under threat and anxious, as if I were on high alert, I learned that a common symptom of PTSD is avoidance. Sonya explained to me that I was sidestepping anything that might trigger painful memories, the most agonising of those, in my case, being of the happier variety. I had become quite the expert at ducking and diving, though that was something I wasn't supposed to be proud of.

I consciously tried to avoid anything that reminded me of the good old days. Top of that list was music. In the past, there were always sounds playing in my home, in fact I loved to belt out the odd tune myself. Now, music just made me feel sad, reminding me of everything I'd lost. The radio was banished entirely, especially Radio Nova, our favourite station. Brian and I had listened to it for hours, singing along to random 1980s tracks, competing over who could guess the song or singer first. Recalling these moments even now still jabs at my heart.

Then there was a lifetime of musical moments with my dad and remembering those was just as painful. When I was a kid, he used to drive me to school and we'd spend the journey belting out songs together – everything from Abba harmonies to the very finest Neil Sedaka medleys. We did an excellent rendition of 'Calendar Girl'. The Sedaka tape was jammed in the cassette player for over a month, so we learned all his songs by heart. We sang every song on that album dozens of times, hollered them out every morning together without a care in the world. That memory hurts like I cannot explain. Sonya had her work cut out on this one as I was adamant that all music was a no-go zone.

It was the same with TV programmes, movies and televised sporting events. Brian was obsessed with rugby, never missed a game, and together with Caroline and Ferg we had watched countless matches in our local pub. To this day, I still don't have a clue what the actual rules of the game are, but I was happy to join in the festivities. As a little gang, watching rugby became our thing. We'd always bet on who would score the first try. I'd inevitably back the cutest-looking player, which was often a good tactic. Mind you, these days all the Irish players are easy on the eye. We'd laugh together, yell at the big screen, and basically have a good time. Over a year after Brian had passed I accidentally caught the tail end of a game on TV and actually felt the room swirl. It was too much to bear. I switched off the TV and vowed never to watch rugby again.

My ever-expanding taboo list included food and drink. I no longer ate our home-cooked favourites like kedgeree or paella. Brian did most of the cooking, so my versions would have been poor copies anyway. There were also certain local pubs and restaurants we had frequented together that were barred. That was a handy excuse sometimes because if I had my way, I'd never leave my apartment at all.

Given the many challenges, I wasn't the easiest of patients and could be quite uncooperative. On occasions, I'd refuse to open up or to be open-minded enough to listen to Sonya's solutions. Sometimes I was so angst-ridden, all I could do was cry. Sometimes I was so angry or entrenched in self-pity that there was no talking to me. We didn't exactly argue, but we would come close when I refused to work with her (dang mule stubbornness), but we always came 'good' in the end and slowly things started to improve. I respected Sonya because she never lied to me, never treated me like a child or pretended things were better than they actually were. She just wanted me to try and accept the good things that I still had in this life and to work on coping with the problems that I couldn't escape.

It felt good when I started ticking things off my to-be-avoided list. Listening to songs on Spotify for the first time brought me surprising joy – so long as I avoided 1980s tunes, I was safe. Visiting my parents' house was a higher mountain to climb. Twelve months after the fire, I had yet to return there. That caused me great emotional conflict and was one of my most important goals. Mum constantly begged me to visit, but I couldn't bring myself to do it. She always had to come to mine instead. The prospect of seeing all of my father's possessions, with his art adorning the walls, of smelling the paints in his studio, an aroma I've loved my whole life long ... I was sure I'd fall apart completely. I made every excuse under the sun not to go there for as long as I could, and it took some serious work with Sonya to get me through the front door, but eventually I (or we) succeeded. I sat in Dad's studio, inhaling the bitter-sweet scent of oil paint, and felt a true sense of achievement and love.

Sleep remained the biggest issue. It's truly impossible to keep hold of your marbles when you're not sleeping. Even with all my meds, anything over two hours was still unattainable. It wasn't just the nightmares that I found difficult; often the happier dreams of Brian caused me more distress. Pain would often wake me and, in truth, there were many nights when it was just easier to stay awake. That was when I discovered the joys of late-night TV, and to this day I can dictate by heart the adverts that rolled out in the early hours on the latest wonder mop, must-have toaster oven or all-round fitness equipment. I'd watch any old rubbish as a distraction. Today, while getting shut-eye still gives me trouble, the situation has vastly improved and I might get a whole five hours on the trot. I've learned how to handle the bad nights and make the most of the good ones.

My body image is also still an issue. At first, I was repulsed by my reflection, so much so that nobody, bar the doctors and nurses, was permitted to see any of my skin, except for my face, of course, but that was only because they wouldn't let me wear a paper bag over my head. The truth is, I've had to live with the fact that I am scarred all over and will probably be for my remaining days. My face, luckily, was the least damaged place. In my heyday I wasn't a bad-looking chick and it still takes some getting used to, knowing that girl is long gone, but I'm working on accepting this new version of me.

When you have a toothache, you can put off the dentist for

a while, but eventually you'll need root-canal treatment. Like that, I knew at some stage that Sonya would one day have to address the source of all my problems: the day of the fire. This was the biggie and we took some time to work up to it. She explained that by going back there in detail repeatedly, in a safe setting like our little therapy room, I would eventually feel desensitised to those events. It didn't mean I could erase the pain or consequences of that day, but it could help me to unload some of the survivor's guilt I was carrying (that I lived and Brian died was a source of constant torment) and dispel some of the fears and false beliefs that shadowed me every day since that disaster. In other words, in order to help me conquer my demons, we had to go back to their birthplace.

The first time Sonya asked me to run through the sequence of events of that day was an incredibly harrowing experience. I had spoken about 23 July with her several times before, but never in such precise detail. I closed my eyes firmly and, in a trance-like state, went back there, starting with when we woke up. I relived each moment, describing the beautiful morning I spent with my lovely new husband, our excitement as we changed our Facebook status to Married, making love in the afternoon. Suddenly it all shifted into a rapid spiral: we were in hell, fighting fire. I felt it all: the terror, panic and agony as Brian took his last tortured breath. It was a horrific task and ended with me crying hysterically, begging Sonya to let it end.

It did end, of course, when I opened my eyes, but this was a process that I would have to get used to. We did it week after week, describing 'that day' repeatedly. I began to skip events in my story that were less significant and focus on moments that had greater impact, carrying on until I reached the first moment when I truly felt safe after the fire, when I arrived at the Mitera hospital and met Mr Moutoglis. It was only when he assured me that I was protected in his care that I truly believed I was out of mortal danger.

It may sound like a cruel assignment, revisiting the worst day of my life again and again and again, but the truth is this exercise quickly began to take effect. By unpicking the 'hotspots' (an unfortunate psychology term for the most powerful or traumatic moments) and working out how my mind was processing that information, I began to understand how my brain was replaying these moments through flashbacks and affecting my every move in the now. By breaking down every hotspot, emotion and belief, I began to take some of the power out of the event that had ruined my life and to regain some control over my existence as it was in the present day. It didn't take away the pain or the grief I felt, but it helped me to eradicate some of the effects of PTSD. The flashbacks disappeared and I began to live in the present. It was a difficult treatment for sure, but ultimately a powerful and successful one.

37

AND NOW FOR A RANTING
INTERLUDE

The time came when I could no longer avoid the colossal list of practicalities I'd been ignoring, the most pressing of which was addressing the mile-high pile of paperwork and bills. Having been stuck in hospital for months and with Brian's death to cope with, the post and the debts for both of us had mounted up. I began to wade through it all, contacting banks, businesses and utility companies, prioritising those that had sent final demands. I quickly found myself drowning in the same horrific conversation over and over again: first, I had to clarify my situation and explain to total strangers why bills were overdue, where I had been for nearly six months and why my (now dead) husband hadn't settled his invoices. I begged companies to put these letters in my name, as seeing those envelopes addressed to Brian opened a fresh wound every time. Brian never owed anyone a penny and it hurt seeing his name attached to these communications.

Truthfully, some companies and their employees were wonderful. Many people had heard of my situation and handled the call with great sensitivity. While these conversations were always difficult, it was a lot easier when the person on the other end of the line showed empathy and understanding. Sadly, however, there were corporations that were downright diabolical to deal with and only added to the trauma. I would dearly love to name and shame two, in particular, but I've decided to err on the side of caution. A little rant is good for the soul, mind you, so with that in mind allow me to introduce you to Company A and Company B.

Company A. I was attempting to pay a bill, one of Brian's direct debits that was, to be fair, considerably overdue. The amount owing was substantial and I wanted to pay it in full over the phone and cross it off the list, while ensuring that Brian's name was removed from any future correspondence. I phoned Company A and, after hopping from one department to another and spending an inordinate amount of time on hold (sweet Jesus, that tinky-tonky hold music would drive you to drink), I was eventually put through to a service operative who could only be described as an insensitive young muppet. Let me clarify that his age was not the problem here. I couldn't care less if he was generation X, Y or Z, the problem was that he had the emotional maturity and understanding of a dung beetle. Not only was he incapable of processing the payment, which I tried to do three times (his computer said no, apparently), but he also clearly didn't have a sensitive bone in his body. The phone call was emotionally exhausting.

He asked why the bill was six months overdue and I explained that my husband had passed away in tragic circumstances and that, with his bank account frozen, his direct debits had been cancelled. He asked me why I had left it so long to contact them, so I explained that I'd been in hospital myself, had been fighting for my own life and therefore unable to see to these bills. I reiterated that I wanted to clear the debt completely, but he was having too much fun playing twenty questions. I couldn't decide if he had a sadomasochist streak or was simply trying to make up his daily quota of call-sheet minutes. Either way, everything I was trying to communicate fell on deaf ears. He asked me twice more about my personal circumstances, and then asked if I would like to hear about his new payment plans. I begged him to just take the payment and let me go, desperate to get off the phone before I started to cry.

Clearly muppet boy wanted to use this call as a sales opportunity – Company A had lots of new utility packages available, blah, blah, blah – but this was not the time or place. After his third, unsuccessful attempt at taking the payment, he actually had the nerve to ask me if I had any future plans for my property now that my husband was deceased. That was the final straw: I couldn't believe how crass and cruel he was. After spending nearly an hour on that call, including over thirty minutes on hold, I had enough and finally hung up. My blood was boiling to such a degree, however, that I phoned back the following day to make an official complaint. Amazingly, I also managed to get the bill paid in one fell swoop.

Two weeks later I received a letter saying that Company A took my complaint very seriously and that, having listened to the call in question (these calls *are* actually recorded for training purposes), they were shocked by the content. The employee (muppet) in question was reprimanded and sent on a training course on how to deal with such sensitive situations. A fob off, perhaps, though I truly hope it was a punishingly boring course.

My revenge, naturally, in true Irish style, was telling all and sundry never, ever to use this company's services!

Company B. Then there was the unfortunate scenario where a financial institution, Company B, 'misplaced' some paperwork and effectively turned my tragic loss into a farce. Brian's bank account was frozen as soon as I officially reported his death. I was assigned an assistant to deal with the situation and within days of leaving hospital, I went to meet her at the bank. Initially, I thought she seemed more than capable. At her bequest I brought with me a file full of paperwork. Gathering these documents had been a challenge in itself. It was deeply upsetting to obtain copies of Brian's death certificate and our marriage licence on the same day, the issue dates being only four days apart. However, the bank assistant assured me that a swift resolution would be met, that it would take a month at most and that all my paperwork looked in good order. Naively, I took her at her word. I soon discovered that I was dealing with a liar and a useless, ineffective tosser who promptly set to work doing pretty much nothing at all.

Four months later, while I was struggling to meet my financial burdens and clear Brian's bills, the banker (tosser) had managed to perform a disappearing act that would rival Houdini's greatest achievements. Not only was she nowhere to be found – she was either on holiday, sick leave, coffee break or in the toilet – she also managed to make most of the paperwork I had left with her evaporate into thin air. I lost weeks of my life making phone calls and leaving numerous, no doubt ignored, messages and writing dozens of emails, which were likewise left unanswered. When I eventually managed to track down her colleague (tosser never actually responded to me at all), I was met with a tissue of lies and a list of excuses as long as my arm. Company B claimed they hadn't received half of the items of paperwork. When I explained that I had handed them in personally due to their sensitive nature, they passed the buck, placing the blame on another department.

My breaking point was when I received a final demand from the same financial institution (same company, different department) regarding overdue direct debits for business charges. The wording was threatening, a court appearance was inferred, yet the same company was holding onto Brian's funds. On top of all that, it was the first I'd heard of these charges, which had accrued substantial interest over time. As they couldn't get hold of Brian, they wanted to sue me. I was livid. The very bank that was sitting on his account was suing me for funds owed from that account. I called the department in question and had what one could only describe as an epic meltdown on the phone. The person on the other end of the line appeared mortified once I explained the whole situation and promised to set wheels in motion to rectify the 'miscommunication'.

My brother John got involved at this stage. He happened to phone me a few minutes after that call, and he offered his help. Ireland is so small, I sometimes think that while the six-degrees-of-separation theory applies elsewhere in the world, you could cut that number in half here. John put the word out amongst his contacts, and within 48 hours the bank had assigned me a special case worker to sort it all out. This manager achieved in a remarkably short period of time what her predecessor hadn't managed to do in nearly six months. The missing paperwork, which I had since re-sent, was miraculously located. The department that had threatened to sue me was suitably chastised, and I received a formal apology in writing. At last, everything started to move in the right direction.

Word of my situation reached Company B's PR division. They decided to send me a gift as an act of apology. One afternoon a courier arrived with a huge cardboard box, over a metre high and half that again in width. In a little envelope attached to the box I found a printed note that read: 'From our complaints department, Company B.'

Needless to say, I wasn't exactly overcome with emotion reading those heartfelt words and was thinking that Company B's PR department could use a human touch, but I was curious to see what delights were contained within the parcel. They say curiosity killed the cat; well, it wasn't quite lethal in this case, but I certainly wasn't the cat that got the cream either.

Nestled in the humungous box, wrapped amongst wads of tissue, was a small, measly, half-dead bunch of carnations and daisies. Some of the stems had sadly been decapitated, some were hanging in there, gasping for a drink of water, but the majority were brown, withered and dead as a doornail. How touching, I thought. Nothing speaks more of concern for a recently widowed customer than a bunch of dead flowers.

I promptly threw the dead flowers in the bin. However, all hope was not yet lost because stuck on top of the big box was another, smaller box, wrapped in bright pink paper. In case I'd any doubt as to where this second offering had come from, it too contained a card printed with the same sensitive words: *'From our complaints department.'* Dear God, after working in advertising/marketing for twenty years, what I wouldn't give to shake up their communications team. Once more I found myself less than moved but was willing to give them one more chance. Who knew, this time they may have opted for a more appropriate gift than a bunch of dead flowers. Chocolates, perhaps – everybody loves a nice luxurious box of chocs ...

Behind the feminine wrapping was a box of thoughtfully selected exfoliating soaps and body-scrubbing products. Exfoliating body scrubs: for a woman who had suffered third- and fourth-degree burns all over her body. The very last thing I needed was a box of caustic products designed to strip whatever epidermis I had left. The sheer thoughtlessness of this gift left me speechless. Surely whoever sent this offering must have been made aware of my situation? Surprisingly, though, my initial dismay quickly fizzled into something quite unexpected. I had to admit, it was bloody hilarious. Their shambolic attempt to apologise was so bad, it was actually good – or at least terribly funny. Who knew a bunch of dead flowers and a box of exfoliants could bring such mirth. I laughed so hard, I actually cried. (Tears of laughter made a pleasant change from the other variety.)

I must confess, Company B did eventually come good. The case worker that John was instrumental in finding could not have been more kind or efficient. Apparently when it comes to financial institutions and death, these matters are rarely plain sailing, which was another life lesson I learned the hard way. But in the hands of a real professional the paper trail and comedy of errors were swiftly resolved and I could finally breathe a sigh of relief. Having said that, there's nothing like a good rant every now and then to get things off one's chest!

38

THE KINDNESS OF STRANGERS

You'd be forgiven for thinking, from my previous tirade, that I was turning into a right grump, frustrated by the red tape that was tripping me up and the unfair situation I'd found myself in. I admit it, there were days when I was so overwhelmed by anger, I'd lock myself away and wallow in tears of self-pity and resentment. (Hell, I still have some of those days even now.) However, just when that mood threatened to become all-consuming, the universe would give me a wake-up call, or a kick in the arse, and present me with a reason to keep going. Something magical would happen that would restore my faith in humankind. For all that is cynical and harsh about our world, when you look hard enough, at the heart of it you will find a core of goodness.

While this may sound like I've taken one too many happy pills, allow me to demonstrate some of the random acts of kindness I've experienced.

My first trip to the local supermarket is as good a place to start as any. A stone's throw from home, my local SuperValu store is where I've always done most of my grocery shopping. It was always a friendly store, I knew maybe one or two of the staff by name, but even so I was supremely stressed about my first visit back there after leaving hospital. This was to be my first real venture out of the apartment. Initially, I relied purely on grocery deliveries, being reluctant to step outside my front door. That was all fine and dandy, the service proved really useful, but it just wasn't quite the same as doing my own shop. I like to feel the fruit and veg, to give them a quick sniff when nobody was looking, to squeeze the bread gently, and I'm a total sucker for browsing the special-offers aisle – if it's a bargain, it's going in the basket. It has been said to me on more than one occasion that I'm a control freak, so perhaps the real impetus to break my agoraphobia was that I hated the idea of a total stranger choosing my groceries. If I wanted to take back charge, I'd have to do it myself.

I discussed my dilemma with Sonya, knowing I badly needed to overcome this anxiety. While I wasn't quite reclusive yet, I certainly wasn't embracing any elements of my previous life. Outside visits by family or close pals, I led an isolated existence, avoiding places or situations that could trigger uncontrollable emotions. I was extremely cautious about where I went, what I saw and with whom I spoke. As Sonya had explained during our session, this avoidance tactic was my way of controlling ever-increasing anxiety and was a common symptom of PTSD. Seemingly normal, everyday activities became huge challenges, so I just bypassed them entirely. However, I couldn't avoid my supermarket forever, even though I was terrified of everything from people staring at my strange appearance to songs playing on the tannoy that could remind me of Brian or Dad. I was even worried about how I'd react if I spotted certain items on the shelves (like the damn digestive biscuits Brian inexplicably loved). Sonya decided that this was to be my first big challenge and recommended that I enter the lion's den with a friend in tow. Once again, Caroline stepped up to the plate and after a ludicrous amount of time prepping – I wore so much make-up, my cheek could have been used for fingerprinting – I was eventually coerced out the door. With my crutch and my shopping list firmly gripped in my right hand, off we went.

Initially, the shopping trip was much like any other: we grabbed a trolley and hobbled slowly into the fresh food section. So far, so good! With Caroline in the driving seat, so to speak, we navigated the aisles, while I loaded up with enough groceries to feed an army. There were 'gulp' moments for sure, when I saw Brian's biscuits my stomach did a turn and I closed my eyes entirely. When we reached the pet food section, I couldn't bear the sight of Meow's favourite tins. So we dodged a few molehills for sure, but hadn't yet encountered the mountain, the biggest challenge: the dreaded tills. Once I had completed my shop and moved towards the tills with my overflowing trolley, I realised that I could no longer avoid eye contact with the staff. I had cunningly spent the entire time staring intently at my shopping list, but when we came to pay I could no longer pretend to be the invisible woman. My heartrate sped up with anxiety. Then came the crucial moment that made all the difference.

The shop assistant, who was busy scanning the items, suddenly looked up at me and stopped serving mid-stream. I had known her previously, we'd always passed the time of day, yet in that moment she seemed stunned. Looking at me, unable to speak, she stood up, walked around the till area and hugged me tightly, but very gently, and with tears in her eyes welcomed me back. She used my name. I wondered how she knew it, forgetting about the newspaper coverage. As quickly as she had stood up, she turned on her heel and sat back down to complete her task. Soon another staff member emerged from nowhere, the ever-smiling store manager who always had a joke to hand. He too very cautiously, yet clearly emotionally, welcomed me back. With his voice cracking, he told me they'd been awaiting my return and that if I needed anything at all, they'd be there for me.

I looked around and a few more people had gathered, some offering their respects for Brian, others saying nothing but giving me the nod or tapping me on my back: a show of support and a demonstration of true humanity at its best. They'll probably never know how important that day was, how much their reaction meant. They broke that terrifying spell that hung over my head like a guillotine. Yes, I was still scared, but at least my first escapade out of home had been a successful one. I held my breath and smiled, determined not to cry. As we left the shop, even Caroline exhaled a sigh. I guess she was relieved there were no emotional meltdowns.

After that, my journey back into local life became much easier. I registered with my local pharmacy – goodness knows I'd be spending a lot of time there in the future – and again that visit was filled with hugs and warm wishes. It was comforting to know people were looking out for me. I felt safe in my little village again. These were my neighbours, in every sense. They didn't stare at my wig or bandages and spoke to me as they would anybody else. The only thing that took a bit of getting used to was that everyone seemed to know my name. I heard 'Zoe' everywhere I went. That was okay – ultimately, it reminded me I was still alive.

Something else to get used to was receiving random hugs. I was admiring a woman's dog one afternoon on the street outside my block. I didn't know her personally, though she looked vaguely familiar (the woman that is, not the dog). Anyway, just as I was telling her what an adorable pooch she had, out of the blue she hugged me. She told me that I was very brave and that everyone was behind me and then jogged off at a rapid pace. Perhaps she was embarrassed. I hope she wasn't, it was terribly sweet. Something similar happened when Caroline, Ferg and I went to eat in our local pub. The waitress, who would eventually become a true friend, and who was also touched by great tragedy as she lost her son around the same time as Brian died, offered her condolences and very gently took me by my hand, promising that I would be alright. To some, these experiences may seem intrusive, but to me they were moments of genuine kindness and love. They gave me the strength to keep going.

Then there was the practical help that came from unknown and unexpected sources. A GoFundMe page was set up by a total stranger, a man called Derek Malone. Derek had been in college with Brian when he was studying for an MBA in business. While I was still in Greece, Derek set up this page and the funds, which I only became aware of many months later, were financially a bit of a life-saver. Having been cleaned out after the wedding and honeymoon, I was overwhelmed with bills. Top of the heap were the funeral expenses and related costs. As if by some miracle, just as those debts were getting to an angst-inducing level, Derek got in touch and presented me with the GoFundMe donation. There was enough to cover all of Brian's funeral and transportation costs and a little left over to erase some of the other debts that had been piling up while I was in hospital. I cried with relief as the very patient funeral director was finally paid in full and I wondered if Derek, and all those who donated, would ever know how grateful I am and how their generosity saved the day.

Even my local hair salon, Reba, stepped up. A few days before Brian's memorial, I dropped in with Caroline and sought out the help of my stylist, Jen Redmond. Jen had looked after my hair for the wedding and together with her colleague, Jenny Daly, styled my hair and that of my two bridesmaids, Caroline and Ornaith. We all spent a very happy (and bubbly) few hours getting preened and styled. It was so strange to be back in the same chair, just a few months later, asking Jen to style my wig for Brian's funeral. To say it was an emotionally charged situation wouldn't even touch the surface, but Jen handled it with professional ease, empathy and tenderness. She kept the salon open late for me so that she could see to my needs once all the other customers had left. That way, I wouldn't feel ill at ease around curious eyes.

She styled the wig beautifully on my head (like a normal human) and knew how important it was that I looked as well as I could for Brian. In a way, it was the most important hair style I'd ever had. She got that and treated the occasion with the respect it deserved. Once done, she broke the sombre mood by presenting me with a present: a styling head that looked like a life-size Barbie doll bust, on which I could set my wig. Little did I know – I was new to wig etiquette then – that this was truly a gift from the gods. The styling head was an essential tool in maintaining the wig's shape, especially when it needed to be washed and dried. I dubbed my giant Barbie head 'Dolly', and she became a permanent fixture on my bedside table.

I dropped in to thank Jen for her kindness a few days after the memorial, taking the opportunity to inform her that Dolly had made quite the impression, explaining how she had scared the living daylights out of me the morning after the funeral. Clearly, I had been thrashing around during the night and Dolly had become dislodged from her place on the bedside table. She had rolled off and landed silently on the pillow beside mine in the bed. I woke up with a start to find myself face to face with a smiling, decapitated, life-size Barbie, her painted blue eyes staring intently right back at me. If you thought the head of a horse was a sinister bedfellow, try a life-size doll's head! Anyway, on the morning that was in it, Dolly scared the bejasus out of me, but it was almost worth it when I recounted the story to my wonderful stylist. It felt really good to laugh out loud in that salon again.

That was my little village, my fortress of safety and kindness. There couldn't be a better locality and I dearly love all those who showed me such tender care. Sadly, I couldn't stay there all the time and there were occasions when I would have to wander out into the big bad world, where I'd have to get used to less pleasant encounters. Out there, strangers did stop and stare at me in the street, as though I were a freak of nature. It could have been the scars on my face that caught their eye, the bandages or, more than likely, the wig that had gone temporarily astray. They can be cantankerous little creatures, these wigs. Whatever caused them to goggle, initially it made me terribly upset. In time, though, I worked out that unwelcome glances were just par for the course.

I knew that when it all became too much, I could always retreat to my village, where I was safe and accepted. The kindnesses I had been shown there made it just that little bit easier to face the rest of the world – scars, wigs and all!

39

STUPID PEOPLE SOMETIMES SAY STUPID THINGS

The safe space of my little village was a huge comfort, but even in that safe space there were still moments that I can only describe as challenging and, having lost so much of my confidence, I didn't always handle these scenarios in the best way. Not for the first time I thought of my young nephew, Theo, born without hands, who had faced many difficult situations in his short life, always with dignity and maturity beyond his years. As I said before, he was quite the little warrior. I had to admit that even many months after the fire, with my left 'new' hand concealed in a special pressure-bandaged glove, I could have used some of Theo's skillset to deal with awkward encounters.

One such brush happened in my local newsagents. I had ventured out on my crutch to pick up some essentials, the shop being just a short walk from my apartment. There, I found myself having to resort to one of Theo's tried-and-tested coping strategies – although I believe he was only four or five the last time he used it. Initially feeling quite brave in the shop alone,

I was hobbling around the aisles, carefully placing items in my basket, when I discovered that I was being shadowed by a particularly inquisitive teenager. I say inquisitive, but cheeky little git would be more accurate. As I was in the queue waiting to pay, he came up behind me, poked me in the shoulder and asked, loudly enough to make everybody within earshot turn and stare: 'Missus, what's wrong with your hand?'

I was totally taken by surprise. It was the first time somebody had asked me about my bandages in public, and the fact that so many people were now staring made me deeply uncomfortable. I'd no intention of giving an honest answer, no desire to divulge private details about the fire to a total stranger, and a kid no less. Theo popped into my head and I recalled how he had handled a similar situation when he started national school. Some children had gathered around him in the yard and one particularly curious kid asked him straight out why he had no hands.

'Shark bite,' Theo had quickly responded, no doubt with a beaming smile on his face, if I know my nephew.

The shock factor had the desired effect. Instantly, Theo stood out amongst his peers not because he was without hands but because he carried an air of mystery. He was not a victim, he was a *Crocodile Dundee* adventurer, a mini man of the world. It was a stroke of genius and demonstrates how Theo instinctively knew how to cope with difficult questions and transform what could have been a distressing moment into a victorious one.

Back in my local shop, as a woman in her forties, I was not nearly as brave as my darling nephew, though I did borrow his material. As confidently as I could I said, 'Shark bite,' and then sucked air in through my teeth for added dramatic effect.

The kid stared at me for a split second in astonishment and I hoped that would be an end to it. Unfortunately, my response had the opposite effect: it only encouraged him to ask yet more questions.

The kid shouted at the top of his lungs, 'No wayyyyyy – that's so cool!' and then followed up with a rapid onslaught of questions:

'Where did it happen?'

'Is that why you're on a crutch?'

'Is that a real leg or a fake leg?'

I had no follow-up, no arsenal of smart retorts and frankly had no notion what to say next. So in a moment of mild panic and utter cowardice, I dumped my basket on the floor and swiftly (well, as swiftly as I could, hobbling on my crutch) exited the shop. I left behind the obnoxious kid with his mouth gaping open, minus my provisions I might add, and I didn't even look back. I could have kicked myself for being such a wimp and vowed to tell Theo just how brave I thought he was, now that I'd had a small taste of what he had dealt with so gallantly his whole life.

Now you would be forgiven in thinking that this was just a kid pushing the envelope. Certainly, as time passed, I would learn how to answer those sorts of questions, but back then the whole experience sent me spinning and it was months before I returned to that shop because I was so mortified. And it wasn't just kids that stared or said stupid things. I would discover that adults could be equally insensitive or moronic.

It was during one of my sessions with Sonya, when I was in feisty mood, that I revealed how frustrated I was getting with some people and how hard it was to handle certain situations calmly, when all I secretly wanted to do was blow a gasket. It wasn't as if, all of a sudden, I'd turned into a hothead, flying off the handle at anyone and everyone for no reason. It was just that there were some unfortunate moments when I'd take offense at an idle remark or a thoughtless question and find myself having to cover up my exasperation. I was making great strides in my physical health, but I knew my fuse was growing shorter by the minute and was worried that my anger would explode at an inappropriate moment. Sonya had just the answer.

'Stupid people sometimes say stupid things.'

One of Sonya's seriously ill patients had coined that phrase and often repeated it in her head as a mantra to help her overcome difficult moments when anger threatened to win out. The patient found this little chant prevented her from getting annoyed when 'stupid' people asked questions like, 'Are you better yet?' or 'When will your hair grow back?' Although these queries were never intended to cause upset or offense, they frequently did just that. Sadly, she found herself having to answer them regularly, so she handled these unwelcome scenarios by repeating her incantation in her mind, to help keep her calm. Sonya shared this with me because that woman had learned to control her frustration: who better to take inspiration from?

I was fascinated by this mystery person, though I knew nothing about her other than her coping strategy. In my imagination I referred to her as Superwoman. She was my hero – a young woman bravely battling serious illness while trying to get on with life as best she could. Like me, she didn't have time to waste dealing with daft questions posed by even dafter people. I agreed with Sonya that if she could keep her head, then I could certainly give it a try.

That's when Sonya suggested that Superwoman's chant could come into play.

It really worked for me … most of the time. There was the odd occasion when I repeated it so often in my head it became like a maniacal prayer. *Stupid people, stupid things, stupid people, stupid things.* On bad days I'd have to step back and give myself a firm talking-to – something along the lines of, 'murder is frowned upon in polite society' – but for the most part I was aware of that defined line between fair and unfair reasons for getting annoyed with people and did my utmost not to blur the categories. There were moments I slipped up and snapped, but I think even Superwoman would forgive me those transgressions. Though my reasoning may appear unsound, I've outlined some examples to demonstrate what I believe to be 'valid' (i.e. forgivable) and 'invalid' (i.e. absurd, but hopefully also forgivable) reasons for getting angry into two nifty categories for easy reference.

Valid reasons for feeling angry:
- A certain person, who shall remain nameless, attempting to show me a photo of Brian's remains in the morgue. The reason for doing so remains unclear.
- A particular individual attempting to pull off my burns bandages so she could have a peek at my scars beneath. My scars, my business.
- That muppet in Company A purposely asking me to repeat the details of my husband's death three times on the phone.

- Certain bankers, pension companies and financiers whose sole mission in life is to hold onto people's cash for as long as they can legally, or sometimes illegally.
- Feet swelling to elephantine proportions so that you can't fit into any of your favourite pairs of shoes. If you're of the female persuasion, you will sympathise with this dilemma; if you're a bloke, you're less likely to do so (some guys would kill to have bigger feet ...).
- Being in constant pain – perhaps not so much a valid reason as a useful excuse. Pain makes one terribly cranky.
- Chronic lack of sleep – as above, also a most excellent excuse. Sadly, insomnia also ages one terribly: less Sleeping Beauty, more Sleepless Bitchy.
- 'Friends' selling photos or details of my wedding day to the press. I was amazed to see what some people would do for their fifteen minutes of fame. 'With friends like these ...'

Invalid reasons for feeling angry:
- Normal people doing normal things, like going on sun holidays, wearing T-shirts and shorts, discussing how lovely the hot sunny weather is. I am the summer equivalent of the Grinch: avoiding sunshine at all costs and jealous of everybody who can soak up the rays.
- People having lovely, healthy hair, nails and skin, but insisting on complaining to me about how thin their hair is (while I'm bald), how they just broke a nail (mine all fell off, by the way) and how dry their skin feels (do I need to spell this one out?).
- People staring at my wig and mouthing to each other, 'Is that a wig?'

Answer: Yes, it's a bloody wig and yes, I can bloody well lip-read.

- People asking me, 'Are your burns healed yet?' Most of the time this question comes from a good place but it could be worded better. Each time, I repeat Superwoman's mantra three times in my head before answering with a polite 'Not yet.'

- People saying, 'I know how you feel,' then showing me a picture of a few measly spots on their chin, a bit of sunburn, chapped lips, etc.

  (Note to self: fight urge to punch them in the face repeatedly, say Superwoman's mantra at least six times to avoid responding in an utterly offensive fashion, shake head and say nothing at all.)

- Fashion magazines – I used to pore over these in a past life, but now that I'm no longer the target audience, I find them supremely depressing. Finding nice clothes to wear over all my bandages is challenging, to say the least.

  (Note to self: create new fashion trends like Spring Scar Style, Fab Fashion for Flambéed Forties, Burns Body Bandages – the New Black.)

While most would agree that my first list is perfectly rational – surely anyone would feel irate in those circumstances? – I'm only too aware that the second batch is utterly ridiculous. If I felt annoyed every time somebody in Ireland discussed the weather, well, I'd be permanently annoyed as it's the nation's favourite topic of conversation. I may as well be locked up in a padded cell for life. Likewise, I understand that women, in particular, are only trying to empathise with me by using comparisons of their hair, skin or nails, but I really don't think chapped lips should ever be compared to third-degree burns and it takes an incredibly brave woman to complain about hair breakage when I'm sitting opposite her, bald as a coot.

I explained to Sonya that during each of those instances, my outward reaction was exemplary: I would change the subject entirely or run away rather than admit my true feelings. It was inside me that the Hulk-like reaction, with fury of mammoth proportions, was begging to break free. For most of my life, I've rarely allowed my true feelings to come to the fore in difficult situations. I certainly would never lose my temper in public. Although I had become quite adept at swallowing my anger, as one would ingest an ulcer-shaped pill, I could feel the fiery bitterness begin to burn within me. I'd fantasise about having my moment of retribution. What I wouldn't give for that opportunity to let myself go and give way to a frenzy of screaming frustration, a hole-in-the-wall punching, glass-smashing, toddler-tantrum-stomping release of all my pent-up fury.

Alas, according to Sonya, there were more appropriate ways to deal with these emotions. Talking more openly about my feelings with friends and family would be a good place to start, though it took some time before I could get there. Exercise was another way of working off that frustration, like taking long walks in the open air to blow off some steam – though that in itself was not easy to do either. While I worked on those healthier channels, I could always continue using Superwoman's chant to get me over the rough spots ...

Stupid people sometimes say stupid things.

40

MANOS TSALIAGOS

Official reports say that 102 people died as a result of the wildfires in Athens on 23 July 2018, although some Greek news articles estimate the number was higher. Of the reported fatalities, 48 were women, 43 men and 11 children, including one infant. Only five of those killed were non-nationals: two Polish, one Belgian, one Georgian and, of course, one victim who was Irish, my husband. Thousands of vehicles, homes and buildings were destroyed and during the days that followed 187 people were hospitalised. I was amongst the eleven survivors who were seriously injured, some of whom later passed away in the very hospital where I was being treated. I survived because I was rescued in the nick of time, seconds from death. The man who saved my life is called Manos Tsaliagos.

I discovered his name on my second week in the Mitera. By then, I was obsessed with finding out who had carried me from the boot of the burning car because I couldn't recall if I had thanked him for his heroism. I had no idea what I'd say to him if we met face to face, but I wanted to show my gratitude for his bravery in some way. What do you say to somebody who has saved your life? Would simple words ever be a sufficient way to acknowledge his courage and to express my thanks? I had to start somewhere.

It was Stephen who revealed his name to me, one night in the ICU. I remember studying my brother's handsome face that evening; his dark eyes and furrowed brow displaying the tell-tale signs of anxiety and sheer exhaustion. No doubt he got little sleep in those first few weeks after the fire, travelling between Dublin and Athens, juggling his duties of comforting our parents and doing all he could to help me in my hour of need. I only considered the impact on my brothers months later, when I was back at home. It can't have been easy witnessing their sister, charred and unable to move in that hospital bed. They maintained a calm and gentle demeanour at all times, were so brave and strong, and for that I am immensely proud of them.

That evening I zoned in on Stephen's eyes. His face was covered with a mask (all visitors had to wear them), but his eyes were visible and they looked tormented with worry. He kept clearing his throat and twitching his head, so I guessed he was working his way up to telling me something important. Stephen was apprehensive about bringing up the topic of my rescue, or anything related to the fire, but I knew something was eating away at him, so I told him to spit it out. It was then he revealed that my rescuer had come forward and that his name was Manos.

Stephen knew I'd been hounding hospital staff for information on my rescuer, and Mr Moutoglis had decided it was time to reveal his name. What wasn't revealed was that the story of the hero volunteer who had risked his own life rescuing the Irish bride from the burning car was all over the news in Greece. The first inkling I got of the magnitude of the coverage was a few days later when a young nurse let it slip that I was all over TV. She giggled excitedly as she changed my dressings, whispering that I was her first famous patient. She meant no harm, but I felt uncomfortable, famous for being the burnt bride. Reports revealed that Manos Tsaliagos was a true hero in every sense, not only saving my life that day but also countless others. In fact, he risked his own life to rescue as many people as possible. He had tried to meet me personally in the hospital, but that was not possible while I was in intensive care. I decided the next best thing was to get a written message to him instead.

Stephen offered to help me in that undertaking, transcribing the letter for me, given that my hands were utterly useless at that time. He also promised to track down Manos' address, or at very least that of his fire station, and get my message to him. It was nearly impossible to find the right words to express my feelings. I had learned that Manos was not an employed fire-fighter but a civil volunteer and that he had courageously pushed through the searing flames of those blazing trees to save me. While I had moments when I selfishly wished I had died with Brian in the fire, I still felt incredibly indebted to him for saving me. So writing the letter was not a simple task by any means. Thankfully, Stephen had the patience of a saint. (It's a joke in our family that he's the only Holohan blessed with that virtue, the rest of us being impatient so-and-so's.) I dictated, faltered, and altered the contents several times, while Stephen diligently read and re-read each paragraph back, patiently making the alterations I requested. Eventually, after numerous edits, I decided it was as good as it was going to get. He typed the letter that evening in the apartment that he and John were staying in (courtesy of the embassy) and with that I had some relief, knowing Manos would finally receive my thanks.

My letter wasn't the only missive sent to Manos. Some days later Stephen announced that the Irish Taoiseach, Leo Varadkar, had also written an official letter of thanks, expressing his gratitude to Manos for saving the life of an Irish citizen. That was quite a moment. I was humbled to learn that the leader of our country, a man I admired, had written a letter on behalf of my nation. Many months later, I discovered that the Taoiseach's letter provided a momentous surge of pride and recognition for Manos himself. It wasn't until I eventually managed to converse with him, through the wondrous medium of social media, that I found out just how much it meant to him.

Once back home, I took my time before going anywhere near social media. It was on that long list of scary things I chose to avoid. Beyond attempts to protect my privacy, I found it all too overwhelming. The first time I logged on after the fire, I was met with a barrage of new friend requests and hundreds of messages from total strangers. Nothing to do with my sudden rise in popularity: it was all very strange. The majority of the messages were lovely, containing thoughtful words of condolence, but many were from journalists and TV producers looking for an interview. There were some religious zealots in there too, offering guidance, a few conspiracy theorists about the fire and a couple of all out nut-jobs, one of whom offered romance in my hour of need! Clearly, my security settings were not up to par. Brian would not have been impressed, as he was always nagging me to update them. The invasion into my closeted space alarmed me so much, I immediately logged back out again.

If that was alarming, it wasn't nearly as upsetting as my own homepage. There I discovered photos of our wedding plastered together with articles of Brian's death from a few days later. It was sickening. I was actually physically ill the first time I saw it. These were not my postings. My profile had been hijacked and contained a macabre pastiche of the best and worst days of my life, side by side. Alongside laughing wedding photos, moments of perfect joy that had obviously shared by guests from the wedding, were news clippings of the 'Greek Wildfire Horror', detailing Brian's terrible end. Love and happiness, devastation and death: a noticeboard of my heartbreak, for everyone to see and comment upon.

Even when I made an exception to my avoid-social-media rule on 21 November, I regretted it. I wanted to honour Brian's birthday. I was grief-stricken that day, but I wanted to remember him to all the people who loved him as much as I did. It was my first post since prior to the wedding and it was a deeply personal one. It was a wake-up call to find my message to Brian posted on numerous websites and newspapers shortly after, with one paper managing to pen an entire article around my two brief sentences. Must have been a slow news day. Lesson learned: until I was ready to re-enter that world and grow stronger armour, it was best to either steer clear or accept that my privacy was compromised.

It wasn't until a cold, mid-January morning in 2019 when curiosity, or boredom, got the better of me and I decided to take a sneaky peak once more. Avoiding my homepage, I chose instead to investigate the private message section, and it was there I found a DM from Manos Tsaliagos. By then I was ultra-cautious and wary that this message could be from an imposter, so I spent several hours researching his profile and photos. I read interviews he had given concerning the fire and the recovery mission that took place after the catastrophe and even scanned some of the images from the core of the inferno (many of which, frankly, I wasn't ready to witness). It was only when I found the Taoiseach's letter of thanks proudly displayed on his profile page that I decided it must be the real Manos. This was indeed the man who had saved my life. Eagerly, I answered his brief message with words of thanks and an apology for the delayed response.

Within minutes, Manos responded. Through the helping hand of an online translation tool, we began conversing. He seemed delighted that I had finally answered his mail, which had been sent months before it was seen, unfortunately, and I was excited, if a little overcome, to be finally communicating with him. Language difficulties aside, we managed to interact as best we could. In time, we would develop our own part-written, part-emoji language, for this conversation lasted well beyond that first day.

It took weeks before I could broach the specifics of my rescue with him. Most importantly, I needed to learn the fate of the children that Brian and I had bundled into the car. Manos disclosed that all five children had survived with only minor injuries, as did the adults sitting in the front seats. I was glad to hear it, but it struck home how terribly unfair it was that Brian, the man who carried those children to safety, was the only passenger in that car not to have lived. However, learning that the kids had survived put stop to one particular nightmare. I had been haunted by an image of a wide-eyed toddler in a nappy appearing out of a cloud of smoke, reaching out its hand towards me, only to suddenly disappear again in a flash. Every night this apparition would appear in my sleep and I never reached the child in time to save it. In all those months since the fire, I was convinced the children must have died and that nightmare represented the youngest calling out to me from the other side. Now, in learning that they were all alive, I could rejoice knowing those last few minutes of Brian's life were not in vain. He was a hero for helping those children, and would be always remembered as such.

I'm not sure what my reaction would have been if I'd found out they too had perished in the fire, but asking the question was worth the risk because that night, for the first time, the toddler didn't come to visit me in my sleep.

Manos told me a lot about the day of the fire and what had happened, particularly on that stretch of road. When he discovered me first, he presumed I was dead as I was virtually buried under the burning embers of the tree that had fallen on the car. I was so badly burned and so still, he thought I was gone. It was only when I blinked my eyes and let out a moan that he knew I was alive. How strange, I thought, for in my recollection I was still calling out loudly to Brian when I was discovered, praying that he would answer. Up until then I had believed that it was my shouting that had alerted Manos to my location, but perhaps by then I was only calling out to Brian in my mind.

Many conversations with Manos were difficult, especially about the fire and the aftermath, but even so it was cathartic to talk to somebody who had also visited my little pocket of hell; who had witnessed some of the same sights from that day. Manos also spoke of the horrors of the clean-up mission, which he participated in, and though it may sound macabre, discussing these matters, in truth I was revisiting that road in Mati every time I closed my eyes, so at least this was one way to talk it out.

I began to feel the urge to return to the spot where Brian had perished, where my life was altered forever. Perhaps I needed to mark the place where the man I loved drew his last breath. I decided that as soon as I was well enough to travel, this is what I would do. It would also present me with the opportunity to meet with Manos, a chance to thank the man who had saved my life.

41

RETURN TO GREECE

nevitably, Christmas rolled around again and much like the previous year, I found the season of goodwill difficult to bear. I miss Brian and Dad every day, but for some reason their absence is all the more conspicuous at times of celebration. However, there were some improvements on the previous year and, if I'm honest, I even enjoyed some of the preparations as I decorated my home from top to tail with all things glittering and shiny. I thought Brian would be okay with it after last December's abolition of adornments.

There were the traditional offerings, like the tree, lights, garlands and wreaths, but in pride of place were my cherished, more unusual decorations, like the German flying Christmas cow (it's not Chrimbo without sparkling winged cattle) and the wooden clogged mice and the one-legged troll with the dislocated elbow from Norway. The stand-out best (worst) of all has to be the ugliest porcelain angel you've ever seen. I had bought her for a friend several decades before as a joke. My friend hated the season of goodwill, so I thought she'd appreciate the gesture. But

I became so attached to the ugly angel's delightful wonkiness, I couldn't let her go. She, along with the other members of my eclectic chorus line of decorations, made me surprisingly happy. I'd been collecting them from all over the world since I was a teenager and each had its own funny little tale. This was my attempt to embrace the season and though it didn't all go according to plan (do these festivities ever?), I was proud that I at least gave it a go. I experienced an emotional crash on Christmas night and in the days running up to New Year's I really struggled, but I managed to keep my feelings private, knowing I wasn't the only person on the planet finding that season hard. At least a new decade was waiting just around the corner.

December 2019 was an eventful month for another reason. After much procrastination, I finally decided to take part in legal proceedings in Greece. The case would be part criminal, part civil, though when I began the process I knew nothing of these specifics. All I was after was an explanation for Brian's death and an apology. I realised that the only way I was going to get answers was by returning to Greece and joining the many who were already taking legal action. For over a year I'd obsessively studied reports on the fires in Mati: poring over news clips, watching TV excerpts and following any social posts that related to the events of 23 July 2018. I felt a deep connection to all those victims who had lost their loved ones, their homes, livelihoods and to those who were, like me, branded for life by the fire.

As a result of my research, I discovered that prosecutors had been assigned to an investigation back in March 2019 and that their initial findings reported a series of cataclysmic errors made by the authorities. The report detailed that the mismanagement by police and fire services had resulted in 'chaos and a collapse of the system'. They found 'criminal mistakes and omissions' that had clearly resulted in the eventual death of so many. This went beyond a bungling of operations: there were no warnings, sirens or alarms and certainly no evacuation plan. The blaze was initially ignored entirely by the emergency services. They had all been sent to battle a fire elsewhere and so as gale-force winds whipped up the flames in Mati, where the heat was reported at 50 degrees, the people residing there and in the nearby villages were effectively sitting ducks. They (or we) were left to burn and it was nothing short of a miracle that anybody got out alive. Most of the survivors had decided to pursue a case against the government and I resolved to join them. I wasn't expecting a big monetary outcome: after all, Greece is still in recession, so my expectations were realistic. That wasn't what I was after anyway. This was my last chance to fight for Brian, to demonstrate what a hero he had been and what a great loss his death was to me, his friends and family. It was my opportunity to exorcise some of my demons, to tell my tale in court, explaining exactly what had happened on that terrible day. This was what Sonya and I had been working towards all year in therapy and I was finally ready to embrace the moment.

Before I got to that moment, there were some obstacles to overcome. My solicitor was the aptly named Mr Angelakos. I actually chose him because 'Angel' was in his name ... go figure for an atheist! He informed me out of the blue, in early December, that I had to go to Athens the week before Christmas. It was urgent: the judge of investigation had declared that all those partaking in the case must appear in court before the end of that current year (2019) or they wouldn't be allowed to take part in the proceedings. That really threw a cat amongst the pigeons. As eager as I was to take part, I assumed I'd have many months yet to rehearse, plan and, well, procrastinate. But now Mr Angelakos made it clear that there wasn't a second to lose, or to think for that matter, and that I had one week to book flights and accommodation. Crucially, that also gave only one week to find somebody to travel with me. The idea of returning to Greece was daunting enough; to travel solo was utterly terrifying. I not so subtly put the word out amongst my friends that I needed a chaperone. It was not quite a cap-in-hand request, but it was not far off. The trip was just a few days before the 25th, so this was a big ask. I was overjoyed when Katharine (Lady C) agreed to join me.

In a frenzied fashion I booked flights, hotel rooms and, most importantly, gathered all the paperwork, reports and images Mr Angelakos had requested. My suitcase was filled to the brim with documents by the time I was through. I had one quick therapy session with Sonya before I left, though neither of us really had an iota what lay ahead or what to prepare for. This was a parachute jump if ever there was one. I was hurtling into the unknown. Thankfully, I had Katharine in tow, but she wouldn't be standing with me in court. I felt anxious that some of the Greek victims may resent my taking part in the case, bearing in mind many still had no homes to return to and had yet to receive any compensation. Sonya pointed out that this was an illogical fear, especially given the fact that they had shown me such love and care after the fire, reiterating that I, like all the victims from that tragedy, was just searching for some form of justice for the person I loved and lost. I wanted answers and somebody to be answerable, even though no punishment could take away my pain. At least, with so many involved in the action, I didn't have to take on this fight alone.

Before I knew it, we were ready to head off. I hadn't flown since the medi-plane journey home, which hardly counts as a regular flight given that I was unconscious for the duration. I hadn't left Ireland at all since then and the fact that I was flying back to the place that had altered my life so dramatically was immense. The day swiftly arrived, whether I liked it or not, and before I knew it Katharine's husband, Robbie, was driving us to the airport. We laughed and joked en route as if we were heading off on holiday and by the time we arrived at Dublin airport, I was surprisingly relaxed.

There were, of course, minor wobbles along the way, as there always are in airports. Katharine's boarding pass was the first one. There was an issue with the barcode and she was delayed going through the gates. Oblivious in my own world, I continued ahead of her only to encounter a delightful creature in security who decided I was her victim of choice that day. As I placed my luggage in the tray, the security woman looked at the bandages on my hand and arms and told me to remove them. I laughed, a little surprised, and explained they were burns bandages, not fashion accessories, and couldn't be removed. Unhappy with my response, clearly the laugh was a bad idea, she told me to step aside so that she could perform a body check. I cooperated: always best to take the path of least resistance. She took her merry time performing the task, but I was eventually allowed to pass through the scanner. There her colleague decided to suspiciously rifle through my luggage. I wondered if they had ever seen people with bandages before. I mean, what in God's name did they think I had hidden in there? A little part of me was sorry that I hadn't actually removed them when she'd asked. I would have revelled in her reaction had she seen what lay beneath. As much as I love my new hand, it's still not the prettiest sight you've ever seen. I decided to save my objections for another day. It wasn't worth the aggravation and they were just doing their jobs. Eventually, I made it through to the other side and within minutes Katharine joined me.

After that, the flight itself was a dream, and I mean that literally because I slept for half the journey. I found myself beginning to enjoy the trip. I'd forgotten how much I liked to travel, how excited I used to feel hopping on a flight, wondering what adventures lay in wait. This time, what lay ahead was anybody's guess, but nonetheless I found myself eager to touch down on Greek soil.

We arrived late in the night at the Titania Hotel, dumped our bags and headed straight to the rooftop bar. There we were greeted with a magnificent view of the Acropolis, just a stone's throw from the hotel's terrace. It was the first time I had seen it in all its glory and the sight of this ancient wonder lit up beautifully against the blackened night sky took my breath away. Katharine and I gulped down a bottle of cool white wine and enjoyed the tranquillity, as we were the only customers there that late. We retired shortly afterwards, but neither of us got much sleep. I guess my silent anxiety was catching.

I had arranged to meet Mr Angelakos in the hotel lobby the following morning and Katharine diligently promised not to leave my side. Nervously, we drank coffee and awaited his arrival. My hand shook so much I kept spilling drops into my saucer. On the chair beside me sat a huge folder filled with birth, death and marriage certificates, medical reports and letters from therapists, photographs from surgeries and up-to-date images of all my scars. I kept that folder as close as one would a treasure chest. The thought of anyone seeing the images within filled me with horror, even though I knew very soon several people would be inspecting those pictures closely. I asked Katharine to look away should the images be shown in her presence. It was a ludicrous request, but nobody, bar my medical team, had seen my scars and I wanted to protect my friend as much as my own privacy. Once she had witnessed those images, she would never look at me the same way again.

It wasn't long before Mr Angelakos joined us. He was easy to spot: a tall, sallow, serious businessman in his mid-fifties, looking terribly official in a grey suit and slightly crumpled trench coat. With him he carried a large suitcase and a heavy-duty plastic bag full of papers to rival my own file. Introductions were hurriedly made, and though he had a sober demeanour, when he smiled his face and eyes belied some warmth under the solemn exterior. Mr Angelakos explained that he had just come from court and I got the impression time was of the essence. We only had that day to prepare for my hearing, so every minute counted. He got straight down to the task in hand and asked if I had brought the documents that he had requested. I handed over the folder, knowing that, in doing so, there was no going back.

Minutes later we were joined by a young associate from Mr Angelakos' firm, a young man, probably late twenties or early thirties, who definitely seemed eager to make his mark on the world. He was impeccably dressed in a three-piece suit and, like his boss, was quick to fire off questions in my direction. I'm embarrassed to say that I didn't log his name, although I'm not entirely sure that he actually introduced himself. At that time I was distracted because his boss was poring over the photos in my file. Anyway, the young attorney was trigger-happy to shoot plenty of questions at me and I began to feel intimidated, so I found myself directing my answers at the older man instead. There was something about Mr Angelakos that made me feel more at ease.

After about an hour it was decided that, as we were getting into the nitty-gritty of the case, it would be preferable to move somewhere more private, so we headed to the offices of Nikolaos Angelakos & Associates. It was a short walk away, just behind the hotel, so we went on foot. On our brief trek up the hill we bumped into a superfluity of nuns wearing very long, heavy habits. Amusingly, one chased me for about 20 metres, attempting to press a large wooden crucifix into my hand. I wasn't exactly her target market, but I admired her determination: this was a nun on a mission. Eventually I managed to shake off the habited one and continued the climb along the wobbly cobbled path. The sun was beaming down – even though it was December it had to be in the mid-20s – and immediately I felt discomfort on my skin from the heat. All summer long in Ireland I'd avoided sunshine, and I hadn't expected it to be so hot in Athens at that time of the year. Thankfully, the discomfort was short-lived.

The first thing that struck me as we entered the offices was the mountain of paperwork all over Mr Angelakos' desk. There were piles of paper heaped on every available surface. It reminded me that my case alone was a mere drop in the ocean, though it wasn't until the following day I'd discover that hundreds were involved in this suit. I was introduced to several members of the team and it was explained that we'd spend the afternoon running through my testimony, mapping out the journey we had taken on 23 July and discussing all my surgeries and health issues caused by the fire. My lawyer had done his homework. I learned a lot that I was previously unaware of, like the fact that Manos had discovered me in the boot of the car just metres away from the port. Brian's body was found the following day just a few feet from the burnt-out car, virtually within touching distance of the water. Naturally, I couldn't help thinking that if we'd made it just a few metres further and reached the sea, we both would have been saved. Manos' testimony was to be crucial in establishing exactly where our journey had ended that day.

The junior associate (three-piece-suit guy) was tasked with mapping out our route and I was surprised when he showed me the distance Brian and I had travelled from Villa Aliki to the final crash site. Reliving that journey, even on an on-screen map, was a bit of a shock and I started to wobble. My legs felt as though they might give way and I could feel tears gathering. Quickly, I texted Katharine. She was sitting in one room while I was looking at maps in the lobby. I confessed that I was thinking of 'doing a runner ... but knowing my luck if I did I'd probably be kidnapped by the scary nun'. Nun or no nun, the lift was there right in front of me and it was a pretty tempting option to escape. Katharine immediately walked to the lobby and protectively asked if I needed a break. I shook my head. Just seeing her there gave me the strength to continue. I hastily wiped my eyes, took a deep breath, thanked my lucky stars for having such a good friend, and went back to work.

The next thing I discovered was that the first hospital I was sent to was called Evangelismos and it was confirmed in my notes they had indeed left me without any pain relief for twelve hours. It wasn't until 7.00 a.m. the following morning, on 24 July, that Marianne, my embassy angel, found me hidden behind a curtain on the upper floor. I shudder to think what would have happened had she not helped me escape that place.

I also caught a glimpse of my notes from the Mitera and read that beyond the daily procedures on my eyes, face and body, I had undergone seven crucial operations under general anaesthetic during my four-week stay, including initial grafts on my hand and arms. There were notes about my lung damage, that I was suffering from severe pneumonia and had developed a resistance to thirteen different types of antibiotics and was sensitive to four others. From the mountain of medical documents the Mitera had sent, I was reminded how lucky I was to be alive, not to mention how blessed I was to have been under the care of Mr Moutoglis, as opposed to the alternative venue down the road. After four hours I finally got an understanding of what lay before me and I was very glad to have all that therapy with Sonya under my belt before having to go through this kind of interrogation in a court setting. This was not going to be easy: reliving every moment of that terrible day and the traumas of the months that followed. Like a little mantra in my head, I reminded myself that this was all to seek justice for Brian. I'd managed to get this far already … the court was only a few steps further.

By the time we left Mr Angelakos, both Katharine and I were exhausted and emotionally wrung out. After grabbing a bite to eat in the hotel, we returned to our rooms and fell asleep for a couple of hours. Once awake, we decided to scrap our planned evening out in Athens and opted to stay in and order room service instead. Like a pair of teenagers, we camped out in our pyjamas, watched God only knows what on TV and gossiped the evening away. It was the perfect distraction, with not a mention of the court proceedings the entire evening.

The following morning I was up at the crack of dawn. I took my time doing my burns procedure. On that particular morning I didn't want to feel rushed, so I got up extra early. Breakfast in my room gave me the chance to mentally prepare myself and by the time I met Katharine and Mr Angelakos downstairs in the lobby, I was wide awake and chomping at the bit, ready to go.

We drove a short journey to the courthouse and reached our destination with time to spare. What awaited us was the first surprise of the day. We stepped up to an ordinary, somewhat dated office entrance and passed through the main door. Then we entered what looked like an airport security terminal (thankfully minus the over-eager guard this time round) and once our bags were scanned, walked through another doorway, down some more steps leading us out to a sunny street on the other side. It was like something out of *The Lion, The Witch and The Wardrobe*: what emerged on the street below was entirely unexpected and remarkably different from where we'd just come. Here we were surrounded by many beautiful, ancient courthouses, each built in the classical Greek style, with columns and pillars to beat the band. There were people, so many people rushing around in all directions and there was an energy about the place that was electrifying, as though important decisions were made here on a daily basis. Flanking the path to our left and right were rows of orange trees in full bloom and their cheery amber warmth, along with the sunshine glinting off the pale stone buildings, was mesmerising. Katharine smiled at me and I could tell she was thinking exactly the same thing. We had both studied ancient Greek civilisation in college, though we weren't the most diligent of pupils it has to be said, but this felt like we had stepped back in time to the ancient Athenian senate. We were both spellbound.

Though we would have loved to explore this magic, secret city, there was no time to dilly-dally and we certainly didn't want to be late for the judge. We hurried along to the waiting area outside the courtroom and arrived with just minutes to spare. Suddenly it got real. Sitting there on a hard wooden bench outside the court, waiting for the judge to arrive, my stomach started to churn. I repeated my mantra and tried to stay focused. I couldn't afford to let my emotions win the day. I had a job to do for Brian and I was determined not to bugger it up. The judge of investigations arrived and entered the office to our left. Mr Angelakos explained that I'd be meeting this judge in a private sitting with just the translator and stenographer in attendance. He told me to remain calm and answer all the judge's questions slowly and clearly. My solicitor then handed in my medical reports, certificates and images of my injuries to the judge. My stomach flipped at the thought of him examining those pictures.

Before I entered the court, I was introduced to the translator. That was my second surprise of the day. There are moments in life when you feel you've lucked out and when she arrived and warmly shook my hand, I knew this was one of those times. The translator was an absolute doppelganger of my old friend from Norway called Anne-Kristin, or AK as I had known her. The resemblance was uncanny and instantly I felt as though I had a pal in my corner in that court. It sounds silly, I know, but as it happens, this woman turned out to be just that.

We entered the courtroom, which was effectively a large office: no podium for the judge, just a huge desk at the top of the room. I sat on a comfy chair beside the translator and the stenographer sat at her desk on our left. Even without the official courtroom setting, it was still a pretty intimidating situation. The judge was perhaps a couple of years older than me and, for the most part, communicated only in Greek. The translator (her real name escapes me, so let's call her AK) explained everything that he said. This was a long and complicated process: every question he asked had to be translated and likewise with every answer I gave. The stenographer diligently recorded every word. The entire process would take over three hours.

Given that this was just the beginning of what I now know will be a long legal process, I cannot go into details about what exactly was discussed in that room, but of course it wouldn't take a genius to work out what we covered. There were tears shed, not all from my own eyes, and times when AK held onto my hand tightly to get me through certain harrowing moments. We had one brief ten-minute break, a well-deserved one at that, as the intensity of the testimony was getting to us all, but once that was over we powered through and eventually completed the hearing.

At the end, AK read back my testimony and I had to sign off each page of the detailed log. It was then I heard her relay all the questions and answers, including every detail of that terrible day and what occurred afterwards. She came to the point when Brian and I happened upon those five little children stranded in the middle of the road and she described how we stopped the car and how Brian carried the children and placed them in the back seat. That was the moment I'd been waiting for. There it was, in black-and-white: Brian was a hero. To see this fact stated in an official court document proved to me that he would always be remembered as such. A wave of relief came over me, as though I'd been holding my breath since the day he died and now I could finally breathe again.

'Life is not measured by time – it's measured by moments.'

I'd read that quote recently, before coming to Greece, and it had stayed with me. It struck me then just how momentous that moment in time was for me. AK took my hand, looked me in the eye and, as though she was reading my mind, said, 'You see, everybody will know now that he was a hero.'

That was what I had come back to Greece for, to hear those words honouring Brian and to know that our story had been heard. I left that courtroom with a smile on my face, exhausted for sure, but virtually on a high at the same time. Outside the room I told Katharine and Mr Angelakos, who'd been waiting patiently, that it was done. They both seemed delighted. I guess I wasn't the only one holding my breath. The judge followed us out of the room and after he said a few brief words to my solicitor, he beckoned to me. In an utterly unanticipated move, he embraced me warmly and in perfect English wished me good health and happiness. You could have knocked me over with a feather! I turned to AK and we also hugged for quite some time. It felt as though we'd achieved something great together that day, and I guess we had.

Leaving the court, a smiling, relaxed Mr Angelakos asked me if I would like to see some of the sites in Athens, knowing that my last visit had not exactly been a tourist's dream. He seemed utterly relieved that the hearing was over and as he drove up to the hills overlooking the city, he began to open up about how immense the case actually was. Hundreds were taking part and these private testimony hearings were just the beginning. There would be public court sessions to come and it was unlikely that the entire case would be settled for years. Clearly impassioned by the importance of the suit and how crucial it was that the truth should out, Mr Angelakos stated emphatically that the events of 23 July must never be repeated again.

We continued to drive through the city and for the first time I began to unwind properly, observing the scenery and architecture around us. I wanted to absorb as much as I could, especially as I'd dreamt of visiting Athens since childhood. We drove up to the highest point in the hills and stopped at a small clearing in a forested area. There, Katharine and I gazed down on the stunning views, marvelling at the sprawling vast expanse of Athens below. Mr Angelakos brought us to several other points renowned for their beautiful views and, happy to play tour guide, he eagerly pointed out various monuments and buildings of interest along the way. He was clearly proud of his city and I admired that in him.

Once done with our whirlwind tour he asked us if we were hungry. I answered quite frankly, 'I'm always hungry.' It's a sad truth, I'm afraid to say. (I blame it on my medications, my doctor blames it on my gluttony.) Even if we hadn't been peckish, we all felt as though there was something to celebrate and Mr Angelakos suggested some traditional Greek fare, mentioning his favourite little restaurant just a short walk from the Titania. He drove us back to the hotel and we returned to our rooms to freshen up. I was very happy to lock up those documents and photos back in the hotel safe (out of sight, out of mind) and with that done, I was feeling lighter by the second.

In less than an hour we were sitting in a quaint seafood restaurant with a cool glass of white wine in hand. The young associate, still impeccably dressed, joined us and enthusiastically we worked our way through virtually every dish on the menu. It was a celebratory feast of delicious local specialities. We broke bread, drank wine and shared life stories for several hours and when we finally could eat no more (even I was full), Mr Angelakos insisted on picking up the cheque, although I did put up quite a fight. I had planned that the meal would be my treat, but he was having none of it, explaining in no uncertain terms that in Greece the man always pays the bill. For once I was happy to put my feminist views aside and, in truth, the combination of the delectable food and the numerous glasses of wine, which I had guzzled at quite a rate, was beginning to take effect. I was too tired and too content to argue.

I thanked Mr Angelakos and his apprentice sincerely for transforming what started as such a difficult day into quite a wonderful one. They could not know how cathartic and healing that court hearing was, but no matter, there would be plenty of time to explain: this was, after all, just the beginning of our legal journey. By now I was shattered, and so we bid our companions adieu and once again headed back to the hotel for a siesta. As soon as I closed my bedroom door and kicked off my shoes, I fell into a deep slumber and was it not for my phone ringing an hour later, I probably would have slept the night through.

Katharine was not going to let that happen as this was our last night in Athens, although, to all intents and purposes, this was my first night out in Athens. Sadly, as our trip was so short, we could not meet up with Manos or indeed all my angels at the Mitera as there simply wasn't the time. Those reunions would have to wait until my next trip to Greece, which I was already looking forward to. However, Katharine was determined not to waste those last few precious hours we did have and was eager that we would explore the city. To begin with, she insisted that we check out the Plaka, a pedestrianised part of the city directly under the Acropolis, filled with little curiosity shops, restaurants and bars. As if we hadn't already consumed enough food that day, I decided to treat Katharine to a late dinner in a cute little restaurant, where we whiled away hours chatting and people-watching. I was so relaxed that just for a few hours it felt as though we were on holiday.

To top off the evening, Katharine took me to a fabulous rooftop bar that she had visited the last time she was in Greece, back when she had helped me retrieve my belongings the previous year. The bar was called 360 Degrees and, as the name suggests, the views were breathtaking. It was a panoramic aspect of all that the city by night had to offer, including the magnificent Acropolis, once more lit up in shining glory. There we sat, relaxing in the warm evening air, sipping champagne. She insisted on getting the real McCoy – of course she did, there is a reason why we call her Lady C, you know! There was a sense of achievement in the air. I felt like I'd accomplished what I needed to for Brian and I knew for sure that without my friend by my side on that trip, the outcome could have been a lot different. We smiled and as we sipped our champagne, we toasted Brian to the dark night sky. Closing my eyes briefly, I wiped away a tear and commented: 'He would have loved this place.'

42

RINGING IN A NEW DECADE

t's a little over twelve months since I first put fingers to keyboard (pen and paper are so passé) and I'm not only in a new year but also dipping my toes into a brand-new decade. My friends saw to it that I wouldn't start off 2020 alone. Even though I locked myself away after Christmas for a few weepy days, they interrupted my solitary confinement and basically kidnapped me on New Year's Eve. While they understood that sometimes I need to step away and hide, I'm blessed to have friends who also know when it's time to bulldoze me out of my apartment and drag me back into the real world. And so I toasted in the New Year surrounded by my closest pals, a gaggle of kids and four puppies. I can report that it's very difficult to be sullen when you have a snuggly little pooch in your lap. All things considered, it was a joyful beginning to a new decade and there was even a hint of optimism on the horizon.

As I look back now on my early chapters, I can see just how much has altered over this short period of time. Some things haven't changed: I'm still a lousy typist, for instance. But there have been many developments to report. I have hair on my head for a start (bless you, Jen and Jenny from Reba). It took nine hours over two days to transform my sparse, scouring-pad hair and using every trick in the book – we're talking magic lotions, dark arts and a truck-load of hair extensions – they gave me a full head of shoulder-length hair. I could hardly believe it. No more waking up, rushing for hats, wigs or scarves to disguise my bonce. I felt like a woman again – a woman with hair on her head! To mark the occasion the salon manager, Annemarie, even had a bottle of bubbly on hand and together we toasted the completion of project 'put hair back on Zoe's head'. It had been an uphill battle, but all their work was a resounding success! More than anything, I was ecstatic to wave goodbye to the wigs, those itchy little so-and-sos. For the record, I didn't actually discard them. The good wigs went to a worthy new home, to a fabulous girl who's bravely battling cancer, while the dodgy cheap ones are packed away in my Hallowe'en box for future outings. I was sorry to say goodbye to Dolly, my wig stand, but her work must continue elsewhere: like Mary Poppins, Dolly must go where she's needed most.

Most importantly, I've made vast physical improvements over the last year, bearing in mind that in January 2019 I was still wobbly on my feet. A noteworthy moment was when I finally hit the Phoenix Park, my happy place, for the first time. When I realised that I could do my old trek, even though it took over twice the time to complete, I was exuberant. I remembered lying in my cocoon in Greece, vowing that one day I would walk that same worn-out trail again. All I wanted to do was phone Yiannis and tell him I'd made it at last. He had helped me visualise that trek during the early days in the Mitera, and I had continued to do so every day since. Now that I could walk there once more, I never wanted to stop. Unfortunately, I discovered that running was out because my knees were too badly damaged, but I could still move freely and that was enough for me. For as long as I can, for the rest of my life, I'll continue to walk my socks off.

Likewise, my hand has come on in leaps and bounds. I no longer drop everything I hold, for a start. There was a considerable period of time when no glass jar or bottle was safe in my paw. Why is it always the messiest, stickiest liquids that take a nose dive? Now I can now make a fist and grip with the best of them. The little f***er still rebels and the nerve pain acts up every now and then, but hey – you can't have it all!

Regarding the scars, well, they're something I'm just going to have to get used to. I'm using laser treatment on my chest and back (figure that one out – burning a burn) and so far the results are promising. There will be no complete fix, though. The laser won't make my scars disappear entirely, but they have certainly shrunk in size. These flaws are part of me now and that is something I am trying to accept, one day at a time. Every night I dream I have perfect skin and every morning I wake up disappointed. Mind you, those dreams are preferable to the gruesome ones I used to have nightly, which do still occur, but far less frequently. My patchwork quilt of body burns continues to fade and who knows where I will be at this time next year.

One big win, one I put firmly at Sonya's door, is that I've finally cracked the night-time problem. Any insomniac or new parent will tell you it's very difficult to keep on an even keel with no sleep under your belt. Sleep deprivation is akin to torture and for a long time I got by on two, maybe three hours a night.

Even with pharmaceutical assistance, my brain fought rest with all its might and at my worst, when I was most exhausted and emotionally fractured, my anxiety and PTSD got out of control. Through therapy, Sonya finally broke that spell. CBT is such a powerful tool: it trained my brain to file the horrific incidents of 23 July back where they needed to be, in the past. As I said before, it isn't a magical cure, I haven't forgotten what happened, but those events are no longer on action replay in my mind 24/7. In time the flashbacks faded, the nightmares became less gruesome and my mind finally allowed itself to switch off and sleep. I'll never be a brilliant sleeper and I still need pharmaceutical help to send me off, but at least on waking I'm no longer a perpetual bag of nerves. With a bit of sleep, you can cope with whatever the world throws at you.

The downside to admitting that my CBT has been successful is, inevitably, that the treatment must come to an end. I knew that day would come eventually, but what I didn't foresee is how reluctant I would be to end the process. I'm thoroughly addicted to therapy – who would have thought it! When Sonya broached the topic of a completion date, something along the lines of 'not getting overly dependent', I felt my heart sink. Her job was to get me out of crisis, this I know, and to help me overcome PTSD, or at very least handle it. It never totally disappears. I knew when I sat in that courtroom in Greece, answering all of those questions, peeling back the layers of pain and truth to total strangers, that Sonya's work with me was complete. If I could manage that, well, I could pretty much manage anything. Don't get me wrong, if I had my way, I'd continue our weekly sessions for the rest of my life, but alas there are those in crisis who require her services more urgently than I do. Like any addict, I shall be slowly weaned off my drug of choice and sent back out into the big bad world alone. However, I shall be eternally grateful to this amazing woman for the remainder of my days. She may not know it, but she probably salvaged my sanity – or what parts are worth salvaging.

As for my grief, while Sonya helped me there immensely, too, I've recognised that this one I need to deal with myself. Grief is a very personal injury, one that probably never heals. I don't really buy into the whole time-mends-all-wounds theory, but I do believe that, with its passing, one learns how to better manage the sadness. Perhaps that's the key: acknowledging the loss and learning how to live with it. I accept that Brian and Dad aren't coming back (hate it, but accept it) and that my world will never be the same again, but I also recognise that they would want me to try and start a new life at some stage.

Navigating this 'new life' is tricky. There are days when I'm not quite sure where I belong, when I feel like I'm merely observing the lives of others as opposed to living in my own. In the last year I've watched my friends blossom and progress as they should. Some got engaged, others pregnant, some left their jobs to pursue exciting new career ventures, while others got promoted or went abroad for pastures new. In the meantime, I just froze and played understudy in my own life, too afraid to actually take a lead role.

Brian was a great man for having dreams and making plans. He always told me I needed to look to the future, so in his honour that is what I intend to do: dare to dream some dreams, quit procrastinating and scuttle forward as best I can into this new decade. He constantly nagged me to 'Stop talking about it and write the bloody book'. Now, I don't think this was the actual book Brian had in mind. Somewhere out there he has to be laughing at the irony: that it took this to get me to knuckle down and finally write. I'd been driving him mad talking about writing a book for years, all talk and no action, but at least I'll begin this decade by finally completing what will hopefully be the first of many.

If nothing else, the writing process has been therapeutic and, who knows, perhaps somewhere in my ramblings there might be a screed of advice or a note of hope for others facing sudden loss or difficult physical changes in life.

Things do get better, that I can promise.

Here are a few things they don't teach you in school that I have learned over the last year.

- Always get good legal advice sooner rather than later.

- Stupid people saying stupid things can't help themselves (they are stupid, after all), so best to just laugh it off.

- When someone approaches you with a plastic tube and a ping-pong ball, don't automatically think the worst.

- Never trust a 6ft tall Captain Peanut – he's sure to be up to no good!

- Everybody should try therapy at least once – you get to talk about yourself uninterrupted for an entire hour: what joy!

- It's okay to be sad, and it's also okay to ask for help.

- Time doesn't eradicate grief, but it lightens the load a little day by day.

- Never use the words 'I know how you feel,' not even with the best intentions – nobody knows how anyone else truly feels.

- Wigs are damn itchy things – natural oils, like almond oil, massaged into the scalp really help.

- A good hairdresser is a gift from the gods.

- Nurses are angels on earth and should be treated accordingly, i.e. in their pay cheques.

- You're lucky if you have a handful of good friends – treasure them always and let them know they are treasured.

- Never forget to say the words 'I love you' even when you don't feel like saying it. These could be the last words your person ever hears.

- Just because everybody else's life seems to be moving on doesn't mean yours is frozen to a standstill. We all move at a different pace!

- Be grateful for love, if you're lucky enough to have it in your life.

- Be grateful you had love because once it touches your soul, it will never let you go.

EPILOGUE: BRIAN

The matters of life and death never preoccupied me until the day of the fire. In fact, before I met Brian, I lived life haphazardly, day by day, and hardly planned anything in advance. In the year that followed his death I found myself not only pondering my own future and legacy but also, since he left this world so abruptly, how Brian would want to be remembered. He no longer had a voice, so the responsibility of how best to mark his name lay in my hands and putting pen to paper was one way I could honour his memory.

When he died, Brian slipped out the door without warning and, beyond funeral instructions, left me without a roadmap to the steps required thereafter. I was totally at sea, unsure of what his expectations would be of me after his passing, and the question of his legacy often rolled around my mind in the early hours of the morning. It became quite my preoccupation. I didn't want to let him down.

That question became pressing when I received certain legal papers in the post.

Several months after Brian's funeral, I finally realised that I could no longer put off the inevitable legalities: there were urgent matters to be dealt with and, with Adey's help, I addressed the mammoth task of sorting out what I'd guess you'd call 'Brian's affairs'. It was a horrible thing to have to do, sifting through somebody's personal papers, even when that somebody happened to be your husband, and my first thought was, 'What an invasion of privacy.' Even though we had no secrets, I couldn't help feeling that I was overstepping the mark, going where I did not belong.

My second thought was, 'What if I find something unsavoury?' We've all heard of those scenarios where the widow or widower discovers an uncomfortable truth after their partner dies: a double life long secreted away in the bottom drawer, only to be revealed after death. My imagination went wild as I rummaged in his beautifully organised filing cabinet for the very first time and started delving into Brian's private world. My emotions were torn between guilt and curiosity, and I confess I was rather relieved not to find any skeletons in that closet. There was no embarrassing stash of pornos carefully hidden under piles of corporate files, no evidence of half-a-dozen secret wives living across the sea, nor did I detect massive gambling debts or a stack of bailiff notices secreted away. He was in the all-clear: Brian was as honest in death as he was in life. It may sound as if I enjoyed my little spot of detective work, but through the whole process I felt like I was intruding, so much so that I constantly apologised out loud to Brian. The funny thing is that he wouldn't have minded. He was quite the open book, though one with a lot of intriguing chapters.

This task, particularly after a sudden death, took time and patience. Months were spent organising paperwork and after my 'sojourn' in hospital, I found it all especially difficult. Eventually I hired a solicitor to take on the lion's share of the work. I probably should have done that much earlier. In fact, that would be my top tip for anybody who finds themselves in a similar situation: get good legal assistance from the get-go.

One morning, a fat registered envelope arrived in the post containing a stack of legal papers. This delivery didn't catch me unawares: I was expecting this probate document, a formal submission to be put to the Inland Revenue. At face value it was merely a balance sheet, a debit and credit statement, detailing Brian's assets and liabilities at the time of his death. I already knew most of its contents, nothing within would be a surprise, yet its arrival hit me like a lead balloon.

In large bold type the title page read: **Brian O'Callaghan Westropp Deceased.**

I couldn't have predicted how badly reading the contents of that envelope would affect me. It was more than just upsetting. I broke into a cold, anxious sweat. I knew Brian was 'deceased', that wasn't it. I knew these papers had to be submitted to the court, that wasn't it either. It was how the document was formulated, lists of items Brian owned and monies he owed. That was when it hit me. All I could think was: is that it? Is this supposed to sum up his life? While this was just a legal document, it felt like it was a declaration of Brian's entire existence and it saddened me that this could be seen as a summary of his 46 years on this earth. Suddenly, it felt crass to be party to this process. I was ashamed to sign the tally sheet, as though I were insulting his memory.

I decided the only way to remedy that feeling would be to ascertain exactly what Brian's true legacy should be and come up with my own list, a true summation of Brian things: his best qualities, achievements and victories. To do this properly, I would enlist the help of those who knew him best. I hadn't far to look for inspiration.

Brian the Adventurer

Without a doubt, Brian left his mark wherever he went. Adey, his closest lifelong friend, perhaps knew him better than anybody on this planet – though I'd like to think I could compete there. Adey was dramatically altered as a result of Brian's death. Pain flashed across his face every time he said his friend's name. He once likened his grief to having his head trapped in an ever-closing vice, that was the closest analogy he could find to match the crushing pain of losing his chosen brother without even having the chance to say goodbye. Beyond the manner of Brian's death, that was the hardest thing to accept.

Yet even as he spoke of his devastation, in the next breath Adey could break into a smile as he started down memory lane, sharing the funniest, happiest moments that belonged only to them two. Brian and Adey travelled all over the world together on their motorbikes, frequently camping as they went. Their adventures, the magical memories of their explorations, are treasures that cannot dull with time. They never argued, well, never with consequence, and like explorers of a bygone era took on their journeys with gusto and a zealous curiosity, even when they accidentally strayed into surprising territory. The nudist campsite they once unwittingly booked into in the middle of the night, for instance, is one tale I'll never tire of hearing. Let's just say they literally had a rude awakening the following morning.

Adey knows his world would have been a far sadder, emptier place without Brian in it and the joys they shared cannot be deleted, even by the pain he now has to endure. Today, in memory of his friend, he rides Brian's motorbike with pride: nobody else deserves that honour. Attached to the frame is a small metal capsule containing some of his trusted travelling companion's ashes. So I guess, in some way, they can continue their adventures and remain road-trip buddies for eternity.

Brian the Carer

Clearly, motorbikes were Brian's great passion. For the record, they weren't mine, but I was happy to join him at the odd biker rally ... mostly for the BBQs and after-parties. What many won't know is that Brian's enthusiasm for bikes drew him close to an even greater passion: that of his chosen charity, Blood Bikes. He was a member of BBE – Blood Bikes East branch. Blood Bikes is a network of amazing people who transport urgent medical supplies on the back of their motorbikes all across the country. They do so in their spare time, free of charge, and provide a life-saving service by assisting hospitals and medical facilities across the length and breadth of Ireland. Not to mention that they save our Health Service Executive a small fortune. They are unsung heroes.

Brian was not only a BBE biker but also an active member of the board (treasurer and organiser extraordinaire). I beam with pride when I think of all the people across this country, total strangers to my husband, who probably owe their lives to Brian and his trusted steed. His work for BBE made a huge impact over the years, from both a practical and a business perspective. Brian was always eager to help people in need whenever he could. Countless nights he'd haul himself out of bed when he got the call and bike crucial supplies, sometimes a vast distance from source to destination, knowing that at the other end somebody was desperate for that delivery. Then he'd return home, grab an hour or two of sleep before embracing a full day's work the following morning without a word of complaint. I don't want to make him sound like a saint, but it's true, he never complained about those late-night treks. Brian wanted to make a difference and knowing that he did, and to so many, was enough thanks for him. To this day his work for BBE makes me immensely proud.

Brian the Fun Uncle

I only had to look to Adey and Lisa's three kids to see what an impact Brian made on their world. They grew up with an uncle who adored them and whom they adored in equal measure. Brian didn't have children of his own, so these were as close as he got. Callum, Evan and Natasha speak often of their uncle Brian (or 'Blian' as he was known when they were babies), convinced he's watching over them, especially when they need him most. He's there every time a goal is scored, a match is won or a birthday candle is blown out and a wish is made. They believe he keeps them safe and watches over them from the next world, just as he did in this one. Three little people convinced he's still in their corner. So much so that when that stray cat turned up on their doorstep shortly after his death, they truly believed it was some feline reincarnation of their uncle. (The fact that the cat was female was irrelevant.) When the moggy disappeared, as strays tend to do, she was replaced with an adorable puppy (a male this time). They christened the pup 'Busta Brian', and I'm sure both Brian and Busta Rhymes are honoured. Naturally the dog is incredibly cute and utterly adored.

The children chose to plant three fruit trees in Brian's honour in their back garden, each with a sprinkle of his ashes at its root. All are flourishing beautifully, the healthiest of which is the plum tree. I'm still not quite sure why Natasha, the youngest, insisted on a plum tree to remember him by, but she was adamant in her choice, claiming it was Brian's favourite. (I don't recall him being an avid fan of plums, only ever witnessing him eating the dried variety, prunes, for 'digestive' purposes.) Perhaps it was their inside joke, goodness knows they used to laugh a lot together, and if she wants to honour Brian with a blooming plum shrub or a pile of prunes, so be it. Of course, Brian would be even more amused to hear that his one great legacy in those children's eyes and, well, stomachs, is the legendary Brian breakfast. It was customary that any time we came to visit the family, his big treat would be cooking them his speciality; it was the best cooked breakfast in town.

The first time I visited the family and met the children, Brian explained that cooking breakfast was a sacrosanct tradition, that he'd always get up early and cook a feast for everyone in the family. Naturally, I brought bags of sweets for the little ones, while Brian came with offerings of sausages, bacon, black and white pudding and a dozen eggs from the local butcher. Much to my astonishment, I quickly learned that Brian's treat was far more popular than mine. I've never seen such excitement over a full Irish. Today, the Brian breakfast has become a monthly fixture in that household, following his exact instructions to the letter. It really is a most suitable honour as this way the best meal of the day, and its creator, can live on for eternity.

Brian the Friend

Other eager contributors to the list are Caroline and Ferg. They continue to commemorate Brian through their shared love of rugby and think of him every time that first try is scored. As a group of four we were inseparable, with pints on a Friday after work and dinner parties at the weekend. We'd often go on trips away, weekends down the country, and nurtured a thriving competitive streak with our own little games nights, which invariably I always won (a mild exaggeration!). The dynamic isn't the same now that we're missing the leader of the pack, but I hope we three will remain close friends nonetheless. I haven't the heart to play silly board games with the same carefree manner anymore, but I hope that someday, when it doesn't hurt so much, we can have a games night once more in Brian's memory.

One way we all continue to toast and remember Brian is through our shared appreciation of a decent bottle of red. Only the good stuff for my fella, he knew his wines. We giggle every now and then, remembering Brian's ceremonious sniffing and swilling of the wine in the glass before tasting it, while we plebs just happily glugged away. On the very odd occasion, usually when Adey is in the mix, we will even raise a glass of Scotch to our lips, a true moment of reverence as none of us can actually stand the stuff.

I'm blessed that Brian brought such amazing people into my life, like Adey and Lisa, Caroline and Ferg. The people he chose as friends share many of his wonderful qualities, and have nurtured and supported me from the immediate aftermath of the fire to the present day, proving that Brian only ever chose the very finest people to have in his close circle. Through his friends, you could say, Brian's spirit lives on.

Brian the Negotiator

One unexpected legacy – and such a pity he didn't hang around long enough to witness it – was that he brought a lot of formerly estranged people back together again after his death. For the most part they had fallen out over silly arguments, and some had even forgotten why they were fighting in the first place. After the fire, when I was hospitalised in Greece, friends forgave and galvanised, they rallied in a moment of strength and grief and perhaps a mutual need for comfort. Brian was quite the problem-solver in life and in business he was an epic negotiator, so he'd happily take the credit for resolving those issues. The truth is that once he was taken from this world, that old adage, 'life is too short', became only too real for us all. It was time to put away petty arguments and come together in a force of love and support.

Brian the Family Man

Brian lost both his father and younger brother in tragic circumstances when he was a young man. Tragedy seemed to follow his line, and his mother, Rosemary, was his only remaining close blood relative. He introduced us quite soon after we started seeing each other and it was heart-warming to see that Brian was always there for his mum. He was very protective of her. They shared a love of good cuisine – like her son she is quite the spectacular chef – and they enjoyed cooking together. Having been just the two of them in that family for over two decades, they would often, quite unintentionally, communicate in their own secret language. It usually happened after they'd spent more than an hour or two together, when they began using colloquialisms or 'O'Callaghan Westropp lingo' only the two of them could comprehend. That always made me laugh. You'd need subtitles to work out what or whom they were talking about half the time.

Though they lived at opposite sides of the country, Brian spoke to Rosemary every few days. He worried about her living so far away and often tried to persuade her to move to Dublin, to be closer to where we lived. He wanted to make sure she was safe, concerned she may grow to be lonely out in the countryside, even though she was, and still is, an energetic active woman with a zeal for worldwide travel. Brian didn't lick that off the stones, as they say. I know he wanted to ensure her safety in her older years. That was Brian: always looking to the future, always making a plan. Today those plans are still in the making, even if the chief planner has moved on.

Long before he became my official husband, Brian became part of my family and by extension so did his mother. We all spent Christmas, Easter and birthdays together – all celebrations in our little world were a family affair. But there were other occasions, outside the hallmark holidays, that proved Brian to be a true family man. The way he spent countless hours with me in hospital while my father had life-saving surgery impressed me more than any grand gesture. He held my hand during those really scary moments, when I didn't know if Dad would survive, and somehow managed to make it better. It was his kindness to my parents that made me realise he was the man I wanted to spend the rest of my life with. How terribly unfair that wasn't to be, but how grateful I am to have had the very best of him in our short years together.

He looked out for my parents as he would his own, often calling in on them when he was over their side of the city, to see if they needed anything. A perfect example was when he dropped by to replace their exploding kettle without even telling me. We Holohans are lackadaisical when it comes to electrical items. Brian, having witnessed the wonky kettle the previous day, was convinced the damn thing would blow up. He just called in, having 'miraculously' found a brand-new kettle in the back of his jeep. Often, he'd drop by for a cup of tea and a chat, to cheer up Dad when he was struggling with the crippling effects of chemotherapy. Brian just had the kind of unpatronising way of making a bad day good, a smile that could turn rain into sunshine. He called my parents Mum and Dad and I knew they loved him too, not only for the way he took care of their daughter but for all the qualities that made up the wonderful man he was. As a family, we were honoured to have him as part of the Holohan clan.

Brian my Love
For my own part, the greatest gift he brought to my world and the one he left behind for me to cherish is true love. That legacy

is carved into my soul. I know for sure that while he has taken the better part of my heart with him, it was his love that filled my heart to the brim in the first place, so perhaps he is the rightful owner of it.

Friendship, love, laughter, protectiveness, joy, generosity and a zeal for adventure and life, all washed down with a taste for fine food and even finer wine (give or take the odd prune here and there), these qualities and traits of character make up the sum total of his parts. Far more edifying than a profit-and-loss report, these are Brian O'Callaghan Westropp's true legacies for which he will never be forgotten.

I still remember …

… how your smile could evaporate all of my worries and woes

… how you held my hand in the car when we were stuck in traffic. Together we'd sing our heads off to dodgy 80s tunes on the radio. We didn't even need to look at each other, you'd just automatically reach out and take my hand

… how you'd puff your chest out when some random bloke would attempt to chat me up at parties (attempt and always fail, of course)

… how proud I was of you the first time you visited Dad in hospital when he was diagnosed with cancer, and how you miraculously managed to make him smile that day. Only I knew the last time you had been in that hospital was when you had said goodbye to your own father

… what a great chef you were – loaves and fishes had nothing on you, you could create a feast from virtually nothing

… how sensible you appeared to be most of the time, while secretly you were just a big child (we must have watched

Despicable Me at least a dozen times)

… how incredibly patient you were – that 'ten-minute countdown' rule you tried to impose to ensure I left parties at a reasonable hour was an epic fail. We were always the last ones to leave and you always managed to laugh about it

… how safe you made me feel every day, and how unsafe I feel without you by my side

… how we had our own private code words, strategies and hiding places that belonged only to you and me (promise to take them to my grave)

… how much I appreciated your romantic gestures – there were always fresh flowers in our home, just because …

… how you put up with my kookiness – Lord knows that 2 a.m. is not the best time to discuss why Meow could be the world's first kitty space explorer or why a three-legged donkey and inebriated monkey would make excellent pets

… how kind you were to my darling cat. Besides myself (I had dibs as I adopted her at only four weeks old) you were one of the few humans she truly loved

… how you told me you loved me every day, without fail

… how your snoring was literally the only thing we ever argued about

… how gentlemanly you were to never bring my snoring into those arguments

… how much your friends adored you – your loss is a great wound to all who ever had the honour of knowing you

… how your memory will live on through Brian breakfasts and silly games nights. I can no longer sleep in until noon at weekends, always switch off lights when I leave the room and even throw away empty cartons from the fridge – all bad habits broken for a lifetime thanks to you

... how all the plans we had made together for the future are lost but not forgotten

... how lost I am without you ...

ACKNOWLEDGEMENTS

Although it is practically impossible to thank everybody who has helped me over the last few years as so many have been instrumental in getting me to this safe place, I'm hoping my little book will speak volumes and express my gratitude for me. I've attempted to show my thanks on virtually every page. To those whose names I've omitted here, I beg forgiveness. I could blame my forgetfulness due to the medicinal fog that swamped me for many months, but, in truth, if I thanked every person who assisted me since July 2018, well, the acknowledgements would be longer than the memoir itself. Bearing that in mind, there are some who I am especially indebted to.

To my brothers, John and Stephen, and my darling mother, Deirdre, thank you for your love, kindness and patience. This has been a rough road for our collective Holohan crew, which includes Fiona, Theo and Oren, and Dad would be proud of all of you for your strength, resilience and ability to keep smiling even when the chips are down.

To my girlfriends, especially Ornaith, Katharine, Marian and Caroline. I can't express my gratitude enough for all that you have done to put this Humpty Dumpty back together again. You are warrior women and I am honoured to call you my friends. I would also like to thank my pals Gill, Nicole, Ffrench, Robbie, Ferg, Rami, Allie and countless others for the continued support, gossip and sustained efforts to keep me sane (though I can't say those efforts were entirely successful – my picnic is still a few sandwiches short).

To my adopted family, Adey, Lisa and the kids. I bless the day Brian brought you into my world, and, I'm afraid to say, you're stuck with me for life. Adey, for all that you have done over the last few years, holding my hand at the most traumatic times in my life, I will be eternally grateful. It's little wonder Brian called you his brother.

To those who toil in the health service, day in and day out, this book is my homage to you all. The kindness, care and dedication I have experienced from surgeons, doctors, therapists and nurses has gone so far beyond the call of duty that it still takes my breath away. You are the unsung heroes performing hidden little miracles, keeping ordinary people like me alive. To all my angels in the Mitera hospital in Athens and St James' Hospital in Dublin, I am indebted to you for your compassion, patience and expertise: Mr Moutoglis, Yiannis, Dr Tsopelas, Mr Shelley, Shane, Michelle, Joanne, 'Bill and Ben', Mr Cahill, Owen, Colm, Kevin, Julie, Ashling, Jackie, Lorraine, Bríd and Anthony. To the many dedicated nurses who showed me tenderness and humanity: Anna, Maria, Dimitra, Dimitri, Vassilis, Aspa, Marie, Maria, Deirdre, Trisha, Maya, Helen, Josette, Dolly, Filipina, Abel … the list is endless. A special word of thanks goes to Dr Sonya Collier, who quashed my terror and gave me one of the greatest gifts of all: a good night's sleep. I also owe immense thanks to Dr Suzanne Kenny for always picking up the phone, Dr Kingston, Dr Mark Hamilton and Ailbhe.

A wise person once said 'It takes a village', so I'd like to extend my thanks to my own villagers for keeping me safe and protected, especially to Jen and Jenny in Reba, all the friendly, warm SuperValu crew, and the wonderful Lloyds staff for making those difficult days that little bit easier. There have been many others who have gone the extra mile and helped me on a personal level when least expected, like P. Tobin and Biddie, Aileen and Julie McCall, Risteard Crimmins, Catriona and Fiach O'Brian, Olive at Bellinter cattery, Derek Malone and the management at Swissport Dublin. I and my family owe so much to the exceptional staff at the Irish embassy in Athens, led by Orla O'Hanrahan, Marianne, Michelle and Aliki. I would also like to thank all the team at INM for their continued support since July 2018, especially Gerry, Karen, Eoin, Terri and Nuala.

To Manos – I still find it difficult to find the right words to express my gratitude. 'Thank you for saving my life' hardly seems to cover it. The same, of course, should be said to Mr Moutoglis and Mr Shelley. I will be eternally grateful to you all. Simply put, I would not be here if it were not for each of you going the extra mile.

To Paul Feldstein, thanks for taking a punt on this newbie. I've discovered your abilities are far-reaching: agent, personal coach and negotiator. Thank you for giving me the confidence to continue on this path.

To Rachel Pierce – it was a pleasure working with you. I sincerely hope this will be the first of many projects together. To

Sarah Liddy, Catherine Gough, Laura King and all the team at Gill Books for keeping me busy during lockdown and occupying my brain during the pandemic. I'll always be grateful.

Finally, to my true love, Brian, and my dad, Colm – for your encouragement and never-ending support, I thank you with all my heart.